BEYOND THE MOON COOKBOOK

ALSO BY GINNY CALLAN

Horn of the Moon Cookbook

BEYOND THE MOON COOKBOOK

GINNY CALLAN

HarperCollins*Publishers*

HarperCollins books may be purchased for educational, business, or sales promotional use. For information please write: Special Markets Department, HarperCollins Publishers, Inc., 10 East 53rd Street, New York, NY 10022.

FIRST EDITION

Designed by Helene Wald Berinsky

Library of Congress Cataloging-in-Publication Data

Callan, Ginny.
    Beyond the Moon Cookbook / by Ginny Callan. — 1st ed.
      p.   cm.
    ISBN 0-06-095195-8
    1. Vegetarian cookery.   2. Horn of the Moon Café (Montpelier, Vt.)   I. Title.
TX837.C318   1996
641.5'636—dc20   96-14268

96 97 98 99 00 ❖/RRD 10 9 8 7 6 5 4 3 2 1

To Cort, Callie, and Carter, who know the kitchen is the first place to look for me and accept my love of cooking as they accept my love for them

Contents

Acknowledgments

I would like to thank Kathy Martin, whose fine editing work tremendously aided in smoothing out the rough edges of this book. Loving thanks to my husband, Cort, who continued to wash yet more sinkfuls of dirty dishes without complaint and happily tried out my cooking experiments, giving me an honest response. Thank you to my editors at HarperCollins, Susan Friedland and her associate editor Jennifer Griffin, for bringing my second book to fruition; to Andrea Warnke, for getting involved again, this time with two children running around while she deciphered my handwriting; to Mason Singer, and all the folks at Laughing Bear Associates, for fine design work; to Andrew Kline, for his photographic talent; to Kathleen Kolb, for her beautiful cover illustration; to Marialisa Calta, for years of professional guidance, friendship, and sending me in the right direction when needed; to Nina Simonds, for taking the time to advise me; to Lee Grutchfield, who came up with *Beyond the Moon Cookbook* as a title for the book in an eating and brainstorming session. Thanks to many friends, who shared food ideas and ate my test meals. Special thanks to all of you who have enjoyed using the *Horn of the Moon Cookbook* and have spoken to, written, and called me. Without your kind words and enthusiasm I would not have written a second cookbook. Thank you all.

BEYOND THE MOON COOKBOOK

Beyond the Moon:
Life After the Café

Nine years ago, I shared an important part of my life with readers like you in the *Horn of the Moon Cookbook,* a collection of recipes and reminiscences from my vegetarian restaurant in Montpelier, Vermont. A lot has changed since then, but not my belief in the value of good food lovingly prepared. And so it's a delight to share this new cookbook—a part of my new life—with you.

My career as a food professional began casually enough, but it grew out of a serious personal commitment I made twenty-five years ago. Along with a whole generation, I had read and been touched by Frances Moore Lappé's vegetarian classic, *Diet for a Small Planet,* and the day I rescued a frantic chicken from a neighbor's hatchet, I knew I couldn't eat meat again. That was in 1971, in Vermont. Finding good, prepared vegetarian food wasn't easy in those days, and not long after college I began selling homemade sandwiches to country stores and health food markets around the state.

Health-minded people, vegetarian or not, were looking for more and better food choices, and in 1977 I opened the Horn of the Moon Café. With staff and customers—my neighbors and friends—I shared the challenges and rewards of turning wholesome local farm products into healthful, delicious meals.

I got involved in grassroots politics, got arrested protesting at nuclear plants, met and married my husband, Cort Richardson, and wrote the *Horn of the Moon Cookbook.* The café grew and changed along with me, but it remained at the center of my life.

Then, in 1988, our daughter, Callie, was born, and like every new mother before me, I discovered that babies arrive with their own full and not very flexible agendas. They're a lot like restaurants in that way: when colic flares, when a cash register jams, it needs tending to—now. For two hectic years, I juggled both sets of demands, but in 1990 I turned over the Horn of the Moon to a new owner and turned the page on a new chapter in my life.

I missed the camaraderie and sense of community the café had provided, but I gained something just as important: time to enjoy my family and friends, my garden, and the beautiful Vermont countryside. In summer, Callie and I picked huge armfuls of dandelions, and watched our garden—and weeds—grow. In winter, we zoomed down our steep driveway in a sled, and made snow women, snow dogs, and snow dinosaurs. (There are already so many snowmen in the world!) Cort and I made room in our lives for another child, too, and in 1991 our son, Carter, was born.

My life still revolves around a kitchen, but now it's my home kitchen. Family meals and get-togethers with friends and their children have provided plenty of opportunities to try out new recipe ideas. (There's nothing like a fussy baby or an active toddler to take the fun out of dining out!) I've enjoyed the challenge of devising kid-pleasing dishes to tempt Callie and Carter out of their tofu-and-pasta rut. Like a lot of people, I've become more conscious of the need to cut back on fats; I use less butter and oil in my cooking than I used to, and I've made good use of the growing array of good-tasting, reduced-fat dairy and soy products available. I've discovered lively new tropical tastes during winter escapes to the British Virgin Islands, and have been happy to find once-exotic produce like tomatillos and an assortment of hot peppers in my grocery store and food co-op at home. Teaching my children to cook—and remembering the rubbery eggs and runny cake batter that my own first, tentative efforts yielded—has reminded me of the importance of beginner-friendly recipes. (You'll find them designated ★ **BEGINNER-FRIENDLY**.) Along the way, I've been delighted to see mainstream nutrition experts begin emphasizing what vegetarians have long known: grains, beans, vegetables, and fruits are the foundation of a healthful diet.

The recipes in this book combine those new influences with my long-standing belief that eating should be a pleasurable experience, and that cooking for others is an expression of love. I hope you, your family, and friends enjoy them in that spirit.

ABOUT BALANCE

We're bombarded with so much seemingly contradictory information about food and health these days that it's difficult to make sense of it all. It seems to me that it all comes down to a matter of balance.

There's no question that a diet low in fat is the most healthful choice. Reducing your fat intake isn't all that difficult. For example, you can easily substitute no- or low-fat sour cream, mayonnaise, tofu, and other dairy and soy products for the regular kind; replace eggs with egg substitutes or egg whites (two whites for one whole egg) in most recipes; steam, bake, or boil foods rather than frying; and use vegetable oil spray instead of oil or butter to coat sauté pans and baking dishes.

But it's also clear that for most of us, life would seem less worth living without an occasional creamy sauce or gooey dessert. That's why I think it's important to pick your battles and—unless you're on a medically restricted diet—indulge yourself once in a while. For me, that means eating low-fat most of the time, and enjoying Santa Cruz Fettuccine or Peach Custard Pie now and then. And I do mean enjoy: there's no need for guilt if you keep things in balance; you can savor your occasional indulgences as the special treats they are.

ABOUT KIDS AND COOKING

There are few life lessons more important, fun, and rewarding to teach your children than how to choose and prepare good food. Like any other skill, cooking isn't something kids learn in an afternoon; you need to make them welcome in the kitchen and involve them in meal planning day in and day out. Here are some tips I've learned from cooking with my daughter and son:

- Keep it simple. Try projects like squeezing fresh orange juice or making lemonade or juice pops on a hot summer day.

- Choose easy recipes that you all will enjoy eating. (The beginner-friendly recipes in this book—designated ★ **BEGINNER-FRIENDLY**—offer lots of delicious possibilities.) That doesn't necessarily mean sweets, which many children's cookbooks seem to emphasize. My children love to make and eat fresh, hot biscuits, muffins, pizzas, and their favorite soups. Your kids may surprise you by trying foods they ordinarily would refuse simply because they helped make it.

- Allow plenty of time, and be patient. Cooking with young "helpers" takes longer and generates more mess—but that's the point! Enjoy the process, and don't rush to get finished.

- Let your kids do as much as they safely can—measuring, stirring, rolling, kneading, pushing the start button on the blender or food processor (after you've made sure the lid is on tight and the container isn't overly full).

- Keep it safe. Remind your children of the safety rules each time you begin a cooking project. Don't let them handle hot pots or sharp knives unless they're old enough to do so safely—and then only under your watchful eye. Keep pot handles away from the edge of the stove, and stove knobs off limits.

- Encourage their sense of wonder. Kids love to see things transform. Let them stir sliced strawberries into white frosting and watch it turn pink, or peek at muffins in the oven to see how they rise.

- Let them know that everybody—even you—learns by making mistakes. My kids love hearing about the time I forgot to put baking powder in a batch of muffins and wound up with banana-bran hockey pucks that even the dog refused to eat.

- Teach them that cleaning up is part of the job. Put on some lively music to make cleanup time more fun.

- Set a good example. Your food choices influence your children's eating habits more than anything else. Explain to them why you buy organic produce rather than chemically treated varieties. Show them how to read the nutrition information on packaged foods, and explain why you choose low-sugar, reduced-fat alternatives. You'll be teaching them to be smart consumers as well as smart eaters.

UNUSUAL INGREDIENTS

Some of the ingredients used in *Beyond the Moon* may be unfamiliar to you. What follows is a quick description of some of the more uncommon foods, where they can be found, and possible substitutions for them.

ARROWROOT is a natural thickening agent which is used in some of the pies and sauces. It is sold in most natural food stores and co-ops and is usually located with the spices. Cornstarch can be substituted in equal amounts.

CAROB POWDER is made from a bean that is similar to chocolate. It is used in baking but unlike chocolate it contains no caffeine. Carob powder is sold in most natural food markets and can be located in the baking section. Cocoa powder may be substituted in equal amounts.

CHILI PASTE WITH GARLIC is made from chili peppers, and blended with salt, oil, and garlic. Chili paste is used to add heat or spice to some of the Asian-style dishes and can be found with other oriental products in natural food and Asian markets. Cayenne (to taste) with a touch of sesame oil could be used as a substitute.

NUTRITIONAL YEAST has a mild flavor and is high in B vitamins. It can be purchased as either large yellow flakes or in a fine yellow powder. Nutritional yeast is used on sautéed tofu and other dishes optionally; you can leave it out if you prefer. It's popular at my house sprinkled on popcorn, salads, scrambled eggs, tofu, vegetables, and rice—almost anything really. It should not be confused with brewer's yeast, which is very bitter. Nutritional yeast can be purchased in most natural food stores.

SEITAN, also known as wheat gluten, is used in some of the soups and main dishes. It can be found in many natural food markets and can be located in the refrigerated section, fresh, in the freezer section, frozen, and often with Asian food products, in cans. Seitan resembles meat in both appearance and taste. Tofu or tempeh may be substituted for seitan in equal amounts.

SESAME OIL is very aromatic and is used in cooking Asian dishes. A little goes a long way, so don't let the price put you off. It is sold in small bottles in the oil section of natural food and Asian grocery stores. Walnut oil can be used as a substitute in equal amounts.

SHIITAKE MUSHROOMS are more expensive then your basic button mushrooms but offer a more interesting flavor and texture. They are used in fresh and dried forms in soups, pastas, stir-fried vegetables, frittatas—anywhere mushrooms might go well. The dried mushrooms must be reconstituted by pouring boiling water over them and allowing them to soak for 20 minutes. The dried mushroom stems are then discarded (they are quite tough) and the caps sliced thinly. The mushroom broth, or soaking liquid, is a fine addition to a soup. Shiitake mushrooms can be found fresh in the produce department of many food stores as well as dried in natural food and Asian markets. Standard button mushrooms may be used as a replacement for shiitake mushrooms in equal amounts.

TAHINI is made from crushed sesame seeds and has a creamy, nutty taste. Tahini is like a nut butter and helps bind foods together. It is sold in natural food and Middle Eastern markets as well as ordinary grocery stores. Smooth almond, sesame, or peanut butter can be used as a replacement in equal amounts.

TAMARI is an aged soy sauce made from fermented soy beans. Tamari adds a salty flavor and rich brown color to foods. It is stronger in taste than commercial soy sauces. It is sold in most food stores, often near the Asian products. Some commercial soy sauces are chemically processed and may contain sugar, coloring, and additives. Soy sauce can be substituted for tamari.

TEMPEH is a cultured soy product that is sold in flat, grainy-looking cakes. It is high in protein and can be found either refrigerated of frozen in natural markets. Tempeh is ideal in stir-fries and sandwiches. Marinating sliced tempeh gives it an extra delicious flavor. Tofu or seitan may be substituted for tempeh in equal amounts.

TOFU is a cheeselike soy food that is very adaptable to many different kinds of cooking. Tofu is a very inexpensive source of protein and is high in calcium. Tofu is available in a variety of textures. Extra firm or firm is fine for all the recipes in this book.

Tofu is sold fresh, and is found in dairy or produce sections of markets; it needs refrigeration, unless it is silken tofu, which is sold in an antiseptic wrapped package. If purchased in bulk at a market, tofu needs to be stored in a water-filled container, refrigerated, and the water must be changed daily. Pre-packaged tofu is stored in an airtight container and needs no rinsing until opened. It has a much longer shelf life then loose tofu but is often less firm in consistency.

Most directions for preparing tofu call for it to be drained and pressed. This firms the tofu up and allows it to absorb more flavorings when cooked. To drain and press tofu: slice the tofu into 3 or 4 slabs and drain on paper or clean cotton towels for 5 to 10 minutes. (Draining and pressing also helps prevent the tofu from splattering when it is added to hot oil.) Tempeh or seitan will work as a substitute for some of the recipes that call for tofu.

Breakfast Mainstays

Morning is my favorite time to cook, eat, and entertain. There's something so comfortable and satisfying about a hearty meal of potatoes, eggs, pancakes, muffins, or French toast—washed down with plenty of coffee, tea, juice, and an occasional mimosa—in the casual, friendly morning hours.

I like to invite friends for mid-morning brunch on the weekend; that way I have plenty of time to cook, and they don't have to hop out of bed too early. I almost always serve fruit—a festive fruit salad, a cut-up pineapple, or a simple bowl of berries, for example. The main dish might be a frittata or other egg dish, brunch burritos, or soy sausages alongside pancakes. Potatoes—home fries, red flannels, or hash browns—are usually on the menu, too. And no brunch would be complete without coffee cake, scones, or something else sweet and wonderful from the oven.

If you're planning a brunch, try to prepare some of the food ahead of time so you can relax along with your guests. You can mix together the dry ingredients for pancakes or muffins and boil or bake the potatoes for hash browns a day or more in advance. (When I'm baking potatoes for dinner, I always put extras in the oven for a future meal.)

Even on a busy weekday morning, make sure to eat something nourishing— a quick bowl of cold cereal, a bagel, a piece of fruit—before rushing out the door. I like to drink a glass of kefir, a fruit and yogurt blend, when time is short. And on a cold morning, there's nothing like a bowl of hot cereal cooked with dried fruit and topped with maple syrup to keep me warm inside.

Stuffed Hash Browns

*S*erve this for brunch with biscuits or muffins, and don't plan on eating again *until supper! You can better control the cooking if you bring the water to a boil before adding the potatoes.*

4 generous servings

4 or 5 large potatoes, scrubbed and quartered
1 cup finely chopped onion (1 large onion)
1 cup finely chopped red bell pepper (1 large pepper)
1 tablespoon olive oil
3 scallions, thinly sliced
2 tablespoons minced fresh parsley or 2 teaspoons dried
1 teaspoon salt
Pepper
6 tablespoons canola oil
8 large eggs
1 cup grated sharp Cheddar cheese (4 ounces)
Paprika

Cook the potatoes in boiling water to cover until barely tender, about 10 to 12 minutes. Drain, rinse with cold water, and drain again. When cool enough to handle, coarsely grate the potatoes into a large bowl. (There should be about 6 cups.)

Add the onion, red pepper, olive oil, scallions, parsley, salt, and pepper to taste, and stir well.

Divide the canola oil between two skillets, and heat over medium heat. Scoop the potato mixture, about ¾ cup at a time, into the hot pans to form eight mounds. Gently flatten into patties with a spatula. Let them brown up nicely, 5 to 8 minutes, and flip over.

Make an indentation in the center of each patty with the back of a large spoon, and crack an egg into it. Cover the pans, and let the eggs cook for 2 minutes.

Sprinkle 2 tablespoons of grated cheese over each egg, cover the pan again, and cook for 2 to 3 minutes more, until the cheese has melted. Sprinkle lightly with paprika, and serve immediately.

Deluxe Hash Brown Potatoes

These hash browns, packed with vegetables and tofu, are a meal in themselves, but melon slices and freshly baked biscuits are fine accompaniments. Sautéing the potatoes in two pans allows them to brown more quickly and evenly.

4 to 6 generous servings

6 large potatoes, scrubbed and quartered
1 teaspoon salt
Pepper
½ cup canola oil
1 pound tofu, drained, pressed, and cubed
2 teaspoons tamari
1 tablespoon nutritional yeast (optional)
1 cup chopped onion (1 large onion)
½ cup diced carrot (1 medium carrot)
5 large garlic cloves, peeled and minced
¾ cup diced red bell pepper (1 medium pepper)
3 cups coarsely chopped fresh spinach (lightly packed)
4 scallions, thinly sliced
Ketchup or salsa for serving (optional)

Cook the potatoes in boiling water to cover until barely tender, about 10 to 12 minutes. Drain, rinse with cold water, and drain again. When cool enough to handle, coarsely grate the potatoes into a large bowl. (There should be about 8 cups.) Toss them with the salt and pepper to taste.

Heat 2 tablespoons of the oil in a skillet over medium heat. Sauté the tofu, stirring occasionally, until lightly browned, about 10 to 15 minutes. Pour on the tamari and nutritional yeast, and stir quickly to coat the tofu. Transfer to a small bowl.

Divide the remaining oil between two skillets, and heat over medium heat. Divide the potatoes between the skillets, and sauté, stirring occasionally, until they begin to brown up, about 10 minutes.

Combine the potatoes in one pan, and stir in the onion, carrot, and garlic. Cook, stirring occasionally, until the onion is tender, about 5 minutes.

Stir in the red pepper, spinach, and tofu, and continue to cook, stirring occasionally, until the spinach is wilted and the pepper is tender, about 5 minutes more.

Add the scallions and toss. Remove from heat. Serve with ketchup or salsa if you like.

New England Red Flannel Home Fries

★ **BEGINNER-FRIENDLY**

Red Flannel Potatoes traditionally include ham, but they're quite wonderful without it. The beets add flavor and color that can't be beat!

4 to 6 servings

5 or 6 medium red potatoes, scrubbed and cubed (about 6 cups)
1 medium beet, peeled and cubed (about 2 cups)
¼ cup canola oil
1 cup chopped onion (1 large onion)
1 cup chopped red bell pepper (1 large pepper)
1 teaspoon salt
Pepper
½ cup minced fresh parsley
1 bunch scallions, thinly sliced

Cook the potatoes and beets in boiling water to cover until just tender, about 8 to 10 minutes. Drain well.

Heat the oil in a large skillet over medium heat. Add the potatoes and beets, and sauté, stirring occasionally, until the potatoes begin to brown and crisp, 10 to 12 minutes.

Stir in the onion, red pepper, salt, and pepper to taste. Cook, stirring occasionally, until the onion and pepper are tender, about 5 minutes. Stir in the parsley and scallions, and serve.

Florentine Eggs

The rich, wine-spiked cheese sauce makes this an elegant dish for a special morning. If you're short on time you can replace the fresh spinach with two 10-ounce packages of frozen spinach, thawed and squeezed dry. The fresh spinach, however, has more flavor and color, and natural food markets often sell organically grown greens.

4 generous servings

8 cups coarsely chopped fresh spinach (lightly packed)
3 tablespoons butter or margarine
3 tablespoons unbleached flour
1 ¼ cups milk
¼ cup dry white wine
¾ cup grated provolone cheese (3 ounces)
¼ cup grated Parmesan cheese (1 ounce)
Pinch of salt
Pepper
1 tablespoon vinegar
4 English muffins, split in half
8 large eggs

Steam the spinach just until tender, about 4 to 5 minutes, drain well, and cover to keep warm. (Warm frozen spinach, thawed and sqeezed dry, in a pan and cover.)

In the top of a double boiler set directly on the burner, melt the butter over low heat. Whisk in the flour, and let it cook for a minute or two.

Add the milk and wine, whisking until slightly thickened.

Add the cheeses, salt, and pepper to taste, whisking until the cheese is melted and the sauce is smooth.

Cover the pan, place it on the water-filled bottom of the double boiler, and set it over low heat to keep warm.

Pour the vinegar and about 1½ inches of water into a large skillet, and bring it to a boil.

Begin toasting the English muffins in batches.

Crack the eggs into the skillet. When the water returns to a boil, lower the heat and simmer for 3 to 4 minutes, covered, until the eggs are firm. (You may cook the eggs ahead of time and rewarm them in a pan of simmering water for about a minute.) *(Continued)*

While the eggs are cooking, finish toasting the English muffins, and place them on a serving plate.

Divide the steamed spinach among the muffins. Using a slotted spoon, place a poached egg on each spinach-topped muffin. Pour on the reserved cheese sauce, and serve immediately.

Sunday Morning Biscuit Pizza

The colorful vegetables and delicate biscuit crust combine to produce a splendid-looking and -tasting brunch main course.

6 servings

TOPPING

2 tablespoons canola oil
1 cup chopped onion (1 large onion)
2 large red bell peppers, seeded and cut into thin strips (2 cups)
2 large yellow bell peppers, seeded and cut into thin strips (2 cups)
½ cup drained and chopped oil-packed sun-dried tomatoes
One 10-ounce package chopped frozen spinach, thawed and squeezed dry,
    or 4 cups fresh, chopped, steamed, and squeezed dry
½ teaspoon salt

DOUGH

1 cup unbleached white flour
1 cup whole wheat pastry flour
2 teaspoons baking powder
1 teaspoon salt
½ cup (1 stick) butter or margarine
½ cup plus 2 tablespoons milk

TO FINISH THE PIZZAS

1 cup grated Monterey Jack cheese (4 ounces)
1 cup grated extra-sharp Cheddar cheese (4 ounces)
6 large eggs

Preheat the oven to 425 degrees. Grease a large baking sheet.

Make the topping

Heat the oil in a large skillet over medium heat. Sauté the onion until soft, about 5 minutes. Add the red and yellow peppers, and sauté just until tender, 3 to 4 minutes.

Remove the skillet from the heat, and stir in the sun-dried tomatoes, spinach, and ½ teaspoon salt.

Make the dough

In a food processor or mixing bowl, mix together the flours, baking powder, and 1 teaspoon salt.

Using the processor's chopping blade or a pastry blender, cut in the butter until the mixture resembles coarse cornmeal.

Add the milk, and mix just until blended. Turn the dough onto a floured surface, and knead it just until smooth, 3 to 5 minutes.

Divide the dough into six balls, and roll each into a 6-inch circle on a floured surface. Place on the prepared baking sheet, and pinch up a 1-inch-high rim around the edge of each one.

Finish the pizzas

Toss the two cheeses together, and sprinkle half of it on the prepared dough.

Top the cheese with the sautéed vegetables. Push back the topping from the center of each pizza to form an indentation big enough to hold an egg yolk.

Crack an egg onto each pizza. Sprinkle on the remaining cheese—most on the vegetables and a little on the eggs.

Bake for about 15 minutes, until the eggs are set. Serve immediately.

 # FRITTATAS

A frittata is an open-faced omelet that's broiled after being partially cooked. This allows the eggs to rise to the occasion—puffy and nicely browned. Serve it for brunch, lunch, or dinner with a green salad and biscuits. Be sure to use an oven-proof skillet with a metal handle for the final step; wood or plastic won't do.

Asparagus Frittata

3 to 4 servings

FILLING
- ½ pound asparagus, tough stems snapped off (1½ cups)
- 2 tablespoons canola oil
- ½ cup chopped onion (1 medium onion)
- 1 teaspoon dried basil
- ½ cup chopped red bell pepper (1 small pepper)
- ⅛ teaspoon salt

EGG MIXTURE
- 4 large eggs
- 1 tablespoon chopped fresh dill or 1 teaspoon dried
- ⅛ teaspoon salt
- Pepper

TO FINISH THE DISH
- 1 scallion, thinly sliced
- ½ cup grated Gruyère cheese (2 ounces)
- ½ cup grated sharp Cheddar cheese (2 ounces)
- 1 tablespoon butter or margarine

Place the oven rack about 3 inches from the heat source, and turn on the broiler.

Cut the asparagus into ½-inch pieces, and steam it just until tender, about 4 to 5 minutes.

Heat the oil in a skillet over medium heat. Sauté the onion, basil, and red pepper until the vegetables are tender, about 5 minutes. Stir in the steamed asparagus. Drain the vegetables, and stir in the salt.

Beat the eggs well with the dill, salt, and pepper to taste.

Toss the scallion with the cheeses.

Melt the butter in an ovenproof skillet over medium heat. Pour in the egg mixture, and cook until it begins to set but is still loose on top, about 4 to 5 minutes. Remove from the heat.

Spoon the vegetable mixture over the eggs, and top with the cheese mixture.

Place the skillet under the broiler, and cook for 4 to 5 minutes, until the eggs are puffy and browned on the edges.

Slice the frittata into eighths, and serve immediately.

Spinach Frittata

3 to 4 servings

VEGETABLE MIXTURE
   2 tablespoons canola oil
   ½ cup chopped onion (1 medium onion)
   2 cups coarsely chopped fresh spinach (lightly packed)
   ½ teaspoon dried thyme
   1 medium tomato, chopped (¾ cup)
   ⅛ teaspoon salt

EGG MIXTURE
   4 large eggs
   ⅛ teaspoon salt
   Pepper

TO FINISH THE DISH
   ½ cup grated Cheddar cheese (2 ounces)
   ½ cup grated Monterey Jack cheese (2 ounces)
   1 tablespoon butter or margarine

Place the oven rack about 3 inches from the heat source, and turn on the broiler.

Heat the oil in a skillet over medium heat. Sauté the onion until soft, about 5 minutes. Stir in the spinach and thyme, and sauté until the spinach is just tender, about 3 minutes.

Remove the skillet from the heat, and stir in the tomatoes. Drain, and season with salt.

Beat the eggs with the salt, and pepper to taste.

Toss together the Cheddar and Jack cheeses.

Complete the dish as directed in the Asparagus Frittata recipe (page 14).

Mushroom-Cheddar Frittata

3 to 4 servings

VEGETABLE MIXTURE

2 tablespoons canola oil

½ cup chopped onion (1 medium onion)

1 small green bell pepper, seeded and cut into 1-inch strips (½ cup)

1½ cups sliced mushrooms (6 ounces)

½ teaspoon dried thyme

1 small tomato, chopped (½ cup)

1½ tablespoons minced fresh dill

⅛ teaspoon salt

Pepper

EGG MIXTURE

4 large eggs

⅛ teaspoon salt

Pepper

TO FINISH THE DISH

1 tablespoon butter or margarine

1 cup grated extra-sharp Cheddar cheese (4 ounces)

Place the oven rack about 3 inches from the heat source, and turn on the broiler.

Heat the oil in a skillet over medium heat. Sauté the onion and green pepper until soft, about 5 minutes. Stir in the mushrooms and thyme, and sauté until the mushrooms are tender, about 3 more minutes.

Remove the pan from the heat, and stir in the tomatoes and dill. Drain, and season with the salt, and pepper to taste.

Beat the eggs with the salt, and pepper to taste. Complete the frittata as directed in the Asparagus Frittata recipe (page 14), substituting the Cheddar for the Gruyère-Cheddar mixture.

Artichoke Frittata

A *dish no artichoke lover can resist!*

3 to 4 servings

VEGETABLE MIXTURE
2 tablespoons olive oil
½ cup chopped onion (1 medium onion)
2 large garlic cloves, peeled and minced
½ teaspoon dried basil
One 14-ounce can water-packed artichoke hearts, drained and sliced (1 cup)
1 medium tomato, chopped (¾ cup)
⅛ teaspoon salt

EGG MIXTURE
4 large eggs
¼ teaspoon dried tarragon
⅛ teaspoon salt
Pepper

TO FINISH THE DISH
1 tablespoon butter or margarine
1 cup grated Cheddar cheese (4 ounces)

Place the oven rack about 3 inches from the heat source, and turn on the broiler.

Heat the oil in a skillet over medium heat. Sauté the onion, garlic, and basil until the vegetables are soft, about 5 minutes. Stir in the artichoke hearts, and cook a few minutes more, until warmed through.

Remove the vegetables from the heat, and stir in the tomatoes. Drain, and season with salt.

Beat the eggs with the tarragon, salt, and pepper to taste.

Complete the dish as directed in the Asparagus Frittata recipe (page 14) substituting the Cheddar for the Gruyère-Cheddar mixture.

Cherry-Orange Cheese Blintzes

Blintzes are an Eastern European version of crepes, and this rich cherry rendition makes a yummy brunch entree. Substitute blueberries for the cherries if you like. You can make the batter and filling a day ahead and refrigerate.

4 to 6 servings

BATTER

3 large eggs
1 tablespoon honey
2 tablespoons butter or margarine, melted
1 ¼ cups milk
¾ cup unbleached white flour
¾ cup whole wheat pastry flour
1 teaspoon ground cinnamon

Butter for cooking

FILLING

16 ounces ricotta cheese
4 ounces cream cheese or Neufchâtel cheese, softened (½ cup)
1 tablespoon grated orange peel
2 tablespoons orange juice
1 teaspoon vanilla extract
½ teaspoon ground cinnamon
2 tablespoons honey
2 cups pitted cherries (rinsed and drained if canned)

Sour cream for garnish

Preheat the oven to 375 degrees. Grease a 9 by 13-inch baking dish.

Process the eggs, honey, and 2 tablespoons melted butter in a food processor or blender until smooth. Add the milk and ¼ cup of water, and process again. Add the flours and cinnamon, and process until smooth, stopping once or twice to scrape down the sides.

Melt about 1 teaspoon of butter in a 10-inch skillet over medium heat, and spread it over the bottom of the pan. Tilt the pan, and pour in ¼ cup of batter, swirling the pan to coat the bottom. Cook for about 2 minutes, until lightly browned on the bottom. Turn and cook until lightly browned on the other side, about a minute more.

Repeat until all the batter is cooked, adding butter to the pan as needed. Stack the crepes as you finish them; you'll have about a dozen.

In a medium-size bowl, beat the ricotta and cream cheese until smooth. Stir in the orange peel, orange juice, vanilla, cinnamon, and honey, mixing well. Fold in the cherries.

Spread about ⅓ cup of filling in a fat line on one side of a crepe, leaving a ½-inch border on each end of it. Fold in the edges, and roll up the crepe. Place it in the prepared baking dish, seam side down. Repeat until you have used all the crepes and filling.

Bake for about 10 minutes, until lightly browned. Serve immediately, garnished with sour cream.

Mushroom-Spinach Breakfast Burritos

Eggs, vegetables, and cheese rolled up in a tortilla make a delectable and uncommon morning meal. Serve these with home fries and fresh fruit. Seed the jalapeño for a milder taste.

4 servings

2 tablespoons canola oil
1 cup chopped onion (1 large onion)
1 small jalapeño pepper, minced
1 teaspoon dried oregano
2 cups sliced mushrooms (8 ounces)
2 cups chopped fresh spinach (lightly packed)
2 tablespoons salsa plus additional for brushing and serving
1 large tomato, diced (1 cup)
½ teaspoon salt
½ teaspoon chili powder
1 tablespoon butter or margarine
6 large eggs, beaten
Four 10-inch flour tortillas
2 cups grated jalapeño pepper jack cheese (8 ounces)
Sour cream for serving

Preheat the oven to 400 degrees. Grease a large baking sheet.

Heat the oil in a skillet over medium heat. Sauté the onion, jalapeño pepper, and oregano until the onion is soft, about 5 minutes. Stir in the mushrooms and spinach, and cook until they are just tender, about 3 minutes more.

Remove the skillet from the heat, and stir in 2 tablespoons salsa, the tomato, salt, and chili powder.

Melt the butter in a skillet over medium heat. Pour in the eggs and scramble until almost set, about 4 to 5 minutes. Stir in the vegetable mixture, and cook until the eggs are done, 2 to 3 minutes more. Remove from the heat.

Lay out the tortillas on the prepared baking sheet. Put ½ cup of grated cheese in the center of each tortilla, and top with the egg mixture.

Roll up the tortillas, folding in the sides first. Brush with salsa and bake for 5 to 7 minutes, until the edges just begin to brown.

Serve immediately with sour cream and more salsa.

Red Potato and Three-Pepper Breakfast Burritos

Cilantro adds a fresh Mexican flavor to this variation on the burrito theme. It's a hearty dish that satisfies my weekend craving for a big, high-protein morning meal.

6 servings

3 tablespoons canola oil
1 cup chopped onion (1 large onion)
1 small jalapeño pepper, minced
4 or 5 large garlic cloves, peeled and minced
½ cup chopped red bell pepper (1 small pepper)
½ cup chopped green bell pepper (1 small pepper)
1½ cups sliced mushrooms (6 ounces)
2 cups diced, cooked red potatoes (2 medium potatoes)
1 large tomato, diced (1 cup)
¼ cup minced fresh cilantro
¼ teaspoon salt
Six 10-inch flour tortillas
1 teaspoon butter or margarine
6 large eggs, beaten
3 cups grated Cheddar cheese (12 ounces)
Sour cream and salsa for serving

Preheat the oven to 300 degrees.

Heat the oil in a skillet over medium heat. Sauté the onion, jalapeño pepper, garlic, red and green peppers, and mushrooms until soft, about 5 minutes. Stir in the cooked potatoes, and heat through. Stir in the tomato, cilantro, and salt. Remove the skillet from the heat, and cover to keep warm.

Wrap the tortillas in foil, and put them in the oven to warm.

Melt the butter in a skillet over medium heat. Pour in the eggs, and scramble until set, 5 to 6 minutes. Remove the skillet from the heat.

Divide the warmed tortillas among six plates. Place ¼ cup of cheese in the center of each tortilla. Top the cheese with the vegetable mixture, and then with the remaining cheese. Spoon on the eggs.

Roll up the tortillas, folding in the sides first. Serve immediately with sour cream and salsa.

Black Bean Huevos Rancheros

Serve this flavorful, protein-packed dish with fresh fruit or a green salad. To save time, substitute 4 cups rinsed and drained canned black beans for the dried. Sautéing the tortillas with butter and salsa gives them better flavor, texture, and color.

4 hearty servings

2 cups dried black beans, rinsed and sorted
2 tablespoons canola oil
1 cup chopped onion (1 large onion)
¾ cup chopped green bell pepper (1 medium pepper)
1 medium jalapeño pepper, minced
5 large garlic cloves, peeled and minced
1 medium tomato, diced (¾ cup)
½ teaspoon salt
1 teaspoon ground cumin
Eight 6-inch corn tortillas
Butter or margarine for coating plus extra for frying
Salsa for coating plus extra for garnish (optional)
2 cups grated jalapeño pepper jack cheese (8 ounces)
8 eggs
Sour cream for garnish
Chopped fresh cilantro for garnish

Soak the beans in 6 cups of water in a large, heavy pot for 6 to 8 hours or overnight.

Drain the beans, cover with 6 cups of fresh water, and bring to a boil. Reduce the heat and simmer, stirring occasionally, until tender, 1½ to 2 hours. Drain and mash.

Preheat the oven to 400 degrees. Grease a large baking sheet.

Heat the oil in a skillet over medium heat. Sauté the onion, green pepper, jalapeño, and garlic until soft, about 5 minutes. Stir the onion mixture into the mashed beans, along with the tomato, salt, and cumin.

Wipe out the skillet, and heat it over low heat. Lightly coat both sides of each tortilla with butter and salsa, and sauté them, one at a time, for about a minute on each side. Place the finished tortillas in a single layer on the baking sheet.

Divide the bean mixture among the tortillas, spreading it evenly. Sprinkle on the grated cheese. Bake for about 10 minutes, until the cheese is nicely melted.

Meanwhile, melt additional butter in a large skillet over medium heat, and fry the eggs the way you like them. (I prefer mine over easy.)

Transfer the baked tortillas to plates, and top each with a fried egg. Garnish with sour cream, cilantro, and additional salsa if you like.

Friends of Maple Syrup

Maple syrup and pancakes—or French toast or waffles—are a winning alliance and a Vermont tradition. I developed a real appreciation for maple syrup one March in Woodbury, Vermont, when I helped my neighbors Val and Leitha with their "sugaring." (The name comes from the days when maple syrup was most often cooked down into maple sugar.)

Val was born in Vermont in the late eighteen hundreds, and when I met him he was in his eighties and going pretty strong. His wife, Leitha, was just a young thing in her sixties and spry as could be. They had been making syrup from their twenty acres of maple trees for fifty years.

The snow was up to our waists that spring, and the sun reflected off it so brightly that it hurt our eyes. Val drove the tractor that pulled a large holding tank through the woods. My job was to wade through the snow from tree to tree, collecting, emptying, and rehanging the sap buckets. Every time we had another spring snowfall (known in Vermont as poor man's fertilizer), I had to pack down the paths to the trees again. It was hard work, but it was a pleasure to be out in the sun after the long, cold winter. Though the temperatures were in the thirties and forties, we got hot enough to work in our shirtsleeves.

When the tank was full, Val and I would drive it over to the sugar house and empty the sap into a huge galvanized metal holding tank. Then Leitha took over, carefully cooking the sap down into syrup that was just the right consistency for all the pancake lovers in town. Val and I dried ourselves by the fire, breathing in the sweet, steamy air of the sugar house, and Leitha boiled eggs in the hot sap for snacks. I always hoped for a cracked one that had a bit of maple flavor cooked into it.

Now when I pour maple syrup out onto my pancakes, I remember how heavy those sap buckets were, and how many gallons of sap (up to forty) it can take to make a single gallon of syrup. That's why I think you ought to drizzle it on, and not drown your breakfast in it; real maple syrup is much too precious to waste!

PANCAKES

Pancakes lend themselves to all sorts of personal interpretations. For starters, there's the consistency. In our household, we begin with a standard batter that produces pancakes about ¼ inch thick. After most of us have had our fill, we radically thin it out for my husband, the crepe eater in the family.

Then there's fruit. It can be added to the batter in just about any form—fresh, dried, frozen, canned, or even fruit butters. If there's a purist in the group who prefers plain pancakes, try sprinkling the fruit on each pancake just after they have gone on the griddle, leaving a few unadulterated. Or you can cook up a few plain pancakes first and add the fruit to the remaining batter.

A blend of flours can also make a simple recipe more interesting. Play around with combinations, adding some cornmeal, buckwheat, soy, or oats to whole wheat and white. Try grinding nuts into the flour, or adding some chopped.

The dry ingredients for pancakes can be mixed and stored for weeks. You can put together the wet mix a day in advance and refrigerate it, and then stir together the batter the next morning for a quick pancake breakfast. Leftover batter loses its rising power over time, but a little extra baking powder will restore its punch. If the batter thins out too much, just stir in a bit of flour.

You'll notice that I use whole wheat pastry flour for pancakes, as well as muffins and quick breads. It's milled from a soft wheat berry, and produces a light texture while still adding fiber. Whole wheat bread flour is ground from harder wheat berries and has a higher gluten content, which makes it good for yeast breads.

Lemon-Cheese Pancakes
with Raspberry Maple Syrup

This high-protein cross between pancakes and blintzes has a lovely custardlike consistency.

9 large or 12 medium pancakes

½ cup whole wheat pastry flour
½ cup unbleached white flour
1 tablespoon baking powder
¼ teaspoon salt
3 large eggs, separated
16 ounces low-fat cottage cheese
3 tablespoons fresh lemon juice
1 tablespoon grated lemon peel
1 teaspoon vanilla extract
3 tablespoons canola oil
¾ cup milk
¾ cup raspberries, fresh or frozen
½ cup maple syrup
Butter or margarine for cooking
Raspberry maple syrup for serving

Stir together the flours, baking powder, and salt in a medium-size mixing bowl.

In another bowl, beat the egg whites until stiff.

In a food processor, process the cottage cheese, lemon juice, and lemon peel until smooth. Add the egg yolks, vanilla, oil, and milk, and mix well.

Add the flour mixture to the liquid and process just until mixed. Gently fold into the beaten egg whites.

Heat the raspberries and maple syrup in a small saucepan over low heat just until the syrup begins to bubble. Turn off the heat, and cover the pan to keep the syrup warm.

Meanwhile, melt about ½ tablespoon of butter in a skillet or griddle over medium heat, spreading it across the bottom.

Ladle batter into the pan, using ⅓ to ½ cup per pancake. Spread the batter gently with the ladle so the pancakes won't be too thick.

Cook until the top is bubbly, 3 to 4 minutes. Flip the pancakes and continue cooking until the bottoms are lightly browned, 1 to 2 minutes more.

Cover the pancakes to keep them warm while you cook the rest of the batter, adding more butter to the pan between batches.

Serve with raspberry maple syrup.

Almond Pancakes

For an intense almond flavor, toast 1 cup whole almonds in a 325-degree oven for 7 to 10 minutes, stirring several times. Then grind the nuts into a fine powder (you will have ¾ cup) in the food processor or blender. (I like to toast some extras for munching, too!)

9 large or 12 medium pancakes

1 cup whole wheat pastry flour
1 cup unbleached white flour
2 teaspoons baking powder
½ teaspoon baking soda
½ teaspoon salt
1 teaspoon ground cinnamon
¾ cup ground almonds
2 large eggs
2½ cups milk
2 teaspoons almond extract
2 tablespoons canola oil
Butter or margarine for cooking
Maple syrup for serving

Stir together the flours, baking powder, baking soda, salt, cinnamon, and ground almonds in a medium-size mixing bowl.

In another bowl, beat the eggs with the milk, almond extract, and oil.

Pour the wet ingredients into the dry, stirring just until blended.

Melt about ½ tablespoon of butter in a skillet or griddle over medium heat, spreading it across the bottom.

Ladle batter into the pan, using ⅓ to ½ cup per pancake. Cook until the top is bubbly, 3 to 4 minutes. Flip the pancakes and continue cooking until the bottoms are lightly browned, 1 to 2 minutes more.

Cover the pancakes to keep them warm while you cook the rest of the batter, adding more butter to the pan between batches.

Serve with maple syrup.

Peach Sourdough Pancakes

This isn't a true sourdough, but it produces a light, deliciously tangy pancake. You need to stir together the yeast mixture the day before so it can rise overnight.

12 medium pancakes

1¼ cups unbleached white flour
1¼ cups whole wheat bread flour
1½ teaspoons active dry yeast
2½ cups milk
1 large egg, beaten
1 teaspoon honey
1 teaspoon baking soda
1 tablespoon canola oil
Butter or margarine for cooking
2 large peaches, chopped
Maple syrup for serving
Yogurt for serving

The night before serving, whisk together ¾ cup of the white flour, ¾ cup of the whole wheat flour, the yeast, and 1 cup of the milk. Let the mixture sit overnight at room temperature, loosely covered.

The next morning, whisk in the remaining 1½ cups milk. Then add the remaining ½ cup of each flour, the egg, honey, baking soda, and oil, and whisk just until smooth.

Melt about ½ tablespoon of butter in a skillet or griddle over medium heat, spreading it across the bottom.

Ladle batter into the pan, using ⅓ cup per pancake. Sprinkle each one with chopped peaches. Cook pancakes until the tops are bubbly, 3 to 4 minutes. Flip and continue cooking until the bottoms are lightly browned, about 2 minutes more.

Cover the pancakes to keep them warm while you cook the rest of the batter, adding more butter to the pan between batches. (Leftover batter will hold fine for a day; just be sure to refrigerate it in a container one-fourth empty to allow room for expansion).

Serve with maple syrup and yogurt.

Apple Oat Pancakes

★ **BEGINNER-FRIENDLY**

Make these old-fashioned pancakes nice and big.

9 large pancakes

1 cup rolled oats
1 cup whole wheat pastry flour
2 teaspoons baking powder
½ teaspoon baking soda
¼ teaspoon salt
1 teaspoon ground cinnamon
¼ teaspoon ground nutmeg
¼ teaspoon cardamom
2 large eggs
1 teaspoon honey
2 cups milk
2 tablespoons canola oil
2 medium apples, cored and grated (2 cups)
Butter or margarine for cooking
Maple syrup for serving
Sour cream or yogurt for serving

Stir together the oats, flour, baking powder, baking soda, salt, cinnamon, nutmeg, and cardamom in a medium-size bowl.

In another bowl, beat the eggs with the honey, milk, and oil.

Pour the liquid ingredients into the dry, stirring just until blended. Let the batter sit for 5 minutes, and then gently stir in the grated apples.

Melt about ½ tablespoon of butter in a skillet or griddle over medium heat, spreading it across the bottom.

Ladle batter into the pan, using ½ cup per pancake. Cook until the tops are bubbly, 3 to 4 minutes. Flip and continue cooking until the bottoms are lightly browned, 1 to 2 minutes more.

Cover the pancakes to keep them warm while you cook the rest of the batter, adding more butter to the pan between batches.

Serve with maple syrup and sour cream or yogurt.

Three B's
(Banana-Buttermilk-Buckwheat) Pancakes

★ **BEGINNER-FRIENDLY**

Buckwheat flour makes a heavy pancake on its own, but it adds texture and flavor to this blend. The tangy buttermilk sets off the sweet bananas nicely.

8 medium pancakes

⅓ cup unbleached white flour
⅓ cup whole wheat pastry flour
⅓ cup buckwheat flour
¼ teaspoon salt
1 teaspoon baking powder
¼ teaspoon baking soda
1 large egg
½ cup mashed banana (1 medium banana)
1 cup buttermilk
¼ cup milk
2 tablespoons canola oil
Butter or margarine for cooking
Maple syrup for serving

Stir together the flours, salt, baking powder, and baking soda in a medium-size bowl.

In another bowl, beat the egg with the banana, buttermilk, milk, and oil.

Pour the wet ingredients into the dry, stirring just until blended.

Melt about ½ tablespoon of butter in a skillet or griddle over medium heat, spreading it across the bottom.

Ladle batter into the pan, using about ⅓ cup per pancake. Cook until the tops are bubbly, 3 to 4 minutes. Flip and continue cooking until the bottoms are lightly browned, 1 to 2 minutes more.

Cover the pancakes to keep them warm while you cook the rest of the batter, adding more butter to the pan between batches.

Serve with maple syrup.

Blueberry Ricotta Pancakes

A *light and cheesy blueberry pancake.*

12 large pancakes

1 cup whole wheat pastry flour
½ cup unbleached white flour
1 tablespoon baking powder
⅛ teaspoon salt
¼ teaspoon ground cinnamon
4 large eggs, separated
1 cup ricotta cheese
⅓ cup yogurt or sour cream
1 teaspoon vanilla extract
2 tablespoons honey
1½ cups milk
1½ cups blueberries
Butter or margarine for cooking
Maple syrup for serving

Stir together the flours, baking powder, salt, and cinnamon in a medium-size bowl.

In another bowl, beat the egg yolks with the ricotta cheese, yogurt, vanilla, honey, and milk.

Pour the wet ingredients into the dry, and stir just until blended.

Beat the egg whites until stiff, and gently fold them into the batter. Fold in the blueberries.

Melt about ½ tablespoon of butter in a skillet or griddle over medium heat, spreading it across the bottom.

Ladle batter into the pan, using ½ cup per pancake. Cook until the top is bubbly, 2 to 3 minutes. (These pancakes brown more quickly than other kinds.) Flip and continue cooking until the bottoms are lightly browned, about a minute more.

Cover the pancakes to keep them warm while you cook the rest of the batter, adding more butter to the pan between batches.

Serve with maple syrup.

Nanny Cay Pancakes

★ **BEGINNER-FRIENDLY**

These colorful pancakes with their tropical spice are named for the beautiful little island in the British Virgin Islands where I first tasted them one warm, sunny morning in March a few years ago. They made such an impression that I set out to duplicate them at home. Serve them with Tropical Fruit Salad (page 118), fresh pineapple, or mango slices.

9 large or 12 medium pancakes

1 cup whole wheat pastry flour
¾ cup unbleached white flour
1 tablespoon baking powder
½ teaspoon salt
2 teaspoons ground cinnamon
½ teaspoon ground ginger
¼ teaspoon ground allspice
¼ teaspoon ground nutmeg
2 large eggs
1 cup pureed pumpkin or winter squash
1 teaspoon vanilla extract
2 cups milk
3 tablespoons canola oil
Butter or margarine for cooking
Maple syrup for serving

Stir together the flours, baking powder, salt, cinnamon, ginger, allspice, and nutmeg in a medium-size bowl.

In another bowl, beat the eggs with the pumpkin puree and vanilla. Beat in the milk and oil until smooth.

Melt about ½ tablespoon of butter in a skillet or griddle over medium heat, spreading it across the bottom.

Ladle batter into the pan, using ⅓ to ½ cup per pancake (it will spread a bit). Cook until the tops are bubbly, 3 to 4 minutes. Flip and continue cooking until the bottoms are lightly browned, 1 to 2 minutes more.

Cover the pancakes to keep them warm while you cook the rest of the batter, adding more butter to the pan between batches.

Serve with maple syrup.

 # FRENCH TOAST

French toast is a quick and satisfying centerpiece for a brunch or family breakfast. You can vary the taste and texture with different types of bread. (Dense breads need more time to soak, and dry breads may need to be pricked a few times with a fork.) You can also make a recipe your own by adding a favorite extract, liqueur, or spice to the liquid.

Orange French Toast

★ **BEGINNER-FRIENDLY**

The orange juice, orange peel, and triple sec liqueur give this French toast triple appeal!

4 servings

3 large eggs
½ cup half and half or milk
2 tablespoons orange juice concentrate (frozen orange juice, thawed, no water added)
⅓ cup orange juice (fresh-squeezed is best)
1 ½ tablespoons grated orange peel
1 ½ tablespoons orange liqueur
Butter or margarine for cooking
8 slices whole wheat or oatmeal bread
Maple syrup for serving

Beat the eggs in a broad, shallow bowl (a pie pan or dish works well). Add the half and half, orange juice concentrate, juice, peel, and orange liqueur, whisking until well blended.

Melt about ½ tablespoon of butter in a skillet or griddle over medium heat, spreading it across the bottom.

Soak the bread in the liquid, turning once, just until soaked through.

Transfer the bread to the skillet, and cook until nicely browned, 2 to 3 minutes per side.

Cover the French toast to keep it warm while you soak and cook the rest of the bread, adding butter to the pan between batches.

Serve with maple syrup.

Almond French Toast

★ **BEGINNER-FRIENDLY**

The heady almond aroma is guaranteed to entice late sleepers out of bed!

4 servings

3 large eggs
½ teaspoon almond extract
½ teaspoon ground cinnamon
⅛ teaspoon ground nutmeg
1 tablespoon almond liqueur (such as Amaretto)
¾ cup half and half or milk
Butter or margarine for cooking
8 slices whole wheat bread
½ cup thinly sliced almonds
Maple syrup for serving

Beat the eggs in a medium-size bowl. Whisk in the almond extract, cinnamon, nutmeg, liqueur, and the half and half.

Melt about ½ tablespoon of butter in a skillet or griddle over medium heat, spreading it across the bottom.

Soak the bread in the liquid, turning once, just until soaked through.

Transfer the bread to the skillet, and cook until nicely browned on one side, 2 to 3 minutes. Sprinkle with almond slices, flip, and cook until the other side is browned, 2 to 3 minutes more.

Cover the French toast to keep it warm while you soak and cook the rest of the bread, adding butter to the pan between batches.

Serve with maple syrup, almond-sprinkled side up.

Baked Blueberry French Toast

This is an ideal brunch dish because you can prepare it ahead of time, and sip mimosas with your guests while it's baking.

6 servings

1 loaf crusty French bread
12 ounces Neufchâtel or cream cheese
8 large eggs, beaten
⅓ cup maple syrup plus extra for serving
½ cup sour cream plus extra for garnish
½ cup plain yogurt
½ cup milk
½ teaspoon ground cinnamon
1 teaspoon vanilla extract
1½ cups blueberries plus extra for garnish

Preheat the oven to 350 degrees. Grease a 3- to 4-quart casserole. Cut the bread into ½-inch squares.

Process the Neufchâtel, eggs, and maple syrup in a food processor until smooth. Add the sour cream, yogurt, milk, cinnamon, and vanilla, and process until smooth.

Place half the bread in a single layer in the bottom of the prepared baking dish. Sprinkle on the blueberries. Pour on half the cream cheese mixture, spreading it evenly. Layer on the remaining bread, and pour on the remaining cream cheese mixture, spreading evenly.

Cover tightly with foil and bake for 30 minutes. Remove the foil and bake for 30 minutes more, until the French bread is well set, puffy, and lightly browned.

Garnish with sour cream and blueberries, and serve with maple syrup on the side.

Simple Pleasures

On Sunday mornings when I was a girl, I loved to go to the neighborhood bakery with my father to buy treats for our family. While he picked out rolls, breads, Danish, cookies, doughnuts, and coffee cake, I would gaze at the goodies in the tall glass display cases, imagining what it would be like to sample each one.

Sweet as those memories are, I learned as I began to bake that commercial baked goods don't compare with homemade. From the irresistible aroma that fills your kitchen soon after you pop a batch of muffins or biscuits into the oven, to that last warm, butter-covered bite, it's a simple yet deeply satisfying pleasure.

The muffins, biscuits, scones, and quick breads in this chapter are just that—relatively quick to stir together. Making yeast breads really doesn't take any more work, just a longer stretch of time, and it dovetails nicely into a stay-at-home day when you have other chores to do.

You can build a simple, satisfying lunch or dinner around your freshly baked treats by adding soup and salad to the menu. If you're cooking for one or two, you can cut the muffin, biscuit, and scone recipes in half for a smaller yield. Or make the whole batch, and freeze leftovers tightly sealed in plastic bags or wrap. They thaw quickly in a toaster oven or microwave, and taste almost as good as fresh baked.

Cinnamon Spice Walnut Coffee Cake

★ BEGINNER-FRIENDLY

T*his coffee cake has a wonderful aroma that makes a fine welcome for brunch guests. It's especially good served with frittatas and other egg dishes.*

10 to 12 servings

¾ cup whole wheat pastry flour
1 cup unbleached white flour
½ cup rolled oats
2 teaspoons ground cinnamon
1 teaspoon ground nutmeg
½ teaspoon ground allspice
½ teaspoon ground ginger
¼ teaspoon ground cloves
½ teaspoon salt
½ cup (1 stick) butter or margarine, softened
1 cup honey
1 large egg
¾ cup buttermilk
1 teaspoon baking soda
1 teaspoon vanilla extract
1 cup chopped walnuts
1 cup raisins

Preheat the oven to 350 degrees. Grease a tubular, 10-inch springform pan.

Stir together the flours, oats, cinnamon, nutmeg, allspice, ginger, cloves, and salt in a medium-size bowl.

In a small bowl, beat the butter with the honey, and stir it into the flour mixture. Mix well, and set aside 1 cup.

In the same small bowl, beat the egg with the buttermilk, baking soda, and vanilla. Pour the wet ingredients into the dry, stirring just until combined. Fold in the walnuts and raisins.

Pour the batter into the prepared pan, and sprinkle it with the reserved flour mixture.

Bake for 45 to 50 minutes, until a toothpick inserted in the center of the cake comes out clean. Let it cool for a few minutes before removing the sides of the pan.

Two-Berry Coffee Cake

This moist, fruity coffee cake produces three layers of flavors and textures. The preparation involves a few extra steps, but the result is wonderful to look at as well as to eat.

10 to 12 servings

1½ cups fresh or frozen raspberries
1½ cups fresh or frozen blueberries
1 tablespoon cornstarch or arrowroot
1 cup unbleached white flour
1½ cups whole wheat pastry flour
¾ cup (1½ sticks) butter or margarine, chilled
½ teaspoon baking powder
½ teaspoon baking soda
1 large egg
½ cup honey
¾ cup buttermilk
2 tablespoons wheat germ
4 tablespoons raw or maple sugar

Preheat the oven to 350 degrees. Grease a flat-bottomed, 10-inch springform pan.

Put the berries in a small saucepan, and sprinkle with cornstarch. Cook over low heat, stirring, until thickened, about 4 to 7 minutes, and remove from the heat.

Stir together the flours in a large bowl, and cut in the butter until the mixture resembles coarse cornmeal. (You can perform this step in the food processor, too.)

Set aside a quarter of the flour mixture (about ¾ cup), and stir the baking powder and soda into the rest.

In another bowl, beat the egg with the honey and buttermilk.

Pour the liquid ingredients into the dry, stirring just until combined.

Pour two-thirds of the batter into the prepared pan. Spread on the fruit filling, and spoon the remaining batter in small mounds over the fruit.

Stir the wheat germ and sugar into the reserved flour-butter mixture, and sprinkle it over the top of the cake.

Bake for about 45 minutes, until golden brown. Let the cake cool for a few minutes before removing the sides of the pan.

Rhubarb-Walnut-Buttermilk Coffee Cake

★ **BEGINNER-FRIENDLY**

Rhubarb is prolific in the hills of Vermont, and this is a delectable way to use it.

10 to 12 servings

TOPPING

¼ cup honey

1 tablespoon butter or margarine, softened

½ cup chopped walnuts

2 tablespoons rolled oats

1 teaspoon ground cinnamon

1 tablespoon grated orange peel

CAKE

1¼ cups unbleached white flour

1 cup whole wheat pastry flour

½ cup rolled oats

1 teaspoon baking soda

1 teaspoon ground cinnamon

⅛ teaspoon salt

1 tablespoon grated orange peel

1 large egg

1 cup honey

⅔ cup canola oil

¾ cup buttermilk

1 teaspoon vanilla extract

2 cups sliced rhubarb (1-inch pieces)

Preheat the oven to 350 degrees. Grease a 9 by 13-inch baking pan.

For the topping, in a small bowl, beat the ¼ cup honey with the butter, and stir in the walnuts, oats, cinnamon, and orange peel. Set aside.

For the cake, in a large bowl, stir together the flours, oats, baking soda, cinnamon, salt, and orange peel. In another bowl, beat the egg with the honey, oil, buttermilk, and vanilla. Pour the wet ingredients into the dry, stirring just until combined. Fold in the rhubarb.

Pour the batter into the prepared pan, and sprinkle it with the topping mixture.

Bake for 40 to 45 minutes, until the cake is lightly browned and a toothpick inserted in the center comes out clean. Let it cool for 15 minutes before cutting.

 **MUFFINS**

Oatmeal-Raisin-Bran Muffins

★ BEGINNER-FRIENDLY

Sweet, chewy, and full of fiber.

12 muffins

¾ cup whole wheat pastry flour
1 cup unbleached white flour
1 cup rolled oats
½ cup bran
1 tablespoon baking powder
½ teaspoon baking soda
¼ teaspoon salt
½ teaspoon ground cinnamon
2 large eggs
½ cup honey
½ cup milk
½ cup canola oil
¾ cup raisins

Preheat the oven to 400 degrees. Grease a 12-cup muffin tin.

Stir together the flours, oats, bran, baking powder, baking soda, salt, and cinnamon in a medium-size mixing bowl.

In another bowl, beat the eggs with the honey, milk, and oil.

Pour the wet ingredients into the dry, stirring just until combined. Fold in the raisins.

Spoon the batter into the prepared muffin cups.

Bake for 15 to 18 minutes, until golden brown. Let the muffins cool for a few minutes before removing them from the pan.

Peach Pecan Muffins

★ **BEGINNER-FRIENDLY**

Bake these early in the morning on what promises to be a hot summer day, and then enjoy them in the sunshine with iced tea or iced coffee. Frozen peaches can be substituted for a wintertime treat.

12 muffins

1 cup unbleached white flour
1¾ cups whole wheat pastry flour
1 tablespoon baking powder
¼ teaspoon salt
½ teaspoon ground cinnamon
2 large eggs
½ cup honey
½ cup canola oil
1 cup milk
1½ cups chopped peaches
1 cup coarsely chopped pecans

Preheat the oven to 400 degrees. Grease a 12-cup muffin tin.

Stir together the flours, baking powder, salt, and cinnamon in a medium-size mixing bowl.

In another bowl, beat the eggs with the honey, oil, and milk.

Pour the wet ingredients into the dry, stirring just until combined. Fold in the peaches and ¾ cup of the pecans.

Spoon the batter into the prepared muffin cups, and sprinkle on the remaining pecans.

Bake for 18 to 20 minutes, until golden. Let the muffins cool for a few minutes before removing them from the pan.

Lemon Raspberry Muffins

★ **BEGINNER-FRIENDLY**

*F*resh *raspberries and lemon juice combine in these tempting summertime muffins.*

12 muffins

1 ¼ cups whole wheat pastry flour
1 ¼ cups unbleached white flour
½ teaspoon salt
1 tablespoon baking powder
2 large eggs
½ cup honey
½ cup canola oil
½ cup fresh lemon juice
½ cup milk
1 teaspoon vanilla extract
1 ½ cups fresh or frozen raspberries

Preheat the oven to 400 degrees. Grease a 12-cup muffin tin.

Stir together the flours, salt, and baking powder in a medium-size bowl.

In another bowl, beat the eggs with the honey, oil, lemon juice, milk, and vanilla.

Pour the wet ingredients into the dry, stirring just until combined. Fold in the raspberries.

Spoon the batter into the prepared muffin cups.

Bake for 18 to 20 minutes, until golden. Let the muffins cool for a few minutes before removing them from the pan.

Sweet Carolina Cranberry Muffins

*T*he tart cranberries and sweet potatoes complement each other beautifully, and produce a muffin that bursts with flavor. Bake a sweet potato the next time you're using your oven, and store it in the refrigerator until you're ready to make these. (It will keep fine for several days.)

12 muffins

1¼ cups whole wheat pastry flour
1¼ cups unbleached white flour
2 teaspoons baking powder
1 teaspoon ground cinnamon
¼ teaspoon ground nutmeg
¼ teaspoon salt
2 large eggs
⅔ cup honey
1 cup mashed, baked sweet potato (1 large)
½ cup canola oil
¾ cup buttermilk
1 cup fresh cranberries (large ones cut in half)

Preheat the oven to 400 degrees. Grease a 12-cup muffin tin.

Stir together the flours, baking powder, cinnamon, nutmeg, and salt in a medium-size mixing bowl.

In another bowl, beat the eggs with the honey, and then beat in the sweet potato, oil, and buttermilk.

Pour the wet ingredients into the dry, stirring just until combined. Fold in the cranberries.

Spoon the batter into the prepared muffin cups, and bake for 18 to 20 minutes, until golden. Let the muffins cool for a few minutes before removing them from the pan.

Banana-Date-Oat Muffins

★ **BEGINNER-FRIENDLY**

A friend told me that these sweet, chewy muffins are my best ones! I buy organic bananas at our food co-op to avoid the pesticides used on commercially grown imports.

12 muffins

1½ cups rolled oats
1 cup milk
½ cup canola oil
½ cup honey
2 large eggs
½ cup mashed banana (1 medium banana)
1 cup whole wheat pastry flour
1 cup unbleached white flour
1 tablespoon baking powder
½ teaspoon salt
1 cup chopped dates

Preheat the oven to 400 degrees. Grease a 12-cup muffin tin.

Stir the oats into the milk in a medium-size bowl, and let them soak for 10 minutes. Stir in the oil, honey, eggs, and mashed banana, mixing well.

In another bowl, stir together the flours, baking powder, and salt.

Pour the wet ingredients into the dry, stirring just until combined. Fold in the dates.

Spoon the batter into the prepared muffin cups, and bake for 18 to 20 minutes, until golden. Let the muffins cool for a few minutes before removing them from the pan.

Zucchini-Raisin-Walnut Muffins

★ **BEGINNER-FRIENDLY**

The grated veggies add color, flavor, moisture, and natural sweetness to these teatime treats. You can substitute grated carrot for some or all of the zucchini.

12 muffins

1¼ cups whole wheat pastry flour
1¼ cups unbleached white flour
2 teaspoons baking powder
¼ teaspoon salt
½ teaspoon ground cinnamon
2 large eggs
½ cup honey
⅓ cup canola oil
1 cup milk
1½ cups grated zucchini
½ cup raisins
¾ cup chopped walnuts

Preheat the oven to 400 degrees. Grease a 12-cup muffin tin.

Stir together the flours, baking powder, salt, and cinnamon in a medium-size bowl.

In another bowl, beat the eggs with the honey, oil, and milk.

Pour the wet ingredients into the dry, stirring just until combined. Fold in the zucchini, raisins, and ½ cup of the walnuts.

Spoon the batter into the prepared muffin cups, and sprinkle with the remaining walnuts.

Bake for 18 to 20 minutes, until golden. Let the muffins cool for a few minutes before removing them from the pan.

Toasted Almond–Bran Muffins

Toasting the almonds gives these muffins a richer flavor and color. If you like the flavor of roasted almonds, try spreading almond butter on toasted bread for a tasty treat!

12 muffins

1 cup sliced or slivered almonds
1 cup whole wheat pastry flour
1 cup unbleached white flour
⅔ cup bran
2 teaspoons baking powder
¼ teaspoon salt
2 large eggs
½ cup canola oil
½ cup honey or maple syrup
1 cup milk
2 teaspoons almond extract

Preheat the oven to 400 degrees. Grease a 12-cup muffin tin.

Spread the almonds on a cookie sheet and toast them in the oven for 5 minutes, until lightly browned. (They burn quickly, so keep checking them.) Grind the almonds into a fine powder in the food processor or blender.

Stir together the ground almonds, flours, bran, baking powder, and salt in a medium-size bowl.

In another bowl, beat the eggs with the oil, honey, milk, and almond extract.

Pour the wet ingredients into the dry, stirring just until combined.

Spoon the batter into the prepared muffin cups, and bake for 18 to 20 minutes, until golden. Let the muffins cool for a few minutes before removing them from the pan.

Pumpkin Pecan Muffins

★ **BEGINNER-FRIENDLY**

These moist, flavorful muffins are a perfect way to use up leftover pumpkin or winter squash.

12 muffins

1¼ cups whole wheat pastry flour
1¼ cups unbleached white flour
½ teaspoon ground cinnamon
½ teaspoon ground nutmeg
1 tablespoon baking powder
½ teaspoon salt
⅔ cup honey
⅓ cup butter or margarine, softened
2 large eggs
1 cup pureed pumpkin or winter squash
¾ cup milk
½ cup chopped pecans

Preheat the oven to 400 degrees. Grease a 12-cup muffin tin.

Stir together the flours, cinnamon, nutmeg, baking powder, and salt in a medium-size bowl.

In another bowl, beat the honey with the butter. Beat in the eggs, pumpkin puree, and milk. (If the puree is thin, reduce the milk to ½ cup.)

Pour the wet ingredients into the dry, stirring just until combined. Fold in the pecans.

Spoon the batter into the prepared muffin cups, and bake for 18 to 20 minutes, until golden. Let the muffins cool for a few minutes before removing them from the pan.

Gingerbread Walnut Muffins

★ BEGINNER-FRIENDLY

12 muffins

½ cup (1 stick) butter or margarine
1 tablespoon peeled and grated fresh ginger
½ cup blackstrap molasses
¼ cup honey
2 large eggs
⅓ cup milk
1½ cups whole wheat pastry flour
1½ cups unbleached white flour
1½ teaspoons baking powder
½ teaspoon baking soda
¼ teaspoon salt
½ teaspoon ground nutmeg
½ teaspoon ground cinnamon
¾ cup chopped walnuts

Preheat the oven to 400 degrees. Grease a 12-cup muffin tin.

Melt the butter in a saucepan, and stir in the ginger. Remove the pan from the heat and stir in the molasses and honey.

In a medium-size bowl, beat the eggs with the milk. Pour in the molasses mixture, and beat again.

In another bowl, stir together the flours, baking powder, baking soda, salt, nutmeg, and cinnamon.

Pour the wet ingredients into the dry, stirring just until combined. Fold in ½ cup of the walnuts.

Spoon the batter into the prepared muffin cups and sprinkle on the remaining walnuts. Bake for 15 to 18 minutes, until golden. Let the muffins cool for a few minutes before removing them from the pan.

Winter Fruit and Oat Muffins

★ BEGINNER-FRIENDLY

Add *your favorite dried fruits—raisins, currants, chopped dried apricots, dates, apples, peaches, etc.—and these muffins will start you off right on a cold morning.*

12 muffins

1½ cups rolled oats
1 cup whole wheat pastry flour
1 cup unbleached white flour
1 tablespoon baking powder
1 teaspoon baking soda
¼ teaspoon salt
2 teaspoons ground cinnamon
2 large eggs
¾ cup honey
⅔ cup buttermilk
½ cup canola oil
1 cup chopped mixed dried fruit
½ cup chopped walnuts (optional)

Preheat the oven to 400 degrees. Grease a 12-cup muffin tin.

Stir together the oats, flours, baking powder, baking soda, salt, and cinnamon in a medium-size bowl.

In another bowl, beat the eggs with the honey, buttermilk, and oil.

Pour the wet ingredients into the dry, stirring just until combined. Fold in the fruit and walnuts, if desired.

Spoon the batter into the prepared muffin cups, and bake for 18 to 20 minutes, until golden. Let the muffins cool for a few minutes before removing them from the pan.

Cranberry-Walnut-Cornmeal Muffins

★ **BEGINNER-FRIENDLY**

The pockets of tart berries and crunchy walnuts are a taste sensation.

12 muffins

1 cup whole wheat pastry flour
1 ¼ cups unbleached white flour
¾ cup yellow cornmeal
1 tablespoon baking powder
½ teaspoon salt
2 large eggs
⅔ cup honey
1 cup milk
½ cup canola oil
1 ½ cups fresh cranberries
½ cup chopped walnuts

Preheat the oven to 400 degrees. Grease a 12-cup muffin tin.

Stir together the flours, cornmeal, baking powder, and salt in a medium-size bowl.

In another bowl, beat the eggs with the honey, milk, and oil.

Pour the wet ingredients into the dry, stirring just until combined. Fold in the cranberries and walnuts.

Spoon the batter into the prepared muffin cups (they will be nearly full). Bake for 18 to 20 minutes, until golden. Let the muffins cool for a few minutes before removing them from the pan.

Chocolate Pecan Muffins

★ **BEGINNER-FRIENDLY**

*T*he bits of bittersweet chocolate play off nicely against the cinnamon and pecans.

12 muffins

1 cup unbleached white flour
1¼ cups whole wheat pastry flour
2 teaspoons ground cinnamon
½ teaspoon salt
2 teaspoons baking powder
½ teaspoon baking soda
2 ounces bittersweet chocolate, chopped
2 large eggs
½ cup honey
¾ cup milk
½ cup canola oil
¾ cup coarsely chopped pecans

Preheat the oven to 400 degrees. Grease a 12-cup muffin tin.

Stir together the flours, cinnamon, salt, baking powder, baking soda, and chocolate in a medium-size bowl.

In another bowl, beat the eggs with the honey, milk, and oil.

Pour the wet ingredients into the dry, stirring just until combined. Fold in ½ cup of the pecans.

Spoon the batter into the prepared muffin cups, and sprinkle with the remaining pecans.

Bake for 15 to 18 minutes, until golden. Let the muffins cool for a few minutes before removing them from the pan.

 SCONES

Scones are quick to prepare, and go well with eggs at breakfast, soup at lunch, or a cup of tea anytime.

Oatmeal Date Scones

*T*he oats and dates create a moist, chewy texture.

8 to 10 large scones

1 cup unbleached white flour
1¼ cups whole wheat pastry flour
1 cup rolled oats
1 tablespoon baking powder
½ teaspoon baking soda
½ teaspoon salt
6 tablespoons butter or margarine, chilled
1 large egg
¾ cup buttermilk
3 tablespoons honey
½ teaspoon vanilla extract
½ cup chopped dates

Preheat the oven to 400 degrees.

Combine the flours, oats, baking powder, baking soda, and salt in a medium-size bowl or a food processor, and mix well.

With a pastry blender or the pulsing action of the processor, cut the butter into the flour mixture until it resembles coarse cornmeal.

In another bowl, beat the egg with the buttermilk, honey, and vanilla.

Pour the wet ingredients into the dry, stirring or pulsing just until combined (the dough will be sticky). Fold in the dates.

On a floured surface, form the dough into a ball, and pat it into a ¾-inch-thick circle. Cut the circle into eight or ten wedges, and transfer them to a large ungreased baking sheet.

Bake for 15 to 18 minutes, until golden. Serve warm.

Ginger Currant Scones

Ginger, molasses, and currants are an unusual and pleasing combination.

10 to 12 scones

1 ½ cups whole wheat pastry flour
1 ½ cups unbleached white flour
½ teaspoon baking soda
1 tablespoon baking powder
½ teaspoon salt
¼ teaspoon ground nutmeg
1 teaspoon ground cinnamon
2 teaspoons ground ginger
1 tablespoon peeled and minced fresh ginger
½ cup (1 stick) butter or margarine
1 large egg
⅓ cup molasses
3 tablespoons honey
½ cup plain yogurt
½ cup currants
1 tablespoon raw sugar for sprinkling

Preheat the oven to 350 degrees.

Combine the flours, baking soda, baking powder, salt, nutmeg, cinnamon, and ground and fresh ginger in a medium-size bowl or a food processor, and mix well.

With a pastry blender or the pulsing action of the processor, cut the butter into the flour mixture until it resembles coarse cornmeal.

In another bowl, beat the egg with the molasses, honey, and yogurt.

Pour the wet ingredients into the dry, stirring or pulsing just until combined (the dough will be sticky). Fold in the currants.

On a floured surface, form the dough into a ball, and pat it into a ¾-inch-thick circle. Cut the circle into ten or twelve wedges, and transfer them to an ungreased baking sheet. Sprinkle with raw sugar.

Bake for 15 to 18 minutes, until golden. Serve warm.

 **BISCUITS**

Raisin Cinnamon Biscuits

★ **BEGINNER-FRIENDLY**

About 15 biscuits

1½ cups whole wheat pastry flour
1¾ cups unbleached white flour
1½ tablespoons baking powder
1 teaspoon salt
1 teaspoon ground cinnamon
6 tablespoons butter or margarine, softened
1 large egg
½ cup honey
½ cup milk
1 cup raisins

Preheat the oven to 400 degrees. Grease one large or two small baking sheets.

Stir together the flours, baking powder, salt, and cinnamon in a medium-size bowl.

In another bowl, beat the butter with the egg, honey, and milk.

Pour the wet ingredients into the dry, stirring just until combined (the dough will be sticky). Fold in the raisins.

On a floured surface, roll the dough to a thickness of ½ inch. Dip a 3-inch biscuit cutter or jar lid in flour, and cut out the biscuits, flouring the cutter again as needed. Reroll the dough, and cut out as many biscuits as you can.

Place the biscuits on the prepared baking sheet 2 inches apart, and bake for 10 to 12 minutes, until lightly browned.

Sour Cream and Dill Biscuits

★ BEGINNER-FRIENDLY

Fresh dill is a must for these irresistible biscuits.

About 15 biscuits

1½ cups unbleached white flour
1½ cups whole wheat pastry flour
1½ tablespoons baking powder
½ teaspoon baking soda
1 teaspoon salt
6 tablespoons butter or margarine
1 teaspoon honey
1 cup sour cream
3 tablespoons chopped fresh dill
¼ cup milk

Preheat the oven to 425 degrees. Grease one large or two small baking sheets.

Combine the flours, baking powder, baking soda, and salt in a medium-size bowl or a food processor, and mix well.

With a pastry blender or the pulsing action of the processor, cut in the butter until the mixture resembles coarse cornmeal.

Beat the honey with the sour cream, dill, and milk.

Pour the wet ingredients into the center of the flour mixture. Using a spoon or the pulsing action of the processor, mix the dough just until combined.

Roll the dough into a ½-inch thickness on a floured surface. Dip a 3-inch biscuit cutter or jar lid in flour, and cut out the biscuits, flouring the cutter again as needed. Reroll the dough, and cut out as many biscuits as you can.

Place the biscuits on the prepared baking sheet 2 inches apart, and bake for 10 to 12 minutes, until lightly browned.

Ethereal Buttermilk Biscuits

hree leavening agents—yeast, baking powder, and baking soda—and a second rising give these biscuits their ethereal lightness of being. Start them the night before so the dough has time to rise for 8 hours in the refrigerator. The biscuits need a second rising of 1 hour after being cut into shape.

16 to 18 biscuits

1½ teaspoons active dry yeast
⅓ cup warm water
1½ cups unbleached white flour
1½ cups whole wheat pastry flour
1 tablespoon baking powder
1 teaspoon salt
½ cup (1 stick) butter or margarine, softened
½ teaspoon baking soda
2 tablespoons honey
1⅓ cups buttermilk

Stir the yeast into the warm water, and set it aside until it foams, about 10 minutes.

Meanwhile, combine the flours, baking powder, and salt in a medium-size bowl, mixing well.

Cut the butter into the flour mixture with a pastry blender until it resembles coarse cornmeal.

In another bowl, beat the baking soda with the honey and buttermilk.

Pour the yeast and buttermilk mixtures into the flour mixture, stirring just until combined. Cover the bowl with plastic wrap and refrigerate for 8 hours or overnight, until doubled in size.

About an hour and a half before serving, knead the dough lightly on a floured surface, and roll it into a ½-inch thickness. Grease two baking sheets.

Dip a 2½-inch biscuit cutter or jar lid in flour and cut out the biscuits, flouring the cutter again as needed. Reroll the dough, and cut out as many biscuits as you can.

Place the biscuits 2 inches apart on the prepared baking sheets, cover with plastic wrap, and let them rise in a warm place for about an hour, until doubled in size.

Preheat the oven to 400 degrees.

Uncover the biscuits, and bake them for 12 to 15 minutes, until golden. Serve warm.

Cornmeal and Cheddar Buttermilk Biscuits

★ BEGINNER-FRIENDLY

A *melt-in-your-mouth kind of biscuit.*

About 15 biscuits

1 cup unbleached white flour
1 cup whole wheat pastry flour
1 cup yellow cornmeal
1½ tablespoons baking powder
½ teaspoon baking soda
1 teaspoon salt
6 tablespoons butter or margarine, softened
1 teaspoon honey
⅞ cup buttermilk (1 cup less 2 tablespoons)
1 cup grated extra-sharp Cheddar cheese (4 ounces)

Preheat the oven to 425 degrees. Grease one large or two small baking sheets.

Stir together the flours, cornmeal, baking powder, baking soda, and salt in a medium-size bowl.

Cut the butter into the flour mixture with a pastry blender until it resembles coarse cornmeal.

Mix the honey with the buttermilk, and pour it into the flour mixture, stirring just until blended. Fold in the cheese.

On a floured surface, roll the dough into a ½-inch thickness. Dip a 3-inch biscuit cutter or jar lid in flour and cut out the biscuits, flouring the cutter again as needed. Reroll the dough, and cut out as many biscuits as you can.

Place the biscuits on the prepared baking sheet 2 inches apart, and bake for 10 to 12 minutes, until lightly browned. Serve immediately.

Cranberry–Sour Cream Biscuits

★ **BEGINNER-FRIENDLY**

These light and buttery biscuits are perfect for Thanksgiving or Christmas.

15 biscuits

1¼ cups unbleached white flour
1 cup whole wheat pastry flour
½ cup yellow cornmeal
½ teaspoon baking soda
1½ tablespoons baking powder
½ teaspoon ground cinnamon
⅛ teaspoon ground nutmeg
6 tablespoons butter or margarine, softened
1 large egg
½ cup honey
¾ cup sour cream
¼ cup milk
1 cup fresh cranberries, coarsely chopped

Preheat the oven to 425 degrees. Grease one large or two small baking sheets.

Stir together the flours, cornmeal, baking soda, baking powder, cinnamon, and nutmeg in a medium-size bowl.

Cut the butter into the flour mixture until it resembles coarse cornmeal.

In another bowl, beat the egg with the honey, sour cream, and milk.

Pour the wet ingredients into the dry, stirring just until combined. Add the cranberries, and knead the mixture until smooth.

Roll the dough into a ½-inch thickness on a floured surface. Dip a 3-inch biscuit cutter or jar lid in flour and cut out the biscuits, flouring the cutter again as needed. Reroll the dough, and cut out as many biscuits as you can.

Place the biscuits on the prepared baking sheet 2 inches apart, and bake for 10 to 12 minutes, until lightly browned. Serve immediately.

★ QUICK BREADS

Lemon–Poppy Seed Bread

★ BEGINNER-FRIENDLY

10 to 12 servings

½ cup milk
⅓ cup poppy seeds
¾ cup honey
¾ cup (1½ sticks) butter or margarine, softened
2 large eggs
1 tablespoon fresh lemon juice
1 tablespoon grated lemon peel
1 cup unbleached white flour
1 cup whole wheat pastry flour
1½ teaspoons baking powder
1½ teaspoons baking soda
½ teaspoon salt

Preheat the oven to 325 degrees. Grease a 9 by 5-inch loaf pan.

In a small saucepan, heat the milk just until the boiling point. Remove the pan from the heat, add the poppy seeds, and set them aside to soak.

In a medium-size bowl, beat the honey with the butter until smooth. Beat in the eggs, lemon juice, and lemon peel.

In another bowl, stir together the flours, baking powder, baking soda, and salt.

Add half the dry ingredients to the honey mixture, and beat just until smooth. Beat in the milk mixture and then the remaining dry ingredients. Pour the batter into the prepared pan.

Bake for 45 to 50 minutes, until a toothpick inserted in the center of the bread comes out clean. Cool on a rack for about 10 minutes before removing from the pan. Serve warm or at room temperature. This bread freezes well and will stay moist when wrapped in plastic and refrigerated for a few days.

Apple Bread with Pecan Filling

*Y*ou may substitute chopped pears for the apples in this moist bread with its heavenly filling.

10 to 12 servings

FILLING

¼ cup honey
½ cup coarsely chopped pecans
2 tablespoons unbleached white flour
2 teaspoons ground cinnamon
¼ teaspoon ground nutmeg
2 tablespoons butter or margarine, softened

BREAD

½ cup (1 stick) butter or margarine, softened
¾ cup honey
2 large eggs
1 teaspoon vanilla extract
½ cup plain yogurt or sour cream
¾ cup whole wheat pastry flour
1 cup unbleached white flour
1 teaspoon baking powder
¾ teaspoon baking soda
½ teaspoon ground cinnamon
¼ teaspoon ground nutmeg
¼ teaspoon ground ginger
1 cup chopped unpeeled apple
¼ cup coarsely chopped pecans

Preheat the oven to 350 degrees. Grease a 9 by 5-inch loaf pan.

For the filling, stir together the honey, pecans, flour, cinnamon, nutmeg, and butter until well combined. Set aside.

For the bread, in a medium-size bowl, beat the ½ cup butter with the ¾ cup honey, eggs, vanilla, and yogurt until smooth.

In another bowl, stir together the flours, baking powder, baking soda, cinnamon, nutmeg, and ginger.

Pour the wet ingredients into the dry, stirring just until combined.

Pour about half of the batter into the prepared pan. Carefully spread on the filling, and sprinkle on the apples. Pour the remaining batter into the pan, and sprinkle it with the chopped pecans.

Bake for 50 to 55 minutes, until a toothpick inserted in the center of the bread comes out clean. Cool on a rack for about 10 minutes before removing from the pan. Serve warm or at room temperature. This bread freezes well and will stay moist when wrapped in plastic and refrigerated for a few days.

Oatmeal-Molasses Soda Bread

★ **BEGINNER-FRIENDLY**

Molasses adds a depth of flavor and color.

8 to 10 servings

1½ cups unbleached white flour, plus additional for sprinkling
1½ cups whole wheat flour
¾ cup rolled oats plus extra for sprinkling
1 teaspoon salt
1½ teaspoons baking soda
½ teaspoon baking powder
1 large egg
1¼ cups buttermilk
¼ cup blackstrap molasses

Preheat the oven to 350 degrees. Grease a 10-inch pie pan.

Stir together the flours, ¾ cup rolled oats, salt, baking soda, and baking powder in a medium-size bowl.

In another bowl, beat the egg with the buttermilk and molasses.

Pour the wet ingredients into the dry, mixing well.

Turn the dough out onto a floured surface, and knead it until smooth, about 5 minutes.

Pat the dough into the prepared pan, and sprinkle it with a little flour and rolled oats, pressing the oats lightly so they stick.

Bake for 30 to 35 minutes, until golden. Allow bread to cool for 5 to 10 minutes. Serve warm with butter or margarine and jam on the side.

Pumpkin Cranberry Bread

★ BEGINNER-FRIENDLY

Bake this moist, flavorful bread in the fall when cranberries and pumpkins abound.

10 to 12 servings

2 large eggs
¾ cup honey
½ cup canola oil
¼ cup (½ stick) butter or margarine, softened
1 teaspoon vanilla extract
1 tablespoon grated orange peel
1 cup pureed pumpkin or winter squash
1 cup whole wheat pastry flour
1 cup unbleached white flour
1 teaspoon baking powder
1 teaspoon baking soda
1 teaspoon ground cinnamon
¼ teaspoon ground nutmeg
¼ teaspoon ground ginger
1 cup fresh cranberries, coarsely chopped
¾ cup coarsely chopped walnuts

Preheat the oven to 350 degrees. Grease a 9 by 5-inch loaf pan.

In a medium-size bowl, beat the eggs with the honey, oil, butter, vanilla, orange peel, and pumpkin puree.

In another bowl, stir together the flours, baking powder, baking soda, cinnamon, nutmeg, and ginger.

Pour the wet ingredients into the dry, and mix just until combined. Fold in the cranberries and ½ cup of the walnuts.

Pour the batter into the prepared pan, and sprinkle with the remaining walnuts.

Bake for 55 to 60 minutes, until a toothpick inserted in the center of the bread comes out clean. Cool on a rack for about 10 minutes before removing from the pan. Serve warm or at room temperature. This bread freezes well and will stay moist when wrapped in plastic and refrigerated for a few days.

Cheddar, Scallion, and Jalapeño Corn Bread

★ **BEGINNER-FRIENDLY**

This spicy corn bread goes great with a steaming bowl of chowder or chili on a cold, damp day. For a tamer but still flavorful bread, seed the jalapeño pepper, or leave it out altogether.

8 to 10 servings

1 cup yellow cornmeal
½ cup unbleached white flour
½ cup whole wheat pastry flour
2 teaspoons baking powder
½ teaspoon baking soda
¼ teaspoon salt
2 large eggs
1 cup buttermilk
2 tablespoons blackstrap molasses
¼ cup (½ stick) butter or margarine, melted
1 small jalapeño pepper, minced
3 scallions, thinly sliced
1 cup grated extra-sharp Cheddar cheese (4 ounces)

Preheat the oven to 350 degrees. Grease a 10-inch pie pan.

Stir together the cornmeal, flours, baking powder, baking soda, and salt in a medium-size bowl.

In another bowl, beat the eggs with the buttermilk, molasses, and butter.

Pour the wet ingredients into the dry, stirring just until combined. Fold in the jalapeño, scallions, and cheese.

Pour the batter into the prepared pan, and bake for 20 to 25 minutes, until a toothpick inserted in the center of the bread comes out clean. Allow the bread to cool for 5 to 10 minutes. Serve warm with butter or margarine on the side.

Dill-Chive Bread

Fresh herbs are a must for this delectable bread. I love to make it when dill is abundant in my garden, or when I find a big, beautiful bunch of it at the market. It's great for sandwiches, or all by itself.

2 loaves or rounds

2 cups warm water
2 teaspoons active dry yeast
1 teaspoon honey
2 cups low-fat cottage cheese
1 teaspoon salt
3 tablespoons finely chopped fresh chives
1 cup minced fresh dill
3½ cups whole wheat bread flour
3½ to 4 cups unbleached white flour

Combine the warm water, yeast, and honey in a large bowl. When the yeast begins to bubble, stir in the cottage cheese, salt, chives, and dill.

Stir in 1½ cups of the whole wheat bread flour and 1½ cups of the unbleached white flour, mixing well. Cover with plastic wrap and set aside in a warm place for about 1 hour, until the dough doubles in size.

Punch down the dough, and stir in the remaining 2 cups of whole wheat flour plus 1½ cups of the unbleached flour.

Turn the dough out onto a floured surface, and knead it for 10 to 15 minutes, adding enough additional unbleached flour (½ to 1 cup) to produce a soft, smooth, elastic dough.

Grease two 9-inch pie pans or two 8 by 4-inch loaf pans. Divide the dough in half, shape the halves into rounds or loaves, and place them in the prepared pans.

Set the dough aside in a warm place to rise for about 1 hour, until doubled in size. After about 45 minutes, preheat the oven to 375 degrees.

Bake for 45 to 50 minutes, until the loaves are golden. Let them cool on a rack for a few minutes before removing them from the pan. Serve warm.

Oatmeal Bread

I love the chewy texture that oats add to baked goods, and the fiber they add to your diet.

2 loaves or rounds

3 cups plus 2 tablespoons rolled oats
4 cups boiling water
2 tablespoons active dry yeast
3 tablespoons canola oil plus extra for brushing
3 cups whole wheat bread flour
3 to 4 cups unbleached white flour
1 tablespoon salt
½ cup honey

Put 3 cups of the oats in a large bowl, and pour the boiling water over them. Stir well, and set aside.

When the oats are just warm to the touch, stir in the yeast, 3 tablespoons oil, 1 cup of the whole wheat flour, and 1 cup of the unbleached flour. Cover the bowl with plastic wrap, and set it aside in a warm place for about 1 hour, until the dough has doubled in size.

Punch down the dough, and stir in the salt and honey. With a spoon or your hands, slowly work in 2 more cups of the whole wheat flour and 2 more cups of the unbleached flour.

Turn the dough onto a floured surface, and knead it for about 10 minutes, adding enough additional unbleached flour (about ½ to 1 cup) to produce a soft, smooth, elastic dough.

Grease two 9-inch pie pans or two 8 by 4-inch loaf pans. Divide the dough in half, shape the halves into rounds or loaves, and place them in the prepared pans. Brush the tops with canola oil and sprinkle a tablespoon of oats onto each loaf, pressing it slightly so it sticks.

Set the dough aside in a warm place to rise for about 1 hour, until doubled in size. After about 45 minutes, preheat the oven to 375 degrees.

Bake for 45 to 50 minutes, until the loaves are golden. Let them cool on a rack for a few minutes before removing them from the pan. Serve warm.

A POTPOURRI

Banana Fritters

Fritters are the Caribbean's answer to doughnuts. They're best eaten fresh, sprinkled with sugar or dipped in sour cream and maple syrup. Or serve them plain on the side with a frittata or other egg dish.

6 to 8 servings

¾ cup whole wheat pastry flour
1 cup unbleached white flour
½ cup yellow cornmeal
1 teaspoon baking powder
½ teaspoon ground cinnamon
½ teaspoon salt
½ cup (1 stick) butter or margarine
1 cup mashed bananas (2 medium bananas)
1 tablespoon rum
1 teaspoon vanilla extract
Canola oil for frying
Maple syrup for dipping
Sour cream for dipping

Combine the flours, cornmeal, baking powder, cinnamon, and salt in a medium-size bowl or a food processor.

Cut in the butter using a pastry blender or the pulsing action of the processor until the mixture resembles coarse cornmeal.

Add the bananas, rum, and vanilla, and mix just until smooth. The dough will be slightly sticky.

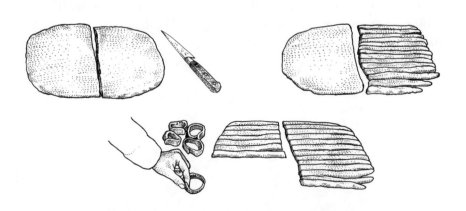

Turn the dough out onto a floured surface, and roll it into a rectangle about 12 inches wide, 16 inches long, and ½ inch thick. Cut the dough in half lengthwise, into two 8 by 12-inch rectangles. Then cut it into strips 8 inches long and ½ inch wide. Pinch the ends of each strip together to form a circle.

Heat 1 to 1½ inches oil in a medium-size saucepan over medium-high heat. To test the temperature, put a tiny piece of dough in the pan; if the oil foams up immediately and the dough bubbles to the surface, it's ready.

Cook two or three dough circles at a time until golden. Drain on paper towels. Serve immediately, with maple syrup and sour cream for dipping.

Crunchy Almond Granola

★ BEGINNER-FRIENDLY

This chewy, sweet-tart granola is a favorite of mine; I can't resist grabbing handfuls to snack on while it's cooling.

6 cups

4 cups rolled oats
¾ cup raw almonds, sliced in half
½ cup sesame or sunflower seeds
¾ cup finely chopped dried apples
½ cup honey
2 tablespoons maple syrup
⅓ cup canola oil
¾ cup currants

Preheat the oven to 325 degrees.

In a large bowl, stir together the oats, almonds, seeds, apples, honey, maple syrup, oil, and 2 tablespoons of water. Mix well, and spread onto a large baking sheet. (The pan should have sides.)

Bake until golden brown, 30 to 35 minutes, stirring well every 5 or 10 minutes. Let the granola cool in the pan. Stir in the currants, and store in an airtight container. The granola will keep for 4 to 6 weeks.

Satisfying Soups

There's nothing like a bowl of hot, steamy soup on a cold, damp day. It warms the kitchen as it simmers in the pot, warms your hands as you wrap them around the soup bowl, and warms you up from the inside out as you eat it. It has a healing quality.

A chilled soup is just as welcome on a hot, muggy summer day. It refreshes you, cools you down, and helps you savor the hot weather before it's gone.

For a first course, choose a soup that complements your meal and doesn't duplicate flavors and ingredients. Light vegetable soups like Creamy Asparagus (page 80) and Potato-Carrot-Spinach (page 91) make excellent starters.

Chilies, chowders, and hearty soups like Nepal Country Vegetable Soup (page 89) and Pennsylvania Cabbage-Mushroom Soup with Dumplings (page 84) need nothing more than good bread and a green salad to make a satisfying meal.

With a well-stocked kitchen, you're ready to make soup anytime. I like to keep dried beans, pasta, grains, canned tomatoes, onions, garlic, celery, potatoes, and carrots on hand. In winter months I stock up on broccoli, winter squash, and other fresh produce at the grocery store or co-op, and in summer I rely on my garden.

To make a good pot of soup, you need a good soup pot. It should be big enough—at least 3 or 4 quarts—so that you can give your soup a good stir without splashing over the sides. It should also have a nice, thick bottom to prevent scorching. I make most of my soups in a 4-quart cast-iron pot that's blackened with use. Other good choices are enamel-coated cast iron and heavy-gauge stainless steel. (Stainless-steel pots need a copper or aluminum bottom or core to spread the heat evenly.)

A blender or food processor takes the place of a pot in most chilled soup recipes. Making a refreshing summer soup is as simple as pureeing bananas, melon, peaches, or any appealing combination of fruits with a little fruit juice and perhaps a dash of cinnamon. Add yogurt or sour cream for a creamy consistency, maple syrup or honey for sweetness, and a garnish of berries or melon balls for color.

Cold vegetable soups are just as easy to improvise. For a garden-fresh gazpacho, start with tomato juice or pureed fresh tomatoes as a base, and add cucumbers, onions, sweet and hot peppers, and cilantro or basil. Let your taste buds and your garden's bounty be your guide.

 **CHILIES**

Black Bean and Lime Chili

★ **BEGINNER-FRIENDLY**

This zesty chili is a favorite of mine. It goes especially well with corn bread or corn muffins. Sour cream, sliced scallions, and grated cheese make fine garnishes.

8 hearty servings

2 cups dried black beans
2 tablespoons canola oil
1 cup chopped onion (1 large onion)
8 large garlic cloves, peeled and minced
1 medium-large jalapeño pepper, minced
1 cup chopped red bell pepper (1 large pepper)
1 teaspoon dried oregano
One 28-ounce can whole tomatoes with their juice, chopped
1 cup fresh or frozen corn kernels
½ cup chopped fresh cilantro
¼ cup fresh lime juice
1 teaspoon salt
Cayenne

Rinse and sort the beans, and soak them in 7 cups of water for 6 to 8 hours or overnight.

Drain and rinse the beans, and bring them to a boil in a large, heavy pot with 7 cups of fresh water. Reduce the heat and simmer, partially covered, for 1½ to 2 hours, until tender.

Working in batches, puree all but 1 cup of the beans with some of their liquid in a blender or food processor, and return them to the pot. (Don't fill the blender more than half full, and leave the top open a crack to let the steam escape.)

Heat the oil in a skillet over medium heat. Sauté the onion, garlic, jalapeño, red pepper, and oregano until the vegetables are tender, about 5 minutes.

Stir the sautéed vegetables into the beans, along with the tomatoes and their juice, the corn, cilantro, lime juice, salt, and cayenne to taste. Simmer for 15 more minutes, stirring occasionally. Ladle into soup bowls and serve.

Four-Bean Chili

*T*his *hearty, protein-rich soup freezes well, so don't hesitate to make a double batch. Discarding the soaking liquid and cooking the beans in fresh water helps eliminate intestinal gas.*

8 hearty servings

⅔ cup dried kidney beans
⅔ cup dried pinto beans
⅔ cup dried black beans
⅔ cup dried lima beans
2 tablespoons canola oil
1½ cups chopped onions (3 medium onions)
6 large garlic cloves, peeled and minced
1 cup chopped green bell pepper (1 large pepper)
1 cup chopped red bell pepper (1 large pepper)
1 to 2 medium jalapeño peppers, minced
One 28-ounce can crushed tomatoes with their juice
One 28-ounce can whole tomatoes with their juice, coarsely chopped
2 teaspoons ground cinnamon
2 teaspoons salt
2 teaspoons cumin seed
1/16 to ¼ teaspoon cayenne (to taste)
1 tablespoon paprika
1 teaspoon ground coriander
Sour cream for garnish (optional)
Chopped fresh cilantro for garnish (optional)

Rinse and sort the beans, and soak them in 8 cups of water for 6 to 8 hours or overnight.

Drain the beans, and put them in a large soup pot with 8 cups of fresh water. Bring the beans to a boil, reduce the heat, and simmer, partially covered, for 1½ to 2 hours, until tender but not mushy.

While the beans are cooking, heat the oil in a large skillet over medium heat. Sauté the onions, garlic, green and red peppers, and jalapeños until soft, about 5 minutes.

When the beans are tender, stir the sautéed vegetables into the pot. Add the crushed and whole tomatoes and their juice, the cinnamon, salt, cumin seed, cayenne, paprika, and coriander. Stir well, and simmer for 15 to 20 minutes, stirring occasionally.

Ladle into soup bowls, and garnish with sour cream and cilantro if you like.

Butternut Chili

★ **BEGINNER-FRIENDLY**

The butternut squash adds a pleasing color and sweetness.

8 hearty servings

3 tablespoons canola oil
1½ cups chopped onions (3 medium onions)
5 large garlic cloves, peeled and minced
1 medium jalapeño pepper, minced
2 teaspoons dried oregano
1 teaspoon dried basil
3 cups chopped fresh broccoli
1 cup chopped green bell pepper (1 large pepper)
1 cup chopped red bell pepper (1 large pepper)
4 cups cubed, peeled butternut squash (1 medium squash)
1 teaspoon salt
1 teaspoon ground cumin
½ teaspoon ground coriander
1½ cups cooked kidney beans
One 28-ounce can whole tomatoes with their juice, chopped
1 cup fresh or frozen corn kernels
Grated Cheddar cheese for garnish (optional)

Heat the oil in a large soup pot over medium heat. Sauté the onions, garlic, jalapeño, oregano, and basil until the onion begins to soften, 2 to 3 minutes.

Stir in the broccoli and green and red peppers, and sauté until just tender, 3 to 4 minutes more.

Add the squash, salt, cumin, coriander, beans, tomatoes and their juice, and 4 cups of water. Bring the soup to a boil, reduce the heat, and simmer, partially covered, for 25 to 30 minutes, stirring occasionally.

Stir in the corn, and cook for a few minutes more.

Ladle the soup into bowls, and garnish it if you like with grated Cheddar cheese.

New England Chili

★ **BEGINNER-FRIENDLY**

Tangy and full-bodied, with a hint of Boston baked beans.

8 hearty servings

2 cups dried pinto beans
2 tablespoons canola oil
2 cups chopped onions (2 large onions)
8 large garlic cloves, peeled and minced
1 cup chopped red bell pepper (1 large pepper)
1 cup chopped green bell pepper (1 large pepper)
2 cups quartered mushrooms (½ pound)
2 teaspoons ground cumin
1 tablespoon chili powder
1 teaspoon salt
1 tablespoon tamari
¼ cup blackstrap molasses
Two 28-ounce cans diced tomatoes with their juice
1 tablespoon cider vinegar
Cayenne

Rinse and sort the beans, and soak them in 7 cups of water for 6 to 8 hours or overnight.

Drain the beans, and put them in a large pot with 7 cups of fresh water. Bring them to a boil, reduce the heat, and simmer, partially covered, for 1 to 1½ hours, until the beans are tender.

When the beans are nearly done, heat the oil in a large skillet over medium heat. Sauté the onions and garlic until soft, about 5 minutes. Stir in the red and green peppers and the mushrooms, and cook until tender, about 5 minutes more.

When the beans are tender, stir the sautéed vegetables into the pot, along with the cumin, chili powder, salt, tamari, molasses, tomatoes and their juice, vinegar, and cayenne to taste. Simmer for 15 minutes, stirring occasionally. Ladle into soup bowls and serve.

 **CHOWDERS**

Monterey Chowder

*T*his colorful, robust chowder is chock-full of vegetables. To reheat it, use a double boiler so the cheese doesn't scorch.

6 to 8 servings

1¼ cups dried lima beans
1 tablespoon butter or margarine
¾ cup chopped onion (1 medium-large onion)
3 large garlic cloves, peeled and minced
½ teaspoon dried dill
¾ cup chopped celery (1½ stalks)
¾ cup chopped red or green bell pepper (1 medium pepper)
1 small jalapeño pepper, minced, or 1 small dried hot pepper, crushed
3 tablespoons unbleached white flour
2 cups milk
1 cup fresh or frozen corn kernels
One 14-ounce can whole tomatoes with their juice, coarsely chopped
1 teaspoon salt
Dash of pepper
1 cup grated Monterey Jack cheese (4 ounces)

Soak the lima beans in 4 cups of water for 2 hours. Drain, put them in a large saucepan with 4 cups of fresh water, and bring them to a boil. Reduce the heat and simmer, partially covered, for about 1 hour, until tender but still whole.

When the beans are nearly done, melt the butter in a large soup pot over medium heat. Sauté the onion, garlic, and dill for about 2 minutes. Add the celery, bell pepper, and jalapeño, and cook for 3 to 4 minutes more, just until tender.

Stir the flour into the vegetables, and let it cook for a minute or two. Slowly pour in the milk, stirring constantly until thickened. Gradually add 2 cups of water, still stirring.

Stir in the corn, the tomatoes and their juice, the lima beans and their cooking water, the salt, and the pepper. Bring the soup to a simmer, and let it cook for 5 to 10 minutes more, stirring occasionally.

A few minutes before serving, add the cheese, and stir until melted. (Don't let the soup return to a boil, or the cheese may scorch.) Serve immediately.

Vegetable Chowder

Vegetable chowder is one of those sustaining soups that helps to get me through the coldest months of winter. I use potatoes as a base and whatever vegetables I have on hand.

8 servings

2 tablespoons canola oil
1 cup chopped onion (1 large onion)
1 cup diced carrots (2 medium carrots)
2 cups chopped fresh broccoli
1 medium green bell pepper, seeded and cut into thin, 1-inch-long strips
  (¾ cup)
1 medium red bell pepper, seeded and cut into thin, 1-inch-long strips
  (¾ cup)
½ cup diced celery (1 stalk)
1 teaspoon dried thyme
3 cups chopped unpeeled potatoes (1 pound)
¼ cup chopped fresh dill or 2 teaspoons dried
1 teaspoon salt
Pepper
4 tablespoons butter or margarine (¼ cup)
4 tablespoons unbleached white flour (¼ cup)
1 cup heavy cream
1 cup milk

Heat the oil in a large soup pot over medium heat. Sauté the onion, carrots, and broccoli until tender, about 5 minutes. Stir in the green and red peppers, celery, and thyme, and cook until tender, 3 to 4 minutes more. Remove the pot from the heat.

Bring 2 cups of water to a boil in a saucepan, and cook the potatoes until just tender, about 10 minutes.

Add the potatoes and their cooking water to the soup pot, along with 4 more cups of water. Bring the soup to a simmer, and stir in the dill, salt, and pepper to taste.

Melt the butter in the saucepan over medium heat, and whisk in the flour. Cook it for a minute or so, and then slowly whisk in the cream and milk.

Stir this white sauce into the soup, and simmer for 15 minutes more, stirring occasionally. Ladle into soup bowls and serve.

★ HOT AND HEARTY

Mushroom Garlic Bisque

The wine adds depth, the bread crumbs add body, and the milk and sour cream add richness to this exceptionally delicious soup.

6 servings

2 cups dry red wine
1 ½ pounds mushrooms, quartered (6 cups)
1 tablespoon butter or margarine
1 ½ cups chopped onions (3 medium onions)
10 large garlic cloves, peeled and minced
½ teaspoon dried leaf thyme
1 ½ cups fresh whole wheat bread crumbs
1 cup sour cream
2 ½ cups milk
2 tablespoons tamari
1 teaspoon salt
2 tablespoons chopped fresh basil
Dash of pepper

Heat 1½ cups of the wine and the mushrooms over medium heat in a large soup pot. Simmer, partially covered, until the mushrooms have absorbed all the wine, about 20 minutes, stirring occasionally.

While the mushrooms are cooking, melt the butter in a skillet over medium heat. Sauté the onions, garlic, and thyme until the onion is soft, about 5 minutes.

Puree the onion mixture in a food processor or blender. Add the bread crumbs, sour cream, and three-quarters of the cooked mushrooms, and process until smooth.

Stir the puree into the soup pot. Whisk in the milk, tamari, salt, basil, pepper, the remaining mushrooms and ½ cup wine, and 2½ cups of water. Heat until warmed through, stirring often. Ladle into soup bowls and serve.

Baked Italian Soup
with Melted Cheese

My Italian version of French onion soup is a savory combination of tender eggplant and tomatoes and crisp red bell peppers topped with croutons and melted cheese.

6 servings

1 medium eggplant, peeled and chopped (about 6 cups)
2 tablespoons canola oil
1 cup chopped onion (1 large onion)
8 large garlic cloves, peeled and minced
1 cup chopped red bell pepper (1 large pepper)
2 teaspoons dried oregano
1 teaspoon dried thyme
¼ cup finely chopped fresh basil
1½ teaspoons salt
1 tablespoon tamari
2 large tomatoes, chopped (2 cups)
½ cup dry white wine
2 cups cubed, sourdough French bread (stale is fine)
1 cup grated mozzarella cheese (4 ounces)
1 cup grated sharp Cheddar cheese (4 ounces)

Cook the eggplant in 6 cups of water in a large soup pot until very soft, 8 to 10 minutes.

Working in batches, puree the eggplant and its cooking water in a food processor or blender. Return it to the pot and set aside.

Heat the oil in a skillet over medium heat. Sauté the onion, garlic, red pepper, oregano, and thyme until the vegetables are tender, about 5 minutes.

Stir the sautéed vegetables into the soup pot, along with the basil, salt, tamari, tomatoes, and wine. Heat the soup to a simmer, and cook, partially covered, for 30 minutes.

About 10 minutes before the soup is done, preheat the oven to 400 degrees.

When the soup is ready, ladle it into six ovenproof bowls. Top the soup with the bread cubes and shredded cheeses. Bake for 10 to 15 minutes, until the cheese begins to brown. Serve immediately.

Bombay Vegetable Soup

A long-ago trip to India inspired this colorful, spicy soup. I especially remember the vendors with their open-air stands piled high with fragrant spices—a necessity for food preservation in a country where many homes don't have refrigerators.

8 to 10 servings

2 cups dried chick-peas, rinsed and sorted (or 5 cups cooked)
2 tablespoons canola oil
1 cup chopped onion (1 large onion)
4 large garlic cloves, peeled and minced
1 cup chopped carrots (2 medium carrots)
2 cups chopped fresh broccoli
1 cup chopped zucchini (1 small zucchini)
1 teaspoon dried thyme
2 tablespoons fresh lemon juice
1 teaspoon ground cumin
1 tablespoon curry powder
⅛ to ¼ teaspoon cayenne (to taste)
1 teaspoon ground coriander
2 teaspoons ground turmeric
1 teaspoon salt
2 tablespoons butter or margarine
2 tablespoons unbleached white flour
1 cup heavy cream
1 cup milk

If using dried chick-peas, soak them in 8 cups of water for 6 to 8 hours or overnight.

Drain the beans, and put them in a large soup pot with 8 cups of fresh water. Bring them to a boil, reduce the heat, and simmer, partially covered, for 2½ to 3 hours, until tender. Stir them occasionally, and add more water if needed.

Drain the beans. Puree half of them with 2 cups of water in a food processor or blender. Return the puree and the whole beans to the soup pot, and set aside.

Heat the oil in a large skillet over medium heat. Sauté the onion, garlic, carrots, and broccoli until tender, about 5 minutes. Add the zucchini and thyme, and cook 2 to 3 minutes more.

Add the sautéed vegetables to the soup pot, along with the lemon juice, cumin, curry, cayenne, coriander, turmeric, and salt. Stir well.

Return the skillet to the stove over low heat. Melt the butter, whisk in the flour, and cook it for a minute or two, stirring constantly. Gradually add the cream and milk, whisking constantly until slightly thickened.

Stir this white sauce into the soup, along with 2 more cups of water. Bring the soup to a simmer over low heat, and cook for 15 to 20 minutes, stirring occasionally. Ladle into soup bowls and serve.

Cauliflower-Mushroom-Cheddar Soup

A *natural vegetarian version of Worcestershire sauce (without anchovies) is available at health food stores.*

6 servings

2 tablespoons canola oil
1 cup chopped onion (1 large onion)
5 large garlic cloves, peeled and minced
1 cup diced carrots (2 medium carrots)
1 cup sliced celery (2 stalks)
1 teaspoon dried thyme
1 teaspoon dried basil
4 cups sliced mushrooms (1 pound)
1/3 cup unbleached white flour
4 cups chopped cauliflower (1 medium head)
1 teaspoon salt
1/2 cup minced fresh parsley or 1 tablespoon dried
1 1/2 cups grated extra-sharp Cheddar cheese (6 ounces)
2 teaspoons Worcestershire sauce

Heat the oil in a large skillet over medium heat. Sauté the onion, garlic, carrots, celery, thyme, and basil until the vegetables are soft, about 5 minutes. Stir in the mushrooms and cook until tender, 3 to 4 minutes more. Stir the flour into the vegetables and remove the skillet from the heat.

Cook the cauliflower in 5 cups of water in a large soup pot until tender, 6 to 8 minutes. Stir in the sautéed vegetables.

Working in batches, puree about one-third of the soup in a food processor or blender, and return it to the pot.

Stir in the salt, parsley, cheese, and Worcestershire. Warm the soup over very low heat for 5 to 10 minutes, stirring occasionally to prevent burning. Ladle into soup bowls and serve.

Creamy Asparagus Soup

*T*his refreshing soup tastes like spring.

4 main-course or 6 first-course servings

2 or 3 medium potatoes, peeled and sliced (about 2½ cups)
2 pounds fresh asparagus
2 tablespoons canola oil
1½ cups diced onions (3 medium onions)
5 large garlic cloves, peeled and minced
2 tablespoons butter or margarine
2 tablespoons unbleached white flour
2½ cups milk
1 teaspoon salt
2 tablespoons chopped fresh basil

Bring 2½ cups of water to a boil in a large soup pot, and cook the potatoes until almost tender, about 6 to 8 minutes.

Meanwhile, trim and discard the tough ends from the asparagus. Trim and set aside the tips, and cut the stalks into 1-inch pieces. (You'll have about 6 cups.)

Add the asparagus pieces to the potatoes, and cook until tender, 6 to 8 minutes more.

While the asparagus is cooking, heat the oil in a skillet over medium heat. Sauté the onions and garlic until soft, about 5 minutes.

Stir the sautéed vegetables into the asparagus and potatoes. Working in batches, puree this mixture in a food processor or blender. Return it to the soup pot, and set aside.

Melt the butter in a saucepan over low heat. Whisk in the flour, and cook it for a minute or two. Gradually add 1 cup of the milk, whisking until slightly thickened.

Add this white sauce to the soup pot along with the remaining 1½ cups milk, the salt, basil, and the reserved asparagus tips.

Bring the soup to a simmer and cook, stirring occasionally, until the asparagus tips are tender, about 5 to 8 minutes. Ladle into soup bowls and serve.

Creamy Tomato-Spinach-Mushroom Soup

★ **BEGINNER-FRIENDLY**

A *quick and easy soup to prepare that you and your guests will relish.*

8 to 10 servings

2 tablespoons canola oil
1 cup chopped onion (1 large onion)
1 teaspoon dried basil
1 teaspoon dried thyme
2 cups sliced mushrooms (½ pound)
One 28-ounce can crushed tomatoes with their juice
One 28-ounce can diced tomatoes with their juice
One 10-ounce package frozen chopped spinach, thawed and drained
1 cup heavy cream
4 tablespoons unbleached white flour (¼ cup)
½ teaspoon salt

Heat the oil in a large soup pot over medium heat. Sauté the onion, basil, and thyme until the onion is soft, about 5 minutes. Stir in the mushrooms and cook until tender, 3 to 4 minutes more.

Stir in the tomatoes and their juices, and the spinach. Reduce the heat and simmer for 10 minutes.

Meanwhile, whisk the cream with the flour in a medium-size bowl until smooth, and stir it into the soup. Add the salt and 2 cups of water.

Heat the soup just to a simmer, stirring occasionally. Ladle into soup bowls and serve.

Dilly Asparagus Leek Soup

I love to make this soup in the spring, when I can harvest wild leeks from the wetter part of the woods near our house.

6 to 8 servings

2 tablespoons canola oil
1½ cups chopped onions (3 medium onions)
1 teaspoon dried thyme
2 cups sliced leeks (2 medium leeks)
2 cups sliced celery (4 stalks)
4 cups sliced cabbage (1 small head)
1 pound fresh asparagus, trimmed and sliced (about 3 cups)
3 tablespoons butter or margarine
3 tablespoons unbleached white flour
2 cups milk
1 teaspoon salt
½ cup minced fresh dill
Pepper

Heat the oil in a large soup pot over medium heat. Sauté the onions, thyme, leeks, celery, cabbage, and asparagus until tender, 6 to 8 minutes. Add 4 cups of water to the pot, and turn off the heat.

Puree half of the soup in a food processor or blender, and return it to the pot.

Melt the butter in a saucepan over medium heat. Whisk in the flour, and cook for a minute or two. Slowly add the milk, whisking until thickened.

Add this white sauce to the pot, along with the salt, dill, and pepper to taste. Warm the soup over low heat for 10 to 15 minutes, stirring occasionally. Ladle into soup bowls and serve.

Tomato-Leek Soup with Stilton Cheese

★ **BEGINNER-FRIENDLY**

Stilton is a rich blue cheese that tastes heavenly with leeks and tomatoes.

8 servings

2 tablespoons canola oil
2 cups sliced leeks (2 medium leeks)
5 large garlic cloves, peeled and minced
¾ cup diced celery (1½ stalks)
½ cup diced carrot (1 medium carrot)
½ teaspoon dried thyme
1 teaspoon dried basil
4 cups sliced potatoes (3 to 4 medium potatoes)
1 cup half and half
1 teaspoon salt
One 28-ounce can peeled and ground or chopped tomatoes with their juice
1½ cups crumbled Stilton cheese (6 ounces)

Heat the oil in a large skillet over medium heat. Sauté the leeks, garlic, celery, carrot, thyme, and basil until the vegetables are tender, 5 to 7 minutes. Remove the pot from the heat.

Bring 2 cups of water to a boil in a saucepan, and cook the potatoes until tender, about 10 minutes.

Working in batches, puree the potatoes, their cooking water, and the half and half in a blender or food processor.

Stir the puree into a soup pot, along with the salt, tomatoes and their juice, sautéed vegetables, and 2 more cups of water.

Bring the soup to a simmer, and cook for 15 minutes, stirring occasionally. Stir in the cheese, and cook just until melted. Ladle into soup bowls and serve.

Pennsylvania Cabbage-Mushroom Soup
with Dumplings

This old-fashioned soup was inspired by a long-ago journey with my mother to Pennsylvania Dutch country, where we enjoyed wonderful dumplings and other kitchen delights. You can make the soup ahead of time, but fix the dumplings at the last minute.

8 servings

DUMPLINGS
- 1 large egg
- ¼ cup unbleached white flour
- ¼ teaspoon baking powder
- Dash of salt

SOUP
- 2 tablespoons canola oil
- 1 cup chopped onion (1 large onion)
- ¾ cup diced carrot (1 medium-large carrot)
- 5 large garlic cloves, peeled and minced
- 4 cups finely chopped cabbage (1 small head)
- 2 cups sliced mushrooms (½ pound)
- 2 tablespoons unbleached white flour
- ¾ cup sour cream
- ½ cup minced fresh parsley
- 2 tablespoons minced fresh dill
- 1 teaspoon salt
- 1 teaspoon paprika
- 1 tablespoon tamari
- Pepper

For the dumplings, stir together the egg, flour, baking powder, and salt, and set aside.

For the soup, heat the oil in a large soup pot over medium heat. Sauté the onion, carrot, and garlic until the onion begins to soften, 2 to 3 minutes. Stir in the cabbage and mushrooms, and cook until tender, 5 to 7 minutes more.

Add 6 cups of water to the pot, bring it to a simmer, and cook for 15 to 20 minutes, stirring occasionally.

Mix the flour with the sour cream, and stir it into the soup along with the parsley, dill, salt, paprika, tamari, and pepper to taste.

Bring the soup back to a simmer. Just before serving, drop in the dumpling batter, a teaspoonful at a time, and simmer, uncovered, for about 5 minutes, until the dumplings are cooked through. Ladle into soup bowls and serve immediately.

Spicy Butternut and Red Lentil Soup

Pureed winter squash and lentils are the creamy base for this mild curried vegetable soup.

8 servings

6 cups cubed, peeled butternut squash (1 large squash)
¾ cup red lentils
2 tablespoons canola oil
1 cup chopped onion (1 large onion)
5 large garlic cloves, peeled and minced
1 cup chopped celery (2 stalks)
1¼ teaspoons salt
2 teaspoons curry powder
½ teaspoon coriander
¼ teaspoon ground nutmeg
Cayenne
3 tablespoons fresh lemon juice
1 medium tomato, diced (¾ cup)
2 cups milk

Cook the squash and lentils in 5 cups of water in a large soup pot until tender, 20 to 25 minutes.

Working in batches, puree the squash, lentils, and cooking water in a food processor or blender. Return the puree to the pot and set aside.

Heat the oil in a skillet over medium heat. Sauté the onion, garlic, and celery until tender, about 5 minutes.

Add the sautéed vegetables to the soup pot. Stir in the salt, curry powder, coriander, nutmeg, cayenne to taste, and lemon juice.

Heat the soup to a simmer. Add the tomato and milk, and simmer for 10 minutes more, stirring occasionally. Ladle into soup bowls and serve.

Southern Sweet Potato Soup

This soup is especially nice for a Thanksgiving or Christmas meal, but its rich and wonderful flavor is welcome anytime.

8 servings

2 tablespoons canola oil
5 large garlic cloves, peeled and minced
1 cup finely chopped onion (1 large onion)
1 cup thinly sliced leek (1 medium leek)
1 teaspoon dried thyme
5 cups vegetable broth or water
1½ cups chopped carrots (3 medium carrots)
6 cups chopped peeled sweet potatoes (2 pounds)
½ cup dry white wine
1 teaspoon salt
1 teaspoon ground ginger
¼ teaspoon ground nutmeg
½ cup minced fresh parsley
3 tablespoons butter or margarine
4 tablespoons unbleached white flour (¼ cup)
2 cups milk
¾ cup tamari-toasted pecans (see Note)

Heat the oil in a skillet over medium heat. Sauté the garlic, onion, leek, and thyme until the vegetables are soft, about 5 minutes. Remove the pan from the heat.

Bring the broth to a boil in a large soup pot, and cook the carrots and sweet potatoes until tender, about 15 minutes.

Working in batches, puree the carrots and sweet potatoes with their cooking liquid in a food processor or blender.

Return the puree to the pot. Stir in the sautéed vegetables along with the wine, salt, ginger, nutmeg, and parsley. Bring the soup to a simmer.

Melt the butter in a saucepan over medium heat. Whisk in the flour, and cook for a minute or two. Slowly pour in the milk, whisking until thickened.

Stir this white sauce into the soup, and let it simmer for a few more minutes.

Ladle the soup into bowls, and sprinkle it with the tamari-toasted pecans.

Note

To toast the pecans, preheat the oven to 375 degrees. Spread ¾ cup chopped pecans on a baking sheet, and bake for 5 minutes. They will begin to turn golden in color. Slide the hot nuts into a small bowl, sprinkle them with 1 teaspoon of tamari, and toss. Spread them out again on the baking sheet, and bake for 2 to 3 minutes more, until crisp but not browned.

Creamy Potato-Vegetable Soup

The contrast of the red tomato and bell pepper with the green spinach makes this a fine soup for the winter holidays.

8 servings

6 cups diced potatoes (2 pounds)
2 tablespoons canola oil
1 cup chopped onion (1 large onion)
2 cups sliced leeks (2 medium leeks)
¾ cup diced red bell pepper (1 medium pepper)
1 pound mushrooms, quartered (4 cups)
1 large tomato, chopped (1 cup)
2 cups chopped fresh spinach (lightly packed)
2 cups milk
1 teaspoon dried parsley
2 tablespoons minced fresh dill
1 to 1½ teaspoons salt

Bring 4 cups of water to a boil in a large pot, and cook the potatoes until tender, about 10 minutes.

Meanwhile, heat the oil in a large skillet over medium heat. Sauté the onion, leeks, and red pepper until tender, about 5 minutes. Add the mushrooms, and cook until tender, 3 to 4 minutes more.

When the potatoes are done, puree them with their cooking water in a food processor or blender, working in batches.

Return the puree to the soup pot, along with the sautéed vegetables, tomato, spinach, milk, parsley, dill, and salt. Bring to a simmer, and cook for 10 to 15 minutes, stirring occasionally. Ladle into soup bowls and serve.

Shiitake Mushroom and Seitan Soup

Sesame oil and tamari add a rich Asian flavor to this quick, nondairy soup. Seitan, made from wheat gluten, is sold in Asian and natural food stores.

6 servings

2 cups boiling water
1 cup dried shiitake mushrooms
1 tablespoon canola oil
1 tablespoon sesame oil
¾ cup finely chopped onion (1 medium-large onion)
5 large garlic cloves, peeled and minced
1 tablespoon peeled and minced fresh ginger
1½ cups sliced broccoli
2 cups chopped bok choy (3 to 4 stalks)
One 10-ounce can curried seitan, rinsed, drained, and diced
3 tablespoons tamari
Cayenne or chili paste with garlic
3 scallions, sliced, for garnish

Pour the boiling water over the mushrooms, and let them soak for 15 to 20 minutes, until soft. Strain them, reserving the water. Discard the stems, and slice the mushrooms into thin strips.

Heat the oils over medium heat in a large soup pot. Sauté the onion, garlic, ginger, and broccoli until the broccoli turns bright green, about 5 minutes. (If the ginger begins to stick, add a tablespoon or two of water.)

Stir in the bok choy, and continue cooking until it's just tender, 3 to 4 minutes more.

Stir in the mushrooms, the reserved soaking liquid, the seitan, tamari, and cayenne or chili paste to taste. Add 4 cups of water.

Bring the soup to a simmer and let it cook for 15 minutes, stirring occasionally. Ladle it into bowls and garnish with chopped scallions.

Nepal Country Vegetable Soup

his gingery, curried vegetable soup will fill your kitchen with enticing aromas. Those same smells greeted me years ago in a restaurant in Nepal, where I enjoyed an intriguing soup that I've tried to duplicate here.

8 servings

5 cups chopped, peeled winter squash
2 tablespoons canola oil
1 cup chopped onion (1 large onion)
6 large cloves garlic, peeled and chopped
2 tablespoons peeled and minced fresh ginger
2 cups chopped fresh broccoli
1 cup chopped carrots (2 medium carrots)
2 medium tomatoes, chopped (1 ½ cups)
1 cup fresh or frozen peas
1 teaspoon salt
2 teaspoons ground coriander
2 teaspoons ground cumin
1 teaspoon ground cardamom
Cayenne

Bring 5 cups of water to a boil in a large pot, and cook the squash until tender, about 15 to 20 minutes.

Working in batches, puree the squash with its cooking water in a food processor or blender. Return the puree to the pot and set aside.

Heat the oil in a large skillet over medium heat. Sauté the onion, garlic, ginger, broccoli, and carrots until tender, about 5 minutes. (If the ginger begins to stick, add a tablespoon or two of water.)

Stir the sautéed vegetables into the soup pot, along with the tomatoes, peas, salt, coriander, cumin, cardamom, and cayenne to taste.

Bring the soup to a simmer and let it cook for 20 minutes, stirring occasionally. Ladle into soup bowls and serve.

Garden Pesto Stew

This soup was inspired by the explosion of summer squash, zucchini, and other garden vegetables that occurs in Vermont each summer. At the height of the harvest, it's not unusual to find a bag of squash by your front door or in your car, left there by a gardening friend. Baskets of zucchini can be seen around town with signs on them saying "FREE SQUASH!" If you don't have access to a garden, look for a farmers' market that sells fresh, inexpensive, organically grown produce.

6 to 8 servings

2 tablespoons olive oil

5 large garlic cloves, peeled and minced

1 cup chopped onion (1 large onion)

1 cup diced carrots (2 medium carrots)

2 cups chopped zucchinis (2 small zucchinis)

2 cups chopped yellow summer squash (2 small squash)

1 cup sliced green beans

1 medium red bell pepper, seeded and cut into thin, 1-inch-long slices (¾ cup)

1½ cups corn kernels (fresh if possible)

2 large tomatoes, chopped (2 cups)

1 teaspoon salt

5 cups vegetable broth or water

PESTO

¼ cup olive oil

3 large garlic cloves, peeled

1 cup fresh basil leaves (lightly packed)

¼ cup chopped fresh parsley

⅛ teaspoon salt

2 tablespoons finely grated Parmesan cheese

Crusty bread for serving

Heat the oil in a large pot over medium heat. Sauté the garlic, onion, and carrots until the onion is tender, about 5 minutes.

Stir in the zucchinis, yellow squash, green beans, and red pepper. Cook until the vegetables are just tender, about 5 minutes more.

Stir in the corn, tomatoes, salt, and broth, and simmer for 15 minutes, stirring occasionally.

While the soup is cooking, process the olive oil, garlic, basil, parsley, salt, and cheese in a blender or food processor until smooth.

When the soup is done, ladle it into bowls, and spoon a dollop of pesto into the center of each one. Serve with warm crusty bread.

Potato-Carrot-Spinach Soup

This quick and easy nondairy soup has a surprisingly creamy taste.

6 to 8 servings

3 tablespoons canola oil
1½ cups chopped onions (3 medium onions)
5 large garlic cloves, peeled and minced
4 cups cubed potatoes (4 medium-large potatoes)
2 cups chopped carrots (4 medium carrots)
1½ teaspoons salt
¼ cup minced fresh dill
3 cups chopped fresh spinach (lightly packed)
Pepper

Heat the oil in a skillet over medium heat. Sauté the onions and garlic until soft, about 5 minutes. Set aside.

Bring 6 cups of water to a boil in a large pot, and cook the potatoes and carrots until tender, about 10 minutes. Stir in the onions and garlic.

Working in batches, puree the vegetables with the cooking water in a blender or food processor.

Return the puree to the pot, and stir in the salt, dill, spinach, and pepper to taste. Bring the soup to a simmer, and let it cook for 15 to 20 minutes, stirring occasionally. Ladle into soup bowls and serve.

Black-and-White Soup

Basil, garlic, and lemon juice give this hearty bean soup its savory flavor. It makes a big batch; you can cut the recipe in half, but leftovers freeze beautifully.

10 to 12 servings

2 cups dried black beans, sorted and rinsed
1 cup dried white (navy) beans, sorted and rinsed
2 tablespoons canola oil
1 cup chopped onion (1 large onion)
5 large garlic cloves, peeled and minced
2 cups diced zucchinis (2 small zucchinis)
¾ cup diced red bell pepper (1 medium pepper)
1 teaspoon dried oregano
2 tablespoons finely chopped fresh basil or 2 teaspoons dried
1 medium tomato, chopped (¾ cup)
¼ cup fresh lemon juice
2 tablespoons chopped fresh parsley or 2 teaspoons dried
1½ teaspoons salt
1 tablespoon tamari
Sour cream for garnish
Sliced scallions for garnish

Put the black beans in a large soup pot with 7 cups of water, and put the white beans in a medium-size pot with 4 cups of water. Let them soak for 6 to 8 hours or overnight.

Drain the beans, and return them to their pots with fresh water (7 cups for the black, 4 cups for the white). Bring the black beans to a boil, reduce the heat, and simmer, partially covered. After 45 minutes, do the same with the white beans. Cook until all the beans are tender, about 45 minutes more.

Working in batches, puree the black beans and their cooking liquid in a food processor or blender.

Return the puree to the pot. Stir in the white beans and their cooking liquid, and set aside.

Heat the oil in a large skillet over medium heat. Sauté the onion, garlic, zucchinis, red pepper, oregano, and basil if dried until the vegetables are tender, about 5 minutes.

Stir the sautéed vegetables into the beans, along with the fresh basil, tomato, lemon juice, parsley, salt, tamari, and 3 to 4 cups of water. Add enough water to give the soup a smooth, medium thickness in consistency.

Bring the soup to a simmer, and let it cook for 15 to 20 minutes, stirring occasionally.

Ladle it into bowls, and garnish with sour cream and scallions.

African Vegetable-Peanut Soup

★ **BEGINNER-FRIENDLY**

Try this deliciously different soup when you're feeling bored with your usual repertoire.

6 generous servings

3 tablespoons peanut oil
6 large garlic cloves, peeled and minced
2 cups chopped onions (2 large onions)
1 large red bell pepper, seeded and cut into thin, 1-inch-long slices
    (1 cup)
1 large green bell pepper, seeded and cut into thin, 1-inch-long slices
    (1 cup)
2 cups sliced mushrooms (½ pound)
One 28-ounce can tomatoes with their juice, chopped
½ cup uncooked brown rice
¼ teaspoon dried red pepper flakes (or to taste)
½ teaspoon salt
¾ cup creamy peanut butter
1 tablespoon fresh lemon juice
Cayenne

Heat the oil in a large soup pot over medium heat. Sauté the garlic and onions until soft, about 5 minutes. Stir in the red and green peppers and mushrooms, and cook just until tender, 3 to 4 minutes more.

Add the tomatoes and their juice to the soup pot, along with the rice, pepper flakes, salt, and 4 cups of water.

Bring the soup to a simmer, and cook, partially covered, until the rice is tender, about 45 minutes, stirring occasionally.

Whisk the peanut butter into the soup until well blended. Add the lemon juice and cayenne to taste. Ladle into soup bowls and serve.

Mushroom, Ginger, and Seashell Pasta Soup

The gingery broth should help chase away winter colds!

6 to 8 servings

1½ cups uncooked shell pasta (about 1-inch shells)
2 tablespoons canola oil
1 cup chopped onion (1 large onion)
½ cup chopped carrot (1 medium carrot)
1 cup sliced celery (2 stalks)
6 large garlic cloves, peeled and minced
1 tablespoon peeled and minced fresh ginger
4 cups sliced mushrooms (1 pound)
¾ cup chopped red bell pepper (1 medium pepper)
3 tablespoons butter or margarine
3 tablespoons unbleached white flour
2 cups vegetable broth
½ cup minced fresh parsley
1 teaspoon salt
1 tablespoon tamari
4 scallions, sliced at an angle
Cayenne

Bring 6 cups of water to a boil in a large pot, and cook the pasta just until tender, about 8 minutes. Remove the pot from the heat.

Heat the oil in a large skillet over medium heat. Sauté the onion, carrot, celery, garlic, and ginger until tender, about 5 minutes. (If the ginger sticks, add a tablespoon or two of water.) Stir in the mushrooms and red pepper, and cook until tender, 3 to 4 minutes more. Add the vegetables to the soup pot.

Melt the butter in a saucepan over medium heat. Whisk in the flour, and let it cook for a minute or two. Slowly add the broth, whisking until thickened.

Stir this sauce into the soup, along with the parsley, salt, tamari, scallions, and cayenne to taste. Bring the soup to a simmer, and cook for 5 to 10 minutes, stirring occasionally. Ladle into soup bowls and serve.

Hot and Sour Soup

This light, gingery soup is a perfect starter for an Asian meal.

6 to 8 servings

1 cup boiling water
10 dried shiitake mushrooms
3 tablespoons peanut oil
2 tablespoons peeled and minced fresh ginger
6 large garlic cloves, peeled and minced
2 medium carrots, sliced into thin, 1-inch-long strips (1 cup)
2 cups sliced cabbage (½ pound)
1 medium red bell pepper, seeded and cut into thin, 1-inch-long slices
    (¾ cup)
2 cups chopped bok choy or napa cabbage (3 to 4 stalks)
8 cups vegetable stock or water
2 tablespoons rice vinegar
2 tablespoons tamari or soy sauce
½ to 1 teaspoon chili paste with garlic
2 tablespoons arrowroot
½ teaspoon salt
2 large eggs, beaten (optional)
1 teaspoon sesame oil
3 scallions, trimmed and thinly sliced, for garnish

Pour the boiling water over the mushrooms, and let them soak until tender, about 15 minutes. Drain them, saving the soaking liquid. Discard the stems, and slice the mushrooms into fine shreds.

Heat the peanut oil in a large soup pot over medium heat. Sauté the ginger, garlic, carrot, and cabbage for a few minutes. (If the ginger sticks, add a tablespoon or two of water.) Stir in the red pepper and bok choy, and cook until barely tender, 3 to 4 minutes more.

Stir the stock into the pot, along with the mushrooms and their soaking liquid, the vinegar, tamari, and chili paste. Bring the soup to a simmer.

Stir the arrowroot into 3 tablespoons of water. Whisk it into the soup, and add the salt.

If using eggs, pour them into the soup, and stir briskly for 2 to 3 minutes. Stir in the sesame oil.

Ladle the soup into bowls, and garnish with scallions.

Mushroom-Leek Matzo Ball Soup

I created this recipe for friends who wanted an alternative to traditional chicken-based matzo ball soup. The matzo batter should sit for at least an hour after mixing, and can be prepared a day ahead.

8 servings

MATZO BALLS

1 cup matzo meal

1 tablespoon chopped chives (fresh or dried)

1 tablespoon chopped parsley (fresh or dried)

1 teaspoon dried thyme

1 teaspoon salt

$\frac{1}{16}$ to $\frac{1}{8}$ teaspoon pepper

$\frac{1}{4}$ cup butter or margarine, softened

2 large eggs, beaten

$\frac{1}{4}$ cup vegetable broth or water

SOUP

2 tablespoons canola oil

1 cup diced onion (1 large onion)

1 teaspoon dried dill

$\frac{1}{2}$ cup diced carrot (1 medium carrot)

2 cups thinly sliced mushrooms ($\frac{1}{2}$ pound)

1 cup thinly sliced leek (1 medium leek)

1 cup diced celery (2 stalks)

8 cups vegetable stock or reconstituted bouillon

2 bay leaves

1 teaspoon salt

1 tablespoon tamari

For the matzo balls, mix the matzo meal, chives, parsley, thyme, salt, and pepper in a medium-size bowl or a food processor. Mix in the butter, eggs, and broth just until blended. Cover and refrigerate the batter for at least an hour.

For the soup, heat the oil in a large skillet over medium heat. Sauté the onion, dill, and carrot for 2 to 3 minutes. Stir in the mushrooms, leek, and celery, and cook until tender, about 5 minutes more.

While the vegetables are cooking, heat the broth to a simmer in a large soup pot. Stir in the sautéed vegetables, bay leaves, salt, and tamari.

While the soup continues to simmer, bring 3 quarts of water to a boil in a large saucepan.

Using your hands, roll the matzo batter into 1-inch balls, and drop them gently into the boiling water. Let them simmer, uncovered, until cooked, about 30 minutes, stirring occasionally. (Spoon one from the pot and slice it in half to check for doneness. The matzo balls should be white inside and cooked through.)

Remove and discard the bay leaves. Drain the matzo balls, add them to the soup, and serve.

 **FOR SUMMER DAYS**

Chilled or Hot Ginger-Carrot Soup

This delicious, gingery soup has a deep orange color and a creamy consistency. Make it ahead and chill it, or serve it hot as soon as it's done.

8 servings

2 tablespoons canola oil
1½ cups chopped onions (3 medium onions)
3 tablespoons peeled and minced fresh ginger
8 cups sliced carrots (2½ pounds)
2 cups sliced potatoes (2 medium potatoes)
1 teaspoon salt
½ teaspoon curry powder
2 tablespoons fresh lemon juice
¼ cup chopped fresh parsley
Chopped fresh chives for garnish

Heat the oil in a large soup pot over medium heat. Sauté the onions and ginger until the onions are soft, about 5 minutes. (If the ginger sticks, add a tablespoon or two of water.)

Add the carrots, potatoes, and 6 cups of water. Bring to a simmer, cover, and cook until the carrots and potatoes are tender, 10 to 15 minutes. Turn off the heat.

Working in batches, puree the vegetables with their cooking liquid in a food processor or blender, and return them to the pot.

Stir in the salt, curry powder, lemon juice, and parsley.

Let the soup cool to room temperature. Cover and refrigerate it until chilled. Serve garnished with fresh chives.

Chilled Avocado-Zucchini Soup
with Jalapeño Pepper

Even zucchini haters should enjoy this creamy, Mexican-flavored soup.

6 to 8 servings

2 tablespoons canola oil
1 cup chopped onion (1 large onion)
1 medium jalapeño pepper, minced
5 large garlic cloves, peeled and minced
8 cups chopped zucchinis (4 medium zucchinis)
1 medium avocado, peeled, pitted, and sliced
¾ cup sour cream or yogurt
1 tablespoon minced fresh cilantro
½ teaspoon salt
½ teaspoon ground cumin
1 tablespoon fresh lemon juice

Heat the oil in a large soup pot over medium heat. Sauté the onion, jalapeño pepper, and garlic until the onion begins to soften, 2 to 3 minutes. Stir in the zucchinis, and cook until soft, 3 to 4 minutes more.

Stir 2 cups of water into the pot, along with the avocado and sour cream.

Working in batches, puree the soup in a food processor or blender, and return it to the pot. Stir in the cilantro, salt, cumin, and lemon juice.

Cool the soup to room temperature. Cover and refrigerate it until chilled.

Cherry Tomato Gazpacho

★ **BEGINNER-FRIENDLY**

This refreshing soup is ideal for a hot summer day.

8 servings

4 large garlic cloves, peeled
1 medium cucumber, peeled and chopped (2 cups)
2 pints cherry tomatoes, halved or quartered (4 or 5 cups)
1 cup diced red onion (1 large onion)
1 cup chopped red bell pepper (1 large pepper)
1 cup chopped green bell pepper (1 large pepper)
⅓ cup minced fresh cilantro
4 cups tomato juice
¼ cup fresh lime or lemon juice
1 teaspoon salt
Cayenne or Tabasco

Puree the garlic and cucumber with 1 cup of water in a blender or food processor.

Pour the liquid into a large bowl. Stir in the tomatoes, onion, red and green peppers, cilantro, tomato juice, lime juice, salt, and cayenne to taste.

Cover and refrigerate until chilled.

Salads

Potato salads and bean salads bring to mind a picnic by the lake, with a warm breeze softly blowing, children happily running around, and sailboats gently bobbing in the distance. The salads people typically tote to picnics and barbecues are smothered in mayonnaise or drowned in dressing, but in this chapter you'll find tastier and more healthful versions of those summertime favorites. For example, Doubly Red Potato Salad (page 104) is brightened by both beets and red potatoes; Brussels Sprout–Potato Salad (page 102) is spiked with Dijon mustard, and Yukon Gold Potato Salad with Green Beans (page 103) is dressed with balsamic vinegar and olive oil.

You'll also find bean-, grain-, and pasta-based dishes like Cauliflower–Black Bean Salad with Buttermilk-Parmesan Dressing (page 106) and Asparagus Pasta Salad with Sesame-Ginger Dressing (page 112) that are meals in themselves. When creating your own main-dish salads, choose vegetables, beans, grains, and pasta in contrasting colors and shapes. Use red and yellow bell peppers as well as green ones for more visual appeal, and balance tender vegetables like asparagus with crisp ones like carrots for a more interesting texture. When you're pressed for time, putting together a salad meal is as easy as combining rinsed and drained canned beans with leftover rice or pasta, steamed or raw vegetables, and a dab of dressing.

Salads, of course, don't always take center stage. At the end of the chapter, check out the tempting side-dish salads and dressings. I like to keep the salad and dressing simple for an elaborate meal, and save more complex combinations for meals with fewer competing tastes and textures.

To make a green salad more interesting, combine two or three kinds of salad greens; home gardeners have an advantage here, but packaged mixtures are available in most produce departments. Wash the greens well; some, like spinach, require two or three changes of cold water, but it's worth the effort: nothing detracts from a beautiful salad like the crunch of grit when you bite into it!

Drying the greens is just as important; the dressing won't cling if they're wet. A salad spinner does a fine job. For an especially big salad, put the washed greens in a pillow case, take it outside, and swing it around your head until the water spins out. (That's how we used to dry greens at the café; once in a while the pillowcase would rip, festooning the parking lot with a layer of lettuce!)

Tear rather than cut your greens to prevent browning around the edges, and serve the salad as soon as it's dressed. Don't overdo the dressing; too much will drown out the flavors of the vegetables, and add unnecessary calories.

With so many bottled dressings on the market, you may not be in the habit of making your own. But most commercial dressings are loaded with sweeteners, chemical additives, salt, and fats. And the selection of healthful ones gets boring after a while. Treat yourself to a homemade dressing. With the wide selection of oils like sesame and seasoned olive oils and vinegars like balsamic and fresh herb varieties, the possibilities are endless. Experiment with flavorings, too: mustard, herbs, horseradish, ketchup, salsa, Worcestershire sauce, tamari, garlic, ginger, and scallions, to name just a few. To make creamy dressings, add yogurt, buttermilk, tofu, or sour cream, or Parmesan, blue, or cottage cheese.

For a finishing touch, look to your flower beds. Edible flowers like daylilies, nasturtiums, honeysuckle, and violets make gorgeous garnishes.

BEYOND THE MOON COOKBOOK

 **POTATO SALADS**

Brussels Sprout–Potato Salad

Brussels sprouts are one of the season's last gifts from the garden. They mature in late fall, long after almost everything else has been harvested. I've had to shake snow off my long, spindly Brussels sprout plants, and even then the tiny, cabbage-like heads hang on for dear life.

6 to 8 servings

6 cups cubed potatoes (2 pounds)
½ pound Brussels sprouts, heads sliced in half
2 hard-cooked eggs, coarsely chopped
1 cup chopped red onion (1 large onion)
¼ cup minced fresh dill or 1 tablespoon dried
1 medium red bell pepper, seeded and cut into thin, 1-inch-long strips
   (¾ cup)
¼ cup sour cream
½ cup mayonnaise (light or tofu variety is fine)
¼ cup plain yogurt
1 tablespoon Dijon or horseradish mustard
1 teaspoon salt
Pepper

Cook the potatoes in boiling water to cover just until tender, about 10 minutes. Drain and set aside to cool.

Steam the Brussels sprouts just until tender, 6 to 8 minutes. Drain and cool.

Gently combine the potatoes, Brussels sprouts, eggs, onion, dill, and red pepper in a medium-size bowl.

Whisk together the sour cream, mayonnaise, yogurt, mustard, and salt. Fold the dressing into the salad, and season to taste with pepper. Serve chilled or at room temperature.

Yukon Gold Potato Salad
with Green Beans

You'll never think of potato salad as boring again after you try this flavorful combination of tender Yukon Gold potatoes and crisp green beans accented by Greek olives and red onions.

8 to 10 servings

8 cups cubed unpeeled Yukon Gold potatoes (2⅔ pounds)
1 pound green beans
1 cup chopped red onion (1 large onion)
18 Greek olives, pitted and sliced
1 medium red bell pepper, seeded and cut into thin, 1-inch-long strips
   (¾ cup)
¼ cup balsamic vinegar
2 garlic cloves, peeled
1 teaspoon salt
1 teaspoon prepared mustard
½ teaspoon dried thyme
1 tablespoon tamari
½ cup olive oil

Cook the potatoes in boiling water to cover just until tender, about 10 minutes. Drain and cool.

Trim the beans, and cut them diagonally into 1-inch pieces. (You'll have about 4 cups.) Steam until barely tender, about 5 minutes. Cool.

Gently combine the potatoes and green beans in a large bowl, along with the onion, olives, and red pepper.

Process the vinegar, garlic, salt, mustard, thyme, and tamari in a blender or food processor until smooth. Reduce the speed to low, and slowly pour in the oil.

Fold the dressing into the vegetables. Serve chilled or at room temperature.

Doubly Red Potato Salad

★ **BEGINNER-FRIENDLY**

The beets turn this salad a slightly outrageous but quite beautiful red. Beet juice can also color your hands and cutting board; use lemon juice or a mild bleach solution to remove it.

8 to 10 servings

6 cups quartered small red potatoes (2 pounds)
1 pound beets, tops trimmed (4 cups)
1 teaspoon salt
1 cup diced red onion (1 large onion)
½ cup minced fresh dill
18 to 24 pitted black olives, sliced in half lengthwise
½ cup mayonnaise or mayonnaise substitute
¼ cup plain yogurt
¼ cup sour cream

Cook the potatoes in boiling water to cover just until tender, about 10 minutes. Drain and cool.

Cook the beets in boiling water to cover until tender, 12 to 15 minutes. Drain, cool, and slip off or peel the skin. Cut the beets into 1-inch cubes.

Gently combine the potatoes and beets in a large bowl, along with the salt, onion, dill, and olives.

Whisk together the mayonnaise, yogurt, and sour cream. Fold the dressing into the salad. Serve chilled or at room temperature.

Black-Eyed Pea Salad

★ **BEGINNER-FRIENDLY**

My friend Maureen, a transplanted Southerner, told me I did black-eyed peas justice with this simple but delightful salad.

6 to 8 servings

2 cups dried black-eyed peas
¾ cup diced red onion
3 large garlic cloves, peeled and minced
¾ cup diced red bell pepper (1 medium pepper)
5 scallions, thinly sliced
½ cup minced fresh parsley
⅓ cup balsamic vinegar
⅓ cup olive oil
1 tablespoon tamari
¾ teaspoon salt

Soak the black-eyed peas in 6 cups of water for 6 to 8 hours or overnight.

Drain the beans, put them in a pot with 6 cups of fresh water, and bring them to a boil. Reduce the heat and simmer, partially covered, for 20 to 25 minutes, just until tender.

Drain the beans, and transfer them to a medium-size bowl. Stir in the red onion and garlic.

When the peas are cool, stir in the red pepper, scallions, and parsley.

Whisk together the vinegar, olive oil, tamari, and salt. Stir the dressing into the salad, and serve at room temperature.

Cauliflower–Black Bean Salad with Buttermilk-Parmesan Dressing

The white cauliflower makes a striking backdrop for the black beans and red and green bell peppers. The simple, tangy dressing is one you'll want to use on other salads, too.

6 servings

6 cups cauliflower florets (1 large head)
1 cup cooked black beans
6 scallions, thinly sliced
1 medium red bell pepper, seeded and cut into thin, 1½-inch-long strips (¾ cup)
1 medium green bell pepper, seeded and cut into thin, 1½-inch-long strips (¾ cup)
3 or 4 large garlic cloves, peeled
5 tablespoons cider vinegar
2 tablespoons canola oil
¼ cup buttermilk
¼ cup finely grated Parmesan cheese (1 ounce)
¼ teaspoon salt
Freshly ground pepper

Steam the cauliflower just until tender, 5 to 7 minutes. Let it cool.

Combine the cauliflower, beans, scallions, and red and green peppers in a serving bowl.

Process the garlic, vinegar, oil, buttermilk, Parmesan, salt, and pepper to taste in a blender or food processor until smooth.

Toss the salad with the dressing, and serve immediately.

Barley-Lentil Salad

★ BEGINNER-FRIENDLY

This hearty, wholesome salad is a favorite of mine. Black olives and cherry tomatoes make handsome garnishes.

6 to 8 servings

1 cup barley
1 cup green lentils
5 large garlic cloves, peeled and minced
1 cup chopped red onion (1 large onion)
2 cups diced celery (4 stalks)
¾ cup minced fresh parsley
¼ cup olive oil
⅓ cup fresh lemon juice
1 tablespoon Dijon mustard
½ teaspoon salt

Bring the barley and 2½ cups of water to a boil in a saucepan. Reduce the heat and simmer, partially covered, until the water is absorbed and the barley is tender, about 45 minutes.

Meanwhile, bring the lentils and 2 cups of water to a boil in a saucepan. Reduce the heat and simmer, partially covered, until the water is absorbed and the lentils are tender, 20 to 30 minutes.

Transfer the barley and lentils to a medium-size bowl, and stir in the garlic.

When the barley and lentils have cooled, stir in the onion, celery, and parsley.

Whisk together the olive oil, lemon juice, mustard, and salt. Stir the dressing into the salad, and serve at room temperature.

Asparagus, Rice, and Black Bean Salad

★ **BEGINNER-FRIENDLY**

*T*his cilantro- and citrus-scented salad makes a refreshing meal on a hot summer's evening.

8 servings

1 cup brown basmati rice
1½ cups cooked black beans
2 tablespoons olive oil
1 pound fresh asparagus
4 large garlic cloves, peeled and minced
1 large red bell pepper, seeded and cut into thin, ½-inch-long slices (1 cup)
5 scallions, thinly sliced
¼ cup minced fresh cilantro
⅓ cup fresh lemon or lime juice
½ teaspoon salt
1 teaspoon ground cumin
1 tablespoon tamari

Bring the rice and 2 cups of water to a boil in a saucepan. Reduce the heat, and simmer, partially covered, until the rice is tender, 30 to 40 minutes.

Combine the rice in a serving bowl with the black beans and olive oil. Set aside.

Trim the tough ends from the asparagus, and cut it diagonally into slices. (You'll have about 3 cups.) Steam the asparagus until barely tender, about 5 minutes.

Stir the asparagus into the rice, along with the garlic, red pepper, scallions, and cilantro.

Whisk the lemon juice with the salt, cumin, and tamari.

Stir the dressing into the salad, and serve at room temperature.

Curried Rice Salad with Apples and Chick-Peas

★ **BEGINNER-FRIENDLY**

I first enjoyed this delightful salad on board a sailboat in the Caribbean after hours of sun and snorkeling. When we had our fill, we tossed leftovers overboard to the fish, and watched them gobble it up as eagerly as we had.

8 to 10 servings

1½ cups brown basmati rice
5 scallions, sliced
1 medium apple, seeded and chopped
½ cup raisins
¾ cup chopped red bell pepper (1 medium pepper)
1 cup cooked chick-peas
¼ cup minced fresh cilantro
1 teaspoon ground turmeric
1 teaspoon curry powder
½ teaspoon salt
2 tablespoons mayonnaise or mayonnaise substitute
2 teaspoons Worcestershire sauce or vegetarian variety (see page 79)
¼ cup fresh lemon juice
¼ cup olive oil

Bring the rice and 3 cups of water to a boil in a saucepan. Reduce the heat and simmer, partially covered, until the water is absorbed and the rice is tender, 40 to 45 minutes. Fluff the rice with a fork, and set it aside to cool.

Combine the cooled rice in a medium-size bowl with the scallions, apple, raisins, red pepper, chick-peas, and cilantro.

Whisk together the turmeric, curry powder, salt, mayonnaise, Worcestershire, lemon juice, and olive oil.

Stir the dressing into the salad, and serve at room temperature.

Barley-Feta Salad

★ **BEGINNER-FRIENDLY**

*S*erve this Middle Eastern salad with pita bread on the side and a chilled glass of white wine or iced tea.

6 servings

1 cup barley
2 tablespoons canola oil
5 large garlic cloves, peeled and minced
2 cups chopped broccoli
1 medium red bell pepper, seeded and cut into thin, 1½-inch-long pieces (¾ cup)
1 medium green bell pepper, seeded and cut into thin, 1½-inch-long pieces (¾ cup)
5 scallions, thinly sliced
½ cup minced fresh parsley
12 Greek olives, pitted and sliced
6 tablespoons olive oil
1 teaspoon salt
1 teaspoon ground cumin
¼ cup fresh lemon juice
1½ cups crumbled feta cheese (6 ounces)
Spinach leaves

Bring the barley and 2½ cups of water to a boil in a saucepan. Reduce the heat and simmer, partially covered, until the water is absorbed and the barley is tender, 35 to 45 minutes.

Heat the canola oil in a skillet over medium heat. Sauté the garlic and broccoli until just tender, about 5 minutes. (Add a tablespoon or two of water if needed to prevent sticking.)

Combine the barley in a medium-size bowl with the broccoli, red and green peppers, scallions, parsley, and olives.

Whisk together the olive oil, salt, cumin, and lemon juice.

Stir the dressing into the salad, and toss with the feta cheese. Serve on a bed of spinach leaves.

Cashew Rice Salad

★ **BEGINNER-FRIENDLY**

*A*sian *flavors and vibrant colors.*

6 servings

1½ cups basmati rice
1 tablespoon canola oil
2 heaping tablespoons peeled and minced fresh ginger
½ cup finely chopped carrot (1 medium carrot)
2 cups diagonally sliced green beans (½ pound)
1 large red bell pepper, seeded and cut into thin, 1½-inch-long slices
    (1 cup)
5 scallions, diagonally sliced
¼ cup minced fresh cilantro
¾ cup coarsely chopped roasted cashews
3 tablespoons tamari or soy sauce
3 tablespoons sesame oil
¼ cup rice vinegar
½ teaspoon salt

Bring the rice and 3 cups of water to a boil in a saucepan. Reduce the heat and simmer, partially covered, until the water is absorbed and the rice is tender, 35 to 40 minutes. Transfer the rice to a medium-size bowl.

Heat the canola oil in a skillet over medium heat. Sauté the ginger, carrot, and green beans, adding 2 tablespoons of water after a minute or two. After 2 to 3 minutes more, stir in the red pepper, and continue to cook until the beans are just tender, 2 to 3 minutes.

Stir the sautéed vegetables into the rice, along with the scallions, cilantro, and half the cashews.

Whisk the tamari with the sesame oil, vinegar, and salt.

Stir the dressing into the salad. Garnish with the remaining cashews, and serve at room temperature.

Asparagus Pasta Salad with Sesame-Ginger Dressing

A *combination of spinach and white fettuccine noodles is especially attractive.*

6 servings

12 ounces dry fettuccine
1 tablespoon sesame oil
1 pound asparagus
1 medium red bell pepper, seeded and cut into thin, 1-inch-long slices (¾ cup)
5 scallions, thinly sliced
¼ cup minced fresh cilantro

DRESSING
⅓ cup rice vinegar
2 teaspoons Dijon mustard
2 tablespoons tamari or soy sauce
3 large cloves garlic, peeled
1 tablespoon peeled and minced fresh ginger
¼ teaspoon salt
½ cup peanut oil
2 tablespoons sesame oil

1 tablespoon sesame seeds for garnish

Cook the fettuccine in a large pot of boiling water until *al dente*, 8 to 10 minutes. Drain, transfer to a medium-size bowl, and toss with the 1 tablespoon sesame oil.

Trim the tough ends from the asparagus, and slice it diagonally into 1-inch pieces. (You'll have about 3 cups.) Steam the asparagus just until tender, 5 to 8 minutes.

Toss the asparagus, red pepper, scallions, and cilantro with the fettuccine.

In a blender, process the vinegar, mustard, tamari, garlic, ginger, and salt until smooth on medium-high speed. Reduce the speed to low, and slowly pour in the peanut and sesame oils.

Toss the salad with the dressing. Garnish with sesame seeds and serve.

Blue Cauliflower Salad

This marinated salad is equally delicious made with broccoli. Serve it with chilled white wine or sparkling cider.

4 to 6 generous servings

1 medium head cauliflower, broken into florets (about 4 cups)
¾ cup cider vinegar
1 cup canola oil
¼ cup tamari
¼ cup dry white wine
2 large garlic cloves, peeled and cut in half
1 bunch romaine lettuce, torn into bite-size pieces
1 large Vidalia or red onion, cut in half and thinly sliced (1 cup)
1 large green bell pepper, seeded and thinly sliced (1 cup)
2 large tomatoes, cut into wedges (2 cups)
2 cups crumbled blue cheese (8 ounces)
Croutons for topping

Steam the cauliflower just until tender, 4 to 5 minutes. Rinse with cold water and drain.

In a 2-quart container, whisk together the vinegar, oil, tamari, wine, and garlic. Add the cauliflower and stir to coat. Cover and refrigerate at least 4 hours; overnight is best.

Drain the cauliflower, saving the marinade (discard the garlic). Combine it in a large bowl with the lettuce, onion, green pepper, and tomatoes.

Toss the salad with enough marinade to moisten it. Top it with the cheese and croutons, and serve immediately.

Tomato-Feta Salad

★ BEGINNER-FRIENDLY

Quick and simple yet elegant.

4 servings

2 tablespoons balsamic vinegar
3 tablespoons olive oil
¼ teaspoon salt
Pepper
1 medium cucumber, peeled and diced (2 cups)
1 large green bell pepper, seeded and thinly sliced (1 cup)
½ cup coarsely chopped red onion (1 medium onion)
2 medium tomatoes, cut into chunks (1½ cups)
¼ cup chopped fresh basil
1 cup crumbled feta cheese (4 ounces)

Combine the vinegar, olive oil, salt, and pepper in a small, lidded container, and shake well.

In a medium-size bowl, combine the cucumber, green pepper, onion, tomatoes, basil, and cheese.

Pour the dressing over the salad, toss, and serve immediately.

Zesty Cabbage Salad

★ **BEGINNER-FRIENDLY**

This mildly spicy coleslaw has just a touch of mayonnaise.

4 to 6 servings

6 cups shredded green cabbage (1 medium head)
2 cups grated carrots (4 medium carrots)
6 scallions, sliced
½ cup minced fresh parsley
½ cup currants or raisins
¾ cup chopped red bell pepper (1 medium pepper)
½ cup plain yogurt
¼ cup mayonnaise or mayonnaise substitute
¼ cup sour cream
1 tablespoon hot Dijon or horseradish mustard
2 tablespoons fresh lemon juice
1 tablespoon vinegar
1 teaspoon honey
½ teaspoon salt

Combine the cabbage, carrots, scallions, parsley, currants, and red pepper in a medium-size bowl. Toss well.

Whisk together the yogurt, mayonnaise, sour cream, mustard, lemon juice, vinegar, honey, and salt.

Pour the dressing over the salad, toss well, and serve.

Marinated Artichoke and Vegetable Salad

This crisp and tangy salad is packed with red and green bell peppers, mushrooms, red onion, and artichokes, plus chick-peas for protein.

6 to 8 servings

¾ cup olive oil
¼ cup balsamic vinegar
2 tablespoons tamari
2 teaspoons Dijon or hot mustard
¼ teaspoon salt
One 14-ounce can artichoke hearts, drained and cut into sixths
½ pound mushrooms, quartered (2 cups)
1 medium green bell pepper, seeded and cut into 1-inch-square chunks
     (¾ cup)
1 medium red bell pepper, seeded and cut into 1-inch-square chunks (¾ cup)
1 large red onion, quartered and thinly sliced (1 cup)
1 cup cooked chick-peas

Whisk together the olive oil, vinegar, tamari, mustard, and salt in a medium-size bowl. Add the artichoke hearts and mushrooms, and toss to coat. Cover and refrigerate for about an hour, stirring occasionally.

Drain the vegetables, saving the marinade. Combine them in a bowl with the green and red peppers, onion, and chick-peas.

Toss the salad with half the reserved marinade, and serve. (Save the remaining marinade to use as a dressing another time.)

Broccoli, Cauliflower, Walnut, and Avocado Salad

*T*he avocado adds a rich smoothness to the salad that plays off nicely against the crunchy walnuts. Look for sweet Vidalia onions in your market in the spring.

6 to 8 servings

½ cup chopped walnuts
1 teaspoon tamari
1 medium head cauliflower
1 medium bunch broccoli
1 large red bell pepper, seeded and cut into thin, 2-inch-long strips (1 cup)
¾ cup chopped Vidalia or red onion (1 medium-large onion)
1 medium avocado, peeled, seeded, and cut into ½-inch chunks
¼ cup minced fresh cilantro
¼ cup olive oil
¼ cup fresh lemon juice
1 tablespoon Dijon mustard
¼ teaspoon salt

Preheat the oven to 325 degrees. Spread the walnuts on a baking sheet, and toast them for 3 to 5 minutes, just until they begin to brown.

Slide the nuts into a small bowl, sprinkle them with tamari, and stir to combine. Spread them on the baking sheet again, and toast for 2 to 3 minutes more, until lightly browned. Set aside.

Break off the cauliflower and broccoli florets, and slice the stems. (You'll have about 4 cups each of broccoli and cauliflower.) Steam the broccoli and cauliflower just until tender, 5 to 7 minutes. Transfer to a medium-size bowl.

When the steamed vegetables are cool, stir in the red pepper, onion, avocado, and cilantro.

In a small bowl, whisk together the olive oil, lemon juice, mustard, and salt.

Pour the dressing over the salad, toss gently, top with the toasted walnuts, and serve.

Garden Tomato, Basil, and Mozzarella Salad

★ BEGINNER-FRIENDLY

*T*his simple salad makes a great light lunch served on crusty French bread. Be sure to buy fresh mozzarella; it's softer, so it more readily absorbs the tomato and basil flavors. If you can find golden-yellow tomatoes, they make a gorgeous presentation in combination with red ones.

4 servings

1½ cups cubed fresh mozzarella cheese (6 ounces)
3 or 4 large tomatoes, cut into chunks (3 to 4 cups)
½ cup coarsely chopped fresh basil
10 Greek olives, pitted and sliced
1 tablespoon olive oil (preferably extra-light)
¼ teaspoon salt

Combine the mozzarella, tomatoes, basil, and olives in a medium-size bowl. Pour on the olive oil and toss gently. Sprinkle on the salt and toss again. Let the salad sit for 15 minutes before serving.

Tropical Fruit Salad

★ BEGINNER-FRIENDLY

*T*he ginger adds a delightful zing, but you may want to reduce or eliminate it for children and others with tame taste buds.

6 to 8 servings

1 large fresh pineapple, cored, peeled, and chopped (4 cups)
1 medium mango, peeled, pitted, and sliced (2 cups)
3 or 4 bananas, quartered lengthwise and cut into 1-inch-long strips
2 cups seedless red grapes or halved strawberries
1 to 2 teaspoons fresh peeled and minced ginger (optional)
¼ cup fresh lime juice

Combine the pineapple, mango, bananas, grapes, and ginger in a medium-size bowl. Toss gently. Pour on the lime juice, toss again, and serve immediately.

Creamy Sesame Dressing

★ BEGINNER-FRIENDLY

2 cups

3 large garlic cloves, peeled
4 ounces tofu, drained and pressed
½ cup sour cream or plain yogurt
⅓ cup fresh lemon juice
2 tablespoons sesame oil
2 teaspoons tamari or soy sauce
¼ teaspoon salt
2 scallions, coarsely chopped

Combine the garlic, tofu, sour cream, lemon juice, sesame oil, tamari, salt, and scallions in a blender or food processor. Process until well combined.

Artichoke-Parmesan Dressing

★ BEGINNER-FRIENDLY

Marinated artichoke hearts are a bit costly, but this dressing is worth the splurge.

1½ cups

One 6½-ounce jar marinated artichoke hearts in oil
¼ cup fresh lemon juice
3 large garlic cloves, peeled
2 tablespoons finely grated Parmesan cheese
¼ teaspoon salt
¼ cup olive oil

Combine the artichoke hearts and their oil, the lemon juice, garlic, Parmesan cheese, salt, and olive oil in a blender or food processor. Process until well combined.

Pesto Dressing

★ BEGINNER-FRIENDLY

This pesto dressing—minus the traditional nuts—has a lot of body and a deep green color.

1½ cups

3 large garlic cloves, peeled
⅓ cup cider vinegar
1 cup fresh basil leaves (lightly packed)
½ cup coarsely chopped fresh parsley
1 cup canola oil
¼ teaspoon salt
½ cup finely grated Parmesan cheese (2 ounces)
Dash of pepper

Combine the garlic, vinegar, basil, parsley, and ¼ cup of the oil in a blender or food processor. Process on high speed until smooth.

Reduce the speed to low, carefully lift the lid of the blender, and drizzle in the remaining ¾ cup oil. Add the salt, Parmesan cheese, and pepper, and process until well combined.

Dilly Lemon-Dijon Dressing

★ BEGINNER-FRIENDLY

Fresh dill adds a cooling flavor and refreshing color to summer salads.

1¼ cups

½ cup chopped fresh dill
½ cup chopped fresh parsley
2 large garlic cloves, peeled
¼ cup fresh lemon juice
2 tablespoons Dijon mustard
¾ cup canola oil

Combine the dill, parsley, garlic, lemon juice, and mustard in a blender or food processor. Process until smooth.

Turn off the blender and pour in about ¼ cup of the oil. Turn the blender on, carefully lift the lid, and slowly pour in the remaining oil.

Creamy Dill Dressing

★ BEGINNER-FRIENDLY

This light, creamy dressing is so appealing you'll be sure to add it to your list of favorites.

1½ cups

2 large garlic cloves, peeled
¼ cup chopped fresh parsley
½ cup chopped fresh dill
½ cup sour cream or yogurt
¼ teaspoon salt
¼ cup cider vinegar
½ cup olive oil

Combine the garlic, parsley, dill, sour cream, salt, and vinegar in a blender or food processor. Process until smooth.

With the blender still running, carefully lift the lid, and slowly pour in the olive oil and process until well combined.

Avocado Vinaigrette

★ BEGINNER-FRIENDLY

This thick, creamy dressing goes especially well on a green salad with a Mexican main dish.

1 cup

2 large garlic cloves, peeled
½ medium avocado, pitted and peeled
½ cup chopped fresh parsley
¼ cup cider vinegar
¼ teaspoon salt
Dash of pepper
½ cup canola oil

Combine the garlic, avocado, parsley, vinegar, salt, and pepper in a blender or food processor. Process until smooth.

With the blender still running, carefully lift the lid and slowly add the oil, processing until well combined.

Creamy Lemon-Chive Dressing

★ **BEGINNER-FRIENDLY**

Chives are the perfect perennial: they require almost no labor, and they produce all summer long. Chives add zip to soups, salads, and this flavorful dressing.

1½ cups

¼ cup sour cream or plain yogurt
2 large garlic cloves, peeled
¼ cup fresh lemon juice
2 tablespoons chopped fresh chives
½ cup chopped fresh parsley
¼ teaspoon salt
¾ cup olive oil

Combine the sour cream, garlic, lemon juice, chives, parsley, and salt in a blender or food processor. Process until smooth.

With the blender still running, carefully lift the lid and slowly pour in the olive oil, processing until well combined.

Dijon, Chive, and Honey Dressing

★ **BEGINNER-FRIENDLY**

For a lively variation, add a teaspoon or two of fresh horseradish.

1 cup

1 large garlic clove, peeled
2 tablespoons chopped fresh chives
2 tablespoons Dijon mustard
2 tablespoons honey
¼ cup cider vinegar
½ cup canola oil

Combine the garlic, chives, mustard, honey, and vinegar in a blender or food processor. Process until smooth.

With the blender still running, carefully lift the lid and slowly pour in the oil, processing until well combined.

Mexican Vinaigrette

★ **BEGINNER-FRIENDLY**

Serve this cilantro- and lime-flavored dressing on a green salad as part of a Mexican meal.

1½ cups

2 large garlic cloves, peeled
1 tablespoon chopped chives
¼ cup chopped fresh parsley
½ cup chopped fresh cilantro
⅓ cup fresh lime juice
¼ cup cider or white wine vinegar
1 teaspoon prepared mustard
1 teaspoon chili powder
¼ teaspoon salt
¾ cup canola oil

Combine the garlic, chives, parsley, cilantro, lime juice, vinegar, mustard, chili powder, and salt in a blender or food processor. Process until smooth.

With the blender still running, carefully lift the lid and slowly pour in the oil, processing until well combined.

Lunch

We're lucky to live in a time when flavorful, whole-grain breads are widely available in bakeries and markets. Good bread is the basis for good sandwiches—the original portable lunch.

To pack extra nutrition and appeal into those lunch boxes and brown bags, add grated raw vegetables, chopped fresh herbs, capers, sliced olives, or pickled or marinated peppers to your sandwiches. For protein, include hummus, tofu, nut butter, or sliced, hard-cooked egg. Layer sliced cheese or lettuce leaves next to the bread to keep sandwiches from getting soggy, and pack chutney or dressing in a separate container for flavor and moistness. For a change of pace, fill pita bread halves with leftover stir-fried vegetables and rice, or low-fat cottage cheese mixed with nuts and raisins.

Any of the sandwiches in this chapter make a fine at-home meal as well. Try a hot sandwich like the Balkan Sandwich (page 128) with sautéed cabbage, red pepper, and onions topped with soy bacon and blue cheese or Texas Tofu Temptation (page 130) for a simple and delicious dinner.

Stuffed baked potatoes also make great light meals. Let your imagination and your leftovers be your guide in improvising your own. Leftover baked potatoes are full of possibilities, too: try chopping and sautéing one with spinach, tomatoes, and tofu for an instant entree.

Fritters are a fun and interesting lunchtime alternative. They're especially good when you're entertaining, because you can prepare the batter in advance and fry the fritters at the last minute. Serve them as a main course with a green salad, or fry bite-size portions as an appetizer.

 **SANDWICHES**

French Bread with Two Cheeses and Vegetables

★ **BEGINNER-FRIENDLY**

The crunchy celery and bell pepper are a nice contrast to the soft cheeses and tomato.

4 servings

1 cup crumbled feta cheese (4 ounces)
1 cup crumbled blue cheese (4 ounces)
10 to 12 Greek olives, pitted and chopped
3 scallions, sliced
¾ cup chopped green bell pepper (1 medium pepper)
½ cup chopped celery (1 stalk)
¼ cup minced fresh parsley
1 tablespoon Dijon or hot mustard
3 tablespoons mayonnaise or mayonnaise substitute
1 loaf sourdough French bread
Fresh spinach leaves
2 medium tomatoes, sliced

Preheat the oven to 400 degrees.

Combine the cheeses, olives, scallions, green pepper, celery, and parsley in a medium-size bowl.

Mix the mustard with the mayonnaise, and stir it into the cheese mixture.

Warm the bread in the oven for 5 minutes. Slice it into four pieces, and slice each piece in half crosswise.

Layer four of the bread slices with spinach leaves. Spread the cheese mixture evenly over the spinach. Top with the tomato and the remaining bread slices and serve.

Open-Faced Tofu-Vegetable Sandwich with Mornay Sauce

Topped with cheese sauce, this hearty hot sandwich is ideal for a cold day.

4 servings

4 tablespoons canola oil
1 pound tofu, drained, pressed, and cubed
2 tablespoons nutritional yeast (optional)
2 tablespoons tamari
5 large garlic cloves, peeled and minced
1 cup chopped green bell pepper (1 large pepper)
2 cups sliced mushrooms (½ pound)
1 teaspoon dried basil
½ teaspoon salt
1 medium tomato, chopped (¾ cup)
2 tablespoons butter or margarine
½ cup finely chopped onion (1 medium onion)
3 tablespoons unbleached white flour
1 cup milk
1½ cups grated extra-sharp Cheddar cheese (6 ounces)
½ cup minced fresh parsley
4 thick slices sourdough bread, lightly toasted

Heat 2 tablespoons of the oil in a skillet over medium heat. Sauté the tofu, stirring occasionally, until browned and slightly crisp on all sides, 10 to 15 minutes. Sprinkle on the yeast, pour in the tamari, and toss quickly. Transfer the tofu to a bowl.

Heat the remaining 2 tablespoons oil in the skillet over medium heat. Sauté the garlic, green pepper, mushrooms, and basil until the vegetables are tender, about 5 minutes. Remove the pan from the heat, and stir in ¼ teaspoon of the salt, the tomato, and cooked tofu. Cover to keep warm.

Melt the butter in a saucepan over low heat. Sauté the onion until soft, about 5 minutes. Whisk in the flour, and cook for a minute or two. Slowly pour in the milk, whisking until thickened. Add the cheese, parsley, and remaining ¼ teaspoon of salt, whisking until the cheese is melted. Reheat the vegetables if needed.

Divide the bread among four plates. Spread one-fourth of the tofu-vegetable mixture over each slice, top with sauce, and serve immediately.

Greek Ambrosia Sandwich

★ BEGINNER-FRIENDLY

This sandwich is bursting with flavor and texture: sharp feta cheese, mellow cream cheese, garlic and dill, sun-dried tomato and diced red onion, smooth avocado, and crisp spinach leaves.

6 generous servings

- 1 cup crumbled feta cheese (4 ounces)
- 4 ounces cream cheese or Neufchâtel, softened
- 2 tablespoons mayonnaise or mayonnaise substitute
- 2 large garlic cloves, peeled and minced
- 2 tablespoons finely chopped fresh dill
- ⅛ teaspoon salt
- ¼ cup diced, drained oil-packed sun-dried tomatoes
- ¾ cup diced red bell pepper (1 medium pepper)
- ⅓ cup diced red onion
- 12 slices crusty sourdough bread, lightly toasted
- 1 or 2 medium avocados, peeled, seeded, and sliced
- 2 medium tomatoes, sliced
- 2 cups fresh spinach leaves (lightly packed)

Combine the feta, cream cheese, mayonnaise, garlic, dill, and salt in a food processor, and process until smooth.

Transfer to a bowl, and stir in the sun-dried tomatoes, red pepper, and red onion.

Spread the cheese mixture on six of the bread slices. Top with the avocado, tomato, spinach leaves, and the remaining bread. Cut and serve.

Balkan Sandwich

Serve this savory variation on a Reuben sandwich with dill pickles on the side.

4 servings

4 tablespoons canola oil
1 cup chopped onion (1 large onion)
3 cups thinly sliced green cabbage
¾ cup chopped red bell pepper (1 medium pepper)
1 teaspoon dried thyme
¼ teaspoon caraway seeds
¼ teaspoon salt
1½ cups crumbled blue cheese (6 ounces)
One 6-ounce package soy bacon (8 slices)
8 slices rye bread, lightly toasted
Mustard or mayonnaise

Heat 2 tablespoons of the oil in a skillet over medium heat. Sauté the onion, cabbage, red pepper, and thyme until the cabbage is just tender, about 5 minutes.

Transfer the vegetables to a bowl, and stir in the caraway seeds, salt, and blue cheese. Cover to keep warm.

Heat the remaining 2 tablespoons oil in the skillet over medium heat. Fry the soy bacon until crisp and browned on both sides, about 5 minutes.

Place four slices of the bread on plates, and top with the cabbage filling and soy bacon. Spread mayonnaise or mustard on the remaining bread, and place on top. Serve immediately.

Egg Salad Sandwiches with Sun-Dried Tomatoes

★ **BEGINNER-FRIENDLY**

A *lively, colorful version of a traditional summer sandwich.*

4 servings

4 large eggs
2 tablespoons mayonnaise or mayonnaise substitute
2 tablespoons plain yogurt
2 teaspoons Dijon mustard
8 oil-packed, sun-dried tomato halves, drained and chopped
8 Greek olives, pitted and chopped
4 scallions, thinly sliced
Dash of salt
8 slices whole wheat bread, lightly toasted
4 slices Cheddar cheese (optional)
Fresh spinach leaves
Pickles for serving

Cover the eggs with cold water in a saucepan. Bring to a boil. Boil for 12 minutes. Rinse with cold water. When cool enough to handle, peel and chop.

Stir together the eggs, mayonnaise, yogurt, mustard, sun-dried tomatoes, olives, scallions, and salt in a small bowl.

Spread the egg mixture over four slices of the bread. Top with cheese slices, spinach leaves, and the remaining bread. Serve with pickles on the side.

Texas Tofu Temptation

This spicy sandwich will intrigue your meat-eating friends. Miso, fermented soy bean paste, is available at health food stores.

4 servings

SAUCE
- 1 tablespoon miso
- 1 tablespoon prepared mustard
- 1 tablespoon ketchup
- 1 teaspoon molasses
- ⅛ to ¼ teaspoon Tabasco sauce

- 1 pound tofu, drained and pressed
- 3 tablespoons canola oil
- 2 teaspoons tamari
- 4 large, crusty rolls
- 6 large garlic cloves, peeled and minced
- 1 cup chopped onion (1 large onion)
- 1 medium jalapeño pepper, minced
- 1 medium green bell pepper, seeded and thinly sliced (¾ cup)
- 1 medium red bell pepper, seeded and thinly sliced (¾ cup)

Stir together the miso, mustard, ketchup, molasses, and Tabasco sauce in a small bowl. Set aside.

Preheat the oven to 325 degrees.

Cut the tofu into ½-inch-thick slices that are about 2 by 4 inches square (the size of the slab).

Heat 2 tablespoons of the oil in a skillet over medium heat. Sauté the tofu until browned and slightly crisp on both sides, 10 to 12 minutes. Pour in the tamari, and flip the tofu over to coat the other side. Drain on paper towels.

Put the rolls in the oven to warm.

Heat the remaining tablespoon of oil in the skillet over medium heat. Sauté the garlic, onion, jalapeño, and green and red peppers until soft, about 5 minutes.

Remove the rolls from the oven, and slice them in half. Spread some of the sauce on the bottom of each roll. Top with tofu slices, sautéed vegetables, the remaining sauce, and the roll tops. Serve immediately.

Stuffed French Bread Sandwiches

You've never eaten a more elegant melted-cheese sandwich.

4 servings

1 loaf sourdough French bread
2 tablespoons canola oil
8 large garlic cloves, peeled and minced
1 teaspoon dried oregano
1 teaspoon dried basil
2 cups sliced mushrooms (½ pound)
¾ cup chopped red bell pepper (1 medium pepper)
¾ cup chopped green bell pepper (1 medium pepper)
½ cup chopped red onion (1 medium onion)
10 Greek olives, pitted and chopped
1 large tomato, chopped (1 cup)
½ teaspoon salt
2 tablespoons finely grated Parmesan cheese
8 slices mozzarella cheese

Preheat the oven to 375 degrees.

Cut the bread in half lengthwise, and then in fourths. Pull out enough bread from the inside of each piece to form a 1-inch indentation. (Save it for making croutons or bread crumbs.) Place the slices on a baking sheet.

Heat the oil in a skillet over medium heat. Sauté the garlic, oregano, basil, mushrooms, and red and green peppers until just tender, about 5 minutes.

Drain the vegetables, and transfer them to a bowl. Stir in the onion, olives, tomato, salt, and Parmesan.

Spoon the vegetable mixture onto the prepared bread. Top with the slices of mozzarella cheese, and bake for 10 minutes, until the cheese is melted and the bread is lightly browned on the edges. Put sandwich tops and bottoms together and serve immediately.

Avocado-Tofu Dream Sandwich

★ **BEGINNER-FRIENDLY**

A *wondrous combination of smooth tofu and avocado and crisp onion and bell pepper.*

5 servings

½ pound tofu, drained well
1 medium avocado, peeled and seeded
1 tablespoon minced fresh dill
1 large garlic clove, peeled and minced
⅛ teaspoon salt
2 teaspoons tamari
2 tablespoons mayonnaise or mayonnaise substitute
1 tablespoon fresh lemon juice
⅓ cup chopped red bell pepper
⅓ cup chopped Vidalia or red onion
5 oil-packed, sun-dried tomato halves, drained and chopped
10 slices sourdough rye bread, lightly toasted
Fresh spinach leaves
Cheddar cheese slices (optional)
Mustard

Mash the tofu and avocado together in a medium-size bowl until smooth.

Stir in the dill, garlic, salt, tamari, mayonnaise, lemon juice, red pepper, onion, and sun-dried tomatoes.

Spread five of the bread slices with the filling. Top with spinach leaves and cheese if you like. Spread the remaining bread with mustard, and place on top. Cut and serve.

Tempeh Sandwich with Two Cheeses

Children may shy away from the bold combination of fermented tempeh and tangy blue cheese, but grown-ups will love it.

6 servings

3 tablespoons canola oil
One 8-ounce package tempeh, cut into ½-inch pieces
1 tablespoon tamari
1 cup chopped onion (1 large onion)
¾ cup chopped red bell pepper (1 medium pepper)
¾ cup chopped green bell pepper (1 medium pepper)
1 small jalapeño pepper, minced
2 cups sliced mushrooms (½ pound)
¼ teaspoon dried savory
¼ teaspoon dried thyme
¾ cup finely chopped celery (1½ stalks)
1 tablespoon ketchup
2 tablespoons fresh lemon juice
1 cup crumbled blue cheese (4 ounces)
1 cup grated Cheddar cheese (4 ounces)
12 slices rye or whole wheat sourdough bread, lightly toasted
Fresh spinach leaves
Mustard

Heat 2 tablespoons of the oil in a skillet over medium heat. Sauté the tempeh until browned on all sides, 8 to 10 minutes. Pour in the tamari and stir quickly to combine. Transfer to a medium-size bowl.

Heat the remaining 1 tablespoon oil in the skillet over medium heat. Sauté the onion, red and green peppers, jalapeño, mushrooms, savory, and thyme until the vegetables are tender, about 5 minutes.

Stir the vegetables into the tempeh. Add the celery, ketchup, lemon juice, and cheeses, and mix well.

Spread the filling over six slices of the bread, and top with spinach. Spread the remaining bread with mustard, place on top, and serve.

Artichoke, Tomato, and Feta Sandwich

★ BEGINNER-FRIENDLY

love the combination of sharp and mellow flavors in this sandwich. It goes well with Cherry Tomato Gazpacho on page 99.

4 servings

1 loaf fresh, crusty French bread
Mustard or mayonnaise (optional)
One 6-ounce jar marinated artichoke hearts, drained and chopped
¼ cup halved pimento-stuffed green olives
¼ cup chopped Greek olives
¼ cup chopped roasted red pepper
1¼ cups crumbled feta cheese (5 ounces)
½ cup finely chopped fresh parsley
½ cup finely chopped fresh basil
¼ cup minced red onion
2 medium tomatoes, sliced

Cut the bread in half lengthwise, and then in fourths. Pull out enough bread from the inside of each piece to form a ½-inch indentation. (Save it for making croutons or bread crumbs.) Spread the slices with mustard or mayonnaise if you like.

Stir together the artichoke hearts, olives, roasted peppers, cheese, parsley, basil, and onion in a medium-size bowl.

Spread the filling over four of the prepared bread slices. Layer the tomato slices over the filling, top with the remaining bread, and serve.

Monterey Tortillas

★ **BEGINNER-FRIENDLY**

This was a popular lunch special with customers and staff alike at the Horn of the Moon Café. The trick is not to overcook the tortillas—to keep them soft but still melt the cheese. The crunchy, spicy, coleslaw goes well with the rich, creamy texture of avocado and melted cheese. A combination of red and green cabbage looks especially nice.

4 servings

2 cups sliced cabbage (½ pound)
½ cup sliced red onion (1 medium onion)
2 tablespoons cider vinegar
¼ teaspoon salt
¼ teaspoon chili powder
Dash of cayenne
Four 10-inch flour tortillas
2 medium tomatoes, sliced
1 medium avocado, peeled, seeded, and sliced
12 to 16 slices jalapeño pepper Jack cheese
Salsa for serving

Preheat the oven to 375 degrees.

Mix the cabbage, half the onion, the vinegar, salt, chili powder, and cayenne in a medium-size bowl. Set aside.

Spread out the tortillas on a baking sheet. Place three or four slices of tomato down the middle of each tortilla. Top the tomato with avocado slices, the remaining onion, and the cheese slices, using 3 or 4 slices for each tortilla.

Bake for 5 minutes, until the cheese is just melted.

Top the tortillas with the cabbage mixture, and roll them up. Serve with salsa on the side.

 **PITAS**

Mediterranean Stuffed Pita

★ **BEGINNER-FRIENDLY**

A *fast lunch for two!*

2 servings

2 whole wheat pita breads
Mayonnaise or mustard (optional)
8 to 10 thin slices mozzarella or provolone cheese
4 medium mushrooms, sliced
12 pitted black olives, cut in half
1 large tomato, thinly sliced
Dash of salt
Dash of dried oregano
Dash of dried basil
12 fresh spinach leaves

Preheat the oven to 425 degrees.

Slice the pitas around the outer edges so that when you split open the pitas you have four whole circles of bread.

Spread mayonnaise or mustard on two of the circles if you like.

Place the other two bread circles on a baking sheet, and top them with a few cheese slices. Layer on the mushrooms, olives, and tomato. Season with salt, oregano, and basil. Add a layer of spinach leaves, and a few more slices of cheese.

Bake for about 5 minutes, just until the cheese is melted. Place the remaining bread circles on top, and bake 2 to 3 minutes more, just until warmed through, and serve.

Asparagus Dill Pita

★ **BEGINNER-FRIENDLY**

A *simply wonderful quick lunch.*

4 servings

4 whole wheat pitas
Mustard (optional)
20 asparagus spears, steamed
2 medium tomatoes, sliced
1 tablespoon finely chopped fresh dill
Salt
Pepper
8 thin slices extra-sharp Cheddar cheese
8 thin slices smoked provolone cheese

Preheat the oven to 400 degrees.

Slice the pitas around the outside edges so that when you split open the pitas you have eight whole circles of bread.

Spread mustard on four of the circles if you like.

Place the other four circles on a baking sheet. Place five stalks of steamed asparagus on each one. (Cut the asparagus in half if necessary to make it fit.) Cover the asparagus with tomato slices. Sprinkle with dill, and salt and pepper to taste. Top with slices of Cheddar and provolone.

Bake for about 5 minutes, just until the cheese is melted. Top with the remaining bread circles, bake for 2 to 3 minutes more, just until warmed through, and serve.

Pita Pizzas

★ **BEGINNER-FRIENDLY**

Feel free to vary the vegetable and cheese combinations.

4 servings

2 whole wheat pitas
2 tablespoons canola oil
1 cup chopped onion (1 large onion)
4 large garlic cloves, peeled and minced
1 medium green bell pepper, seeded and cut into thin strips (¾ cup)
1 teaspoon dried basil
1 teaspoon dried oregano
1 cup sliced mushrooms (4 ounces)
10 black olives, cut in half
1 medium tomato, chopped (¾ cup)
Dash of salt
1 cup marinara sauce
1½ to 2 cups grated mozzarella cheese (6 to 8 ounces)
1 tablespoon finely grated Parmesan cheese

Preheat the oven to 400 degrees.

Slice the pitas around the outside edges so that when you split open the pitas you have four whole circles of bread.

Heat the oil in a skillet over medium heat. Sauté the onion, garlic, green pepper, basil, and oregano until the vegetables are soft, about 5 minutes. Stir in the mushrooms and cook until tender, about 3 minutes more.

Drain the vegetables, and transfer them to a bowl. Stir in the olives, tomato, and salt.

Place the pitas on a baking sheet, and bake for 2 to 3 minutes, just until lightly toasted.

Spread ¼ cup marinara sauce over each pita. Top with the sautéed vegetables, grated mozzarella, and a dash of Parmesan cheese.

Bake for 8 to 10 minutes, until the cheese is nicely melted, and serve.

Mexican Stuffed Potatoes

Potatoes are a favorite comfort food of mine. The chili filling gives these extra flavor and protein.

4 servings

4 large baking potatoes, scrubbed
2 tablespoons canola oil
5 large garlic cloves, peeled and minced
¾ cup chopped red bell pepper (1 medium pepper)
1 small jalapeño pepper, minced
½ cup chopped onion (1 medium onion)
1½ cups cooked pinto beans (one 15-ounce can, rinsed and drained)
1 medium tomato, chopped (¾ cup)
¼ cup minced fresh cilantro
1 teaspoon ground cumin
½ teaspoon salt
1 cup grated Cheddar or Monterey Jack cheese (4 ounces)
2 tablespoons butter or margarine

Preheat the oven to 425 degrees.

Prick the potatoes once with a fork and bake for 1 hour, until tender. Remove them from the oven and reduce the temperature to 400 degrees.

When the potatoes are cool enough to handle, slice open the tops and gently scoop out the insides, leaving the shells whole. Transfer the white part to a bowl, and mash with a fork.

Heat the oil in a skillet over medium heat. Sauté the garlic, red pepper, jalapeño, and onion until tender, about 5 minutes.

Stir in the beans, tomato, cilantro, cumin, salt, and cheese.

Set aside 1 cup of this filling. Mix the rest with the reserved potato, along with the butter or margarine.

Spoon the filling back into the potato shells. (They will be very full.) Set the potatoes in an ungreased baking dish, and top each with ¼ cup of the reserved bean mixture. Bake for 15 minutes, until warmed through, and serve.

Greek Stuffed Potatoes

4 servings

4 large baking potatoes, scrubbed
2 tablespoons canola oil
¾ cup chopped red onion (1 medium-large onion)
4 large garlic cloves, peeled and minced
1 teaspoon dried oregano
2 cups chopped fresh spinach (lightly packed)
1 medium tomato, chopped (¾ cup)
½ teaspoon salt
2 tablespoons finely chopped fresh basil
2 tablespoons butter or margarine
1 cup crumbled feta cheese (4 ounces)
1 bunch scallions, chopped

Preheat the oven to 425 degrees.

Prick the potatoes once with a fork and bake for 1 hour, until tender. Remove them from the oven and reduce the temperature to 400 degrees.

When the potatoes are cool enough to handle, slice open the tops and gently scoop out the insides, leaving the shells whole. Transfer the white part to a bowl, and mash with a fork.

Heat the oil in a skillet over medium heat. Sauté the onion, garlic, and oregano until the onion is tender, about 5 minutes.

Remove the pan from the heat, and stir in the spinach, tomato, salt, and basil.

Mix the vegetables with the reserved potato. Stir in the butter, cheese, and scallions.

Spoon the filling back into the potato shells. (They will be very full.) Set them on a baking sheet, and bake for 15 minutes, until warmed through, and serve.

Blue Cheese, Asparagus, and Dill Stuffed Potatoes

A *winning combination.*

4 servings

4 large baking potatoes, scrubbed
2 tablespoons canola oil
4 large garlic cloves, peeled and finely chopped
½ cup chopped onion (1 medium onion)
2 cups sliced fresh asparagus (¾ pound, tough ends discarded)
2 tablespoons finely chopped fresh dill
1 cup crumbled blue cheese (4 ounces)
1 teaspoon salt
Pepper
2 tablespoons butter or margarine
½ cup sour cream

Preheat the oven to 425 degrees.

Prick the potatoes once with a fork and bake for 1 hour, until tender. Remove them from the oven and reduce the temperature to 400 degrees.

When the potatoes are cool enough to handle, slice open the tops and gently scoop out the insides, leaving the shells whole. Transfer the white part to a bowl, and mash with a fork.

Heat the oil in a skillet over medium heat. Sauté the garlic, onion, and asparagus until tender, 5 to 7 minutes.

Stir the sautéed vegetables into the reserved potatoes. Add the dill, cheese, salt, pepper to taste, butter, and sour cream, and mix well.

Spoon the filling back into the potato shells. (They will be very full.) Set them on a baking sheet, and bake for 15 minutes, until warmed through.

 **FRITTERS**

See also recipe for Banana Fritters (page 66).

Black Bean, Corn, and Cheddar Fritters

*F*ritters are best served hot and crispy, right out of the pan. Here's a Mexican version I'm partial to, with corn, red bell pepper, chilies, cilantro, and Cheddar cheese.

4 or 5 servings (about 15 fritters)

½ cup yellow cornmeal
½ cup unbleached white flour
½ teaspoon baking powder
½ teaspoon salt
1 teaspoon chili powder
½ teaspoon ground cumin
Dash of cayenne
½ cup milk
1 egg yolk
1 cup cooked black beans
1 cup grated sharp Cheddar cheese (4 ounces)
½ cup fresh or frozen corn kernels
2 tablespoons minced fresh cilantro
¾ cup chopped red bell pepper (1 medium pepper)
2 tablespoons diced, roasted green chili peppers (available in cans)
2 egg whites
½ cup canola oil
Sour cream for serving
Salsa for serving

Stir together the cornmeal, flour, baking powder, salt, chili powder, cumin, and cayenne in a medium-size bowl.

Beat the milk with the egg yolk, and add it to the dry ingredients, mixing well.

Stir in the beans, cheese, corn, cilantro, red pepper, and green chilies.

In another bowl, beat the egg whites with an electric mixer until stiff. Gently fold them into the batter.

Heat the ½ cup oil in a 10-inch skillet over medium-high heat. (Test the heat by dropping a bit of batter into the oil; it should immediately sizzle and rise to the top.)

Spoon in about ¼ cup of batter for each fritter, making three or four at a time. Fry until golden brown on one side, 3 to 5 minutes. Turn and fry until golden brown on the other side, and drain on paper towels. Fry the rest of the batter in batches.

Serve immediately with sour cream and salsa on the side.

Crispy Ginger and Tofu Fritters

T*hese flavorful fritters are addictive. Look for five-spice powder in the Asian section of your market.*

4 servings (about 12 fritters)

2 tablespoons canola oil plus ½ cup for frying
½ pound tofu, drained, pressed, and cut into ¼-inch cubes
2 large garlic cloves, peeled and minced
1½ tablespoons peeled and minced fresh ginger
2 tablespoons tamari
¾ cup chopped red bell pepper (1 medium pepper)
½ cup chopped water chestnuts
5 scallions, sliced
2 tablespoons minced fresh cilantro
½ cup unbleached white flour
½ cup whole wheat pastry flour
½ teaspoon salt
1 tablespoon five-spice powder
1 large egg
½ cup milk

Heat the 2 tablespoons oil in a skillet over medium heat. Sauté the tofu, stirring occasionally, until browned and slightly crisp on all sides, 10 to 12 minutes. Add the garlic and ginger, and cook, stirring, for another minute. Pour in the tamari, and stir quickly to combine.

Transfer the tofu mixture to a medium-size bowl. Stir in the red pepper, water chestnuts, scallions, and cilantro.

(Continued)

In another bowl, stir together the flours, salt, and five-spice powder. Beat the egg with the milk, and pour it into the flour mixture, stirring well. Stir the flour mixture into the tofu and vegetables.

Heat the remaining ½ cup oil in a 10-inch skillet over medium-high heat. (Test the heat by dropping a bit of batter into the oil; it should immediately sizzle and rise to the top.)

Spoon in about ¼ cup of batter for each fritter, making three or four at a time. Gently pat down the fritters with a spatula. Fry until golden brown on one side, 3 to 5 minutes. Turn and fry until golden brown on the other side, and drain on paper towels. Fry the rest of the batter in batches. Serve immediately.

Caribbean Fritters

Conch fritters are served all over the British Virgin Islands, and conch shells are scattered across many beaches. Here is my vegetarian adaptation of this island specialty, which makes a scrumptious lunch or appetizer.

6 servings (about 36 small fritters)

2 tablespoons canola oil plus 1 cup for frying
1 cup chopped onion (1 large onion)
4 large garlic cloves, peeled and minced
1 medium jalapeño pepper, minced
¾ cup chopped red bell pepper (1 medium pepper)
1 cup chopped zucchini (1 small zucchini)
1 cup whole wheat pastry flour
1 cup unbleached white flour
1 teaspoon baking powder
¾ teaspoon salt
1 teaspoon ground cumin
1 teaspoon chili powder
Dash of cayenne
2 large eggs, beaten
1 tablespoon rum
1 cup mashed, cooked winter squash (butternut is good)
¼ cup minced fresh parsley
Caribbean Dipping Sauce (recipe follows)

Heat the 2 tablespoons oil in a skillet over medium heat. Sauté the onion, garlic, jalapeño, red pepper, and zucchini until tender, about 5 minutes. Remove the pan from the heat.

Stir together the flours, baking powder, salt, cumin, chili powder, and cayenne in a medium-size bowl.

In another bowl, beat the eggs with the rum, squash, and parsley. Stir in the sautéed vegetables.

Stir the vegetable mixture into the flour mixture, combining well.

Heat the remaining 1 cup oil in a saucepan over medium-high heat. (Test the heat by dropping a bit of batter into the oil; it should immediately sizzle and rise to the top.)

Spoon in 1 tablespoon of batter for each fritter, making about eight at a time. Fry until golden brown on one side, 3 to 5 minutes. Turn and fry until golden brown on the other side, and drain on paper towels. Fry the rest of the batter in batches. Serve immediately with dipping sauce on the side.

CARIBBEAN DIPPING SAUCE

½ cup

3 tablespoons mayonnaise or mayonnaise substitute
2 tablespoons chopped fresh cilantro
2 tablespoons sour cream
2 tablespoons fresh lime juice
½ to 1 teaspoon hot sauce

Stir together the mayonnaise, cilantro, sour cream, lime juice, and hot sauce. Serve chilled with hot crispy fritters.

For Starters

When friends or family come for dinner, I like to have something tasty ready for them to eat—and have meal preparations in hand so that I can enjoy eating with them. After initial greetings, it's good to sit down and catch up on one another's lives over appetizers and a glass of wine or sparkling cider.

Think about the whole meal when you plan appetizers, and look for ways to vary ingredients and tastes while keeping dishes compatible. Pesto Cheese Dip (page 148) and crackers, for instance, is a fine prelude to Mushroom Pot Pie with Cheddar Cheese Sauce (page 248), and Mushroom-Leek Turnovers with Blue Cheese (page 160) is an appealing starter for Spicy Seitan and Vegetable Stroganoff (page 200). If you've chosen an ethnic theme, the appetizer course is a good place to introduce it—for instance, Baked Black Bean Dip (page 147) before an entree of Enchiladas with Jalapeño and Cilantro Sauce (page 180) or raw vegetables and Szechuan Eggplant Dip (page 149) before a main course of Oriental Tofu Balls with Fruit Sauce, Stir-Fried Vegetables, and Rice (page 236).

The one pitfall to making delicious appetizers is that your guests will fill up on them, so serve small portions, and whisk leftovers back to the kitchen after everyone has had a taste.

Many of these meal openers also work well as light main dishes. The egg rolls are wonderful on their own or with soup or salad, and a bean or cheese dip with crusty bread and fresh vegetables makes a quick and delicious meal.

Baked Black Bean Dip

*T*he *fresh cilantro makes this dish. You can prepare it a day in advance, and bake it just before serving.*

2½ cups

> 2¼ cups cooked black beans (rinse and drain if canned)
> ¾ teaspoon salt
> 1 tablespoon canola oil
> 4 large garlic cloves, peeled and minced
> 1 medium jalapeño pepper, minced
> 2 tablespoons fresh lime or lemon juice
> 2 tablespoons minced fresh cilantro
> 1 teaspoon chili powder
> ½ cup salsa
> Cayenne
> 2 scallions, thinly sliced
> ½ cup grated Cheddar or soy cheese (2 ounces, optional)
> Corn chips for serving

Puree the beans in a blender or food processor with the salt and ¼ cup of water.

Preheat the oven to 400 degrees.

Heat the oil in a skillet over medium heat. Sauté the garlic and jalapeño just until tender, 2 to 3 minutes.

Remove the pan from the heat, and stir in the beans, lime juice, cilantro, chili powder, salsa, cayenne to taste, and half the scallion slices.

Spoon the dip into a 1-quart baking dish, and top with grated cheese if you like. Bake for about 20 minutes, until hot and bubbly. Garnish with the remaining scallions, and serve with corn chips.

Pesto Cheese Dip

★ **BEGINNER-FRIENDLY**

love to make this quick, creamy dip when my garden is bursting with basil.

2 cups

2 cups fresh basil leaves (lightly packed)
4 large garlic cloves, peeled
1 cup ricotta cheese (8 ounces)
½ cup walnuts
¼ teaspoon salt
¼ cup finely grated Parmesan cheese
Corn chips, crackers, or vegetable dippers for serving

Puree the basil, garlic, and ricotta in a food processor or blender. Add the walnuts, salt, and Parmesan, and process until smooth.

Serve chilled or at room temperature with corn chips, crackers, or vegetable dippers.

Feta and Herb Cheese Dip

★ **BEGINNER-FRIENDLY**

1¾ cups

4 ounces cream cheese or Neufchâtel, softened
½ cup plain yogurt
¾ cup crumbled feta cheese (3 ounces)
1 tablespoon fresh lemon juice
¼ teaspoon salt
2 tablespoons minced fresh dill
1 tablespoon minced fresh basil
1 tablespoon minced fresh parsley
Vegetable dippers for serving

Puree the cream cheese, yogurt, feta cheese, lemon juice, salt, dill, basil, and parsley in a food processor or blender.

Serve chilled or at room temperature with carrot sticks, broccoli florets, red and green bell pepper strips, snow peas, and other vegetable dippers.

Szechuan Eggplant Dip

Serve this smooth, hot dip with crackers or vegetable dippers—and ice-cold beer or juice spritzers to put out the fire! Look for chili paste with garlic (Lan Chi is one brand) in the Asian section of your market.

2 cups

3 tablespoons peanut oil
1 pound eggplant, peeled and chopped (about 6 cups)
2 tablespoons peeled and finely chopped fresh ginger
1 to 2 teaspoons chili paste with garlic
2 tablespoons rice vinegar or white wine vinegar
2 tablespoons tahini
2 tablespoons tamari or soy sauce
1 teaspoon sesame oil
2 scallions, thinly sliced

Heat the peanut oil in a skillet over medium heat. Sauté the eggplant and ginger until the eggplant is tender, 8 to 10 minutes, stirring occasionally. (Add a tablespoon or two of water if needed to prevent sticking.)

Puree the sautéed eggplant in a food processor or blender, along with the chili paste, vinegar, tahini, tamari, and sesame oil.

Spoon the dip into a serving bowl. Stir in half the scallions, and garnish with the other half. Serve at room temperature or chilled.

Cheddar and Sun-Dried Tomato Dip

★ **BEGINNER-FRIENDLY**

This simple dip is bursting with flavor. It's best served the day it's made.

2 cups

4 ounces cream cheese or Neufchâtel, softened
¼ cup sour cream
½ cup plain yogurt
2 cups grated extra-sharp Cheddar cheese (8 ounces)
2 large garlic cloves, peeled and minced
4 scallions, thinly sliced
8 oil-packed, sun-dried tomato halves, drained and minced
Dash of salt
Crackers, chips, or vegetable dippers for serving

Stir together the cream cheese, sour cream, and yogurt in a medium-size bowl. Stir in the Cheddar, garlic, scallions, tomatoes, and salt.

Transfer to a serving dish, and serve with crackers, chips, or vegetable dippers.

Layered Hummus Dip

This lively dip is always popular at parties. The hummus and olive spread can be purchased or homemade.

6 to 8 servings

2 cups hummus
¼ cup Greek olive spread (see Note)
1 cup crumbled feta cheese (4 ounces)
¼ cup sour cream
¼ cup plain yogurt
4 scallions, chopped
1 small tomato, diced (½ cup)
Corn chips, vegetable dippers, or crackers for serving

Spread the hummus in the bottom of a 9- or 10-inch ceramic or glass pie plate. Carefully spread the olive mix over it.

In a bowl, stir together the cheese, sour cream, yogurt, and three-fourths of the scallions. Spread gently over the olive mix, and garnish with the remaining scallions and the tomatoes.

Serve chilled or at room temperature with corn chips, vegetable dippers, or crackers.

Note

To make your own olive spread, puree ¾ cup pitted Greek olives, 1 tablespoon olive oil, 1 teaspoon balsamic vinegar, 1 tablespoon capers, ½ teaspoon dried oregano, and 1 large peeled garlic clove in a food processor or blender. Makes ½ cup. Refrigerate or freeze any extra. The spread will last for 4 to 6 weeks refrigerated.

Hot Cheese and Chili Pepper Dip

★ **BEGINNER-FRIENDLY**

Serving a hot dip fresh from the stove is a sure way to get guests together and talking. This one can be reheated in a double boiler. Look for canned, roasted green chilies in the Mexican section of your grocery store.

1 ½ cups

1 tablespoon butter or margarine
½ cup finely chopped onion (1 medium onion)
3 large garlic cloves, peeled and minced
1 tablespoon unbleached white flour
½ cup tomato juice
¼ cup finely chopped pimento or roasted red pepper
2 tablespoons chopped, roasted green chili peppers
¾ cup grated extra-sharp Cheddar cheese (3 ounces)
¾ cup grated Monterey Jack cheese (3 ounces)
½ teaspoon chili powder
⅛ teaspoon salt
Corn chips for serving

Melt the butter in a saucepan over medium heat. Sauté the onion and garlic until soft, about 5 minutes. Whisk in the flour, and let it cook for a minute or two.

Slowly pour in the tomato juice, whisking until smooth and slightly thickened. Stir in the pimento, green chilies, cheeses, chili powder, and salt. Simmer, stirring, until the cheeses melt.

Serve immediately with corn chips (blue corn chips are especially nice).

FLAVORS OF THE ORIENT

Sesame Noodles

This is my interpretation of a recipe given to me by a wonderful chef, Steve Bogart. Steve says sugar should be used for authentic Chinese flavor, but I found that honey works well. The recipe makes enough sauce for several meals; it stores beautifully in the refrigerator, and is great to have on hand.

6 to 8 appetizer servings

SAUCE
> 2 tablespoons peeled and minced fresh ginger
> 5 or 6 large garlic cloves, peeled and minced
> 2 cups tahini
> 1 cup soy sauce or tamari
> ⅓ cup rice vinegar
> ½ cup honey
> ⅓ cup sesame oil
> 1 tablespoon chili paste with garlic

NOODLES
> 1 pound dry fettuccine noodles
> 1 bunch scallions, trimmed and chopped, for garnish

Puree the ginger, garlic, tahini, and soy sauce in a food processor or blender. Add the vinegar, honey, sesame oil, and chili paste, and process until well mixed. Set aside.

Cook the fettuccine in a large pot of boiling water until *al dente*, about 8 minutes. Drain.

Toss the hot pasta with ½ to ⅔ cup of sauce. Garnish with scallions, and serve. Store leftover sauce in a covered plastic container in the refrigerator.

Asian Stuffed Mushrooms

Mushrooms take on a whole different taste and consistency when they are stuffed and baked. This oriental-flavored version is a good introduction to almost any meal.

4 to 6 appetizer servings

1 pound large mushrooms
2 tablespoons canola oil
3 large garlic cloves, peeled and minced
2 tablespoons peeled and minced fresh ginger
¾ cup finely chopped red bell pepper (1 medium pepper)
1 stalk bok choy, chopped (½ cup)
1 teaspoon sesame oil
1 tablespoon tamari or soy sauce
⅛ teaspoon salt
½ cup fresh bread crumbs
¼ teaspoon chili paste with garlic
3 scallions, thinly sliced
1 tablespoon fresh lemon juice

Preheat the oven to 375 degrees. Grease a baking pan.

Pull the stems from the mushroom caps and chop them finely. Place the caps in the prepared baking pan.

Heat the canola oil in a skillet over medium heat. Sauté the garlic, ginger, and red bell pepper just until tender, about 3 minutes. (Stir in a tablespoon or two of water if the ginger begins to stick.)

Stir in the chopped mushroom stems and the bok choy. Cook until the mushrooms are tender and the liquid has evaporated, about 5 minutes more.

Remove the pan from the heat, and stir in the sesame oil, tamari, salt, bread crumbs, chili paste, scallions, and lemon juice.

Using a teaspoon, stuff the mushroom caps with the filling. Bake for 20 to 25 minutes, until the caps are tender. Serve immediately.

Seven-Vegetable Egg Rolls

Flavorful homemade egg rolls are well worth the effort—especially for vegetarians like me who are frustrated to find only shrimp or pork versions at most Chinese restaurants. Egg rolls and spring rolls are best fresh, when the wrappers are still crisp from frying.

16 egg rolls

4 tablespoons canola oil plus 1 cup for frying
1 pound extra-firm tofu, drained, pressed, and diced
3 tablespoons tamari
1 tablespoon nutritional yeast (optional)
2 cups chopped green cabbage
5 large garlic cloves, peeled and minced
1 cup chopped onion (1 large onion)
1 tablespoon peeled and minced fresh ginger
1 cup chopped celery or bok choy (2 stalks)
½ cup diced carrot (1 medium carrot)
5 scallions, sliced
One 8-ounce can water chestnuts, drained and chopped
1 cup mung bean sprouts
1 teaspoon sesame seeds
½ teaspoon salt
One 1-pound package egg roll wrappers

Heat 2 tablespoons of the oil in a large skillet over medium heat. Sauté the tofu, stirring occasionally, until lightly browned on all sides, 10 to 15 minutes.

Add 2 tablespoons of the tamari and the nutritional yeast, and stir quickly to combine. Drain the tofu on paper towels.

Heat 2 more tablespoons of oil in the skillet over medium heat. Sauté the cabbage, garlic, onion, ginger, celery, and carrot until barely tender, about 5 minutes.

Remove the pan from the heat, and stir in the scallions, water chestnuts, bean sprouts, sesame seeds, salt, and the remaining tablespoon of tamari.

Wrap the Egg Rolls

Place a wrapper on a work surface at a diagonal. (Cover the rest with plastic wrap.)

Place ½ cup of filling in a fat line from one corner to the opposite corner, leaving about 2 inches clear at each end. Fold those two corners over the filling.

Brush the bottom corner and edges with water and fold up over the filling and folded corners.

Brush the top corner and edges with water, and roll the egg roll up over it, patting gently to seal it into a snug log shape.

If necessary, brush the connecting points with more water to form a tight seal; this will prevent the filling from leaking out during frying.

Repeat until the filling is used up.

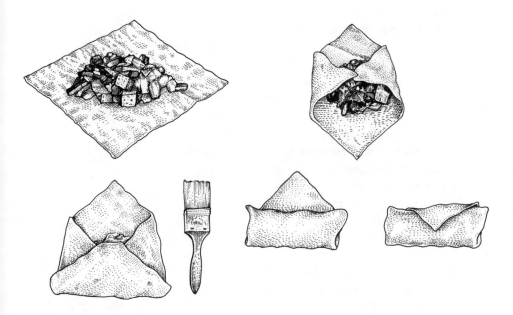

Fry the Egg Rolls

Heat the remaining 1 cup oil in a 1- to 1½-quart saucepan over medium-high heat. (To test the heat, drop a bit of egg roll wrapper into the oil; it should sizzle and come to the top immediately.)

Carefully place one or two egg rolls in the pan. Fry until golden brown and crisp on one side, 3 to 4 minutes. Turn and fry until golden brown on the other side, 1 to 2 minutes more.

Drain on paper towels. Fry the rest of the egg rolls, and serve immediately. They can be rewarmed in a 400-degree oven for 5 to 7 minutes.

Mandarin Dumplings

hese unusual dumplings are wonderfully delicious. If you're lucky enough to have leftovers, they're a great addition to a stir-fry. You can cut any unused wrappers in strips, fry them, and use them as you would chow mein noodles.

48 dumplings

FILLING
- ½ pound tofu, drained and pressed
- 2 tablespoons canola oil plus about ½ cup for frying
- ½ cup finely chopped onion (1 medium onion)
- 3 large garlic cloves, peeled and minced
- 1 tablespoon peeled and minced fresh ginger
- 1 cup finely chopped bok choy or napa cabbage (2 stalks)
- 1 cup finely chopped mushrooms (4 ounces)
- ¾ cup diced red bell pepper (1 medium pepper)
- 4 scallions, chopped
- 1 teaspoon sesame oil
- 1 tablespoon soy sauce or tamari
- Dash of pepper
- ¼ teaspoon salt

- 1 tablespoon unbleached white flour
- One 1-pound package wonton wrappers

DIPPING SAUCE
- ¼ cup soy sauce or tamari
- 3 tablespoons fresh lime juice
- 1 teaspoon sesame oil
- ¼ teaspoon chili paste with garlic

To prepare the filling, mash the tofu in a medium-size bowl, and set aside.

Heat 2 tablespoons of the canola oil in a large skillet over medium heat. Sauté the onion, garlic, ginger, bok choy, mushrooms, and red pepper until the vegetables are tender and the liquid has evaporated, 6 to 8 minutes.

Stir the cooked vegetables into the tofu, along with the scallions, sesame oil, soy sauce, pepper, and salt.

For the dumplings, beat the flour with 2 tablespoons of water in a small bowl, and set aside.

Trim the corners from the stacked wonton wrappers to form an octagonal shape. Place one wrapper on a work surface and cover the rest with plastic wrap.

Using a pastry brush, spread a bit of the flour-water paste on the top edges of the wrapper. Place 1 teaspoon of filling in the center. Fold the wrapper in half, making two small tucks or pleats on each side. Press the edges to seal tightly.

Repeat until you've used all the filling. (Cover the finished dumplings with plastic wrap to keep them from drying out.)

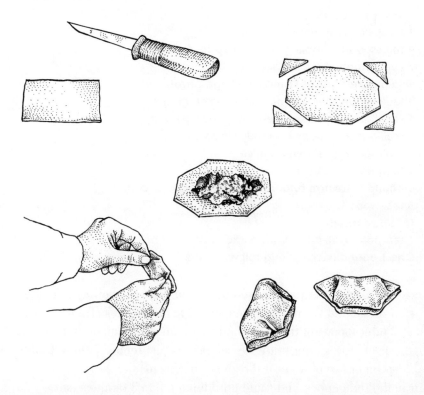

To prepare the dipping sauce, in a small bowl, stir together the soy sauce, lime juice, sesame oil, and chili paste. Set aside.

Wipe out the skillet, and heat 3 tablespoons of canola oil in it over medium-high heat. (Test the oil by dropping in a bit of wonton wrapper; it should immediately sizzle and rise to the top.)

Place ten or twelve dumplings at a time in the hot oil. Fry until golden brown on one side, about 3 minutes. Turn and fry until golden brown on the other side, 1 to 2 minutes more. Drain the fried dumplings on paper towels. Cook the rest in batches, adding more oil to the pan as needed.

Serve hot, with the dipping sauce on the side.

Gingery Vegetable-Barley Egg Rolls

The barley adds a chewy texture to these crisp and spicy egg rolls.

12 egg rolls

½ cup pearled barley
1¼ cups boiling water
4 tablespoons canola oil plus 1 cup for frying
2 cups chopped green cabbage
¾ cup grated carrot (1 medium-large carrot)
3 tablespoons peeled and minced fresh ginger
1 cup chopped red bell pepper (1 large pepper)
4 scallions, trimmed and thinly sliced
1 tablespoon fresh lemon juice
1 teaspoon sesame oil
1 pound extra-firm tofu, drained, pressed, and cubed
3 tablespoons tamari
½ teaspoon salt
1 teaspoon chili paste with garlic
One 1-pound package egg roll wrappers

Cook the barley, partially covered, in 1¼ cups of boiling water until the water is absorbed and the barley is tender, 25 to 30 minutes. Transfer to a bowl.

Heat 2 tablespoons of the canola oil in a skillet over medium heat. Sauté the cabbage, carrot, and ginger until the cabbage is just tender, 3 to 4 minutes. (Stir in a tablespoon or two of water if the ginger begins to stick.)

Stir in the red pepper, and sauté until tender, 2 to 3 minutes more.

Stir the cooked vegetables into the barley, along with the scallions, lemon juice, and sesame oil.

Heat 2 tablespoons more of the canola oil in the skillet over medium heat. Sauté the tofu, stirring occasionally, until lightly browned and slightly crisp on all sides, 10 to 15 minutes. Add 2 tablespoons of the tamari, stirring quickly to combine.

Stir the sautéed tofu into the barley mixture, along with the salt, chili paste, and the remaining 1 tablespoon tamari.

Wrap and fry as directed in the Seven-Vegetable Egg Rolls recipe (page 154). Use ½ cup of filling for each egg roll. Leftover wrappers can be cut into thin strips and fried. The crispy noodles can be snacked on or used as a garnish for a stir-fry.

Spring Rolls

These spring rolls are chock-full of crisp vegetables and fried. They are rolled thinner than traditional egg rolls and are lighter in taste. Egg roll wrappers may be substituted if spring roll wrappers are not available.

22 to 24 spring rolls

8 dried shiitake mushrooms
Boiling water
2 tablespoons canola oil plus 1½ cups for frying
2 cups sliced green cabbage
1 cup chopped onion (1 large onion)
3 tablespoons peeled and minced fresh ginger
¾ cup grated carrot (1 medium-large carrot)
¾ cup chopped red bell pepper (1 medium pepper)
2 cups bean sprouts
4 scallions, trimmed and thinly sliced
One 10-ounce can curried seitan, drained and thinly sliced
½ cup minced fresh cilantro
½ teaspoon salt
1 teaspoon chili paste with garlic
2 tablespoons soy sauce or tamari
1 teaspoon sesame oil
1 large egg
One 1-pound package spring roll wrappers

DIPPING SAUCE
¼ cup soy sauce or tamari
½ teaspoon chili paste with garlic
2 teaspoons honey
¼ cup fresh lime juice

Soak the mushrooms in boiling water to cover for 20 minutes. Drain, discard the soaking water and the stems, and slice the mushroom caps into thin strips.

Heat 2 tablespoons of the canola oil in a large skillet over medium heat. Sauté the cabbage, onion, and ginger until the cabbage is just tender, 3 to 4 minutes. (Add a tablespoon or two of water if the ginger sticks.)

Stir in the carrot and red pepper, and cook until tender, 3 to 4 minutes more.

Remove the pan from the heat, and stir in the bean sprouts, scallions, seitan, cilantro, salt, chili paste, soy sauce, and sesame oil.

(Continued)

Wrap as directed in the Seven-Vegetable Egg Rolls recipe (page 154). Use ¼ cup of filling per roll. Beat the egg with 1 teaspoon of water, and brush it on the finished rolls before frying.

Stir together the soy sauce, chili paste, honey, and lime juice, and set aside.

Fry the spring rolls as directed in the Seven-Vegetable Egg Rolls recipe. Serve immediately with the dipping sauce on the side. Leftover spring rolls may be frozen. When ready to use, thaw and warm in a 400-degree oven for 5 to 7 minutes.

 **PASTRIES**

Mushroom-Leek Turnovers with Blue Cheese

Make this scrumptious appetizer for a special party and watch them disappear.

30 to 35 turnovers (6 to 8 appetizer servings)

2 tablespoons canola oil
4 cups finely chopped mushrooms (1 pound)
½ cup diced onion (1 medium onion)
5 large garlic cloves, peeled and minced
2 cups thinly sliced leeks (1 large leek)
¾ cup diced red bell pepper (1 medium pepper)
1 teaspoon dried dill, plus extra for garnish
¾ teaspoon salt
1 cup crumbled blue cheese (4 ounces)
¼ cup fresh bread crumbs
1 pound phyllo dough (thawed)
½ cup (1 stick) butter or margarine, melted

Preheat the oven to 375 degrees.

Heat the oil in a skillet over medium heat. Sauté the mushrooms, onion, garlic, leeks, red pepper, and dill until the vegetables are tender and the liquid has evaporated, 6 to 8 minutes.

Remove the pan from the heat, and stir in the salt, cheese, and bread crumbs.

Lay out a sheet of phyllo dough on a work surface, and brush it with melted butter. Fold it in thirds lengthwise. Cut the dough in half, forming two rectangles.

Put 1 tablespoon of filling in the bottom left-hand corner of one of the rectangles. Fold the corner up to form a triangle, and continue to fold until the edges are closed (four times). Place the finished triangles on two baking sheets.

Repeat until you have used all the filling.

Brush the triangles with the remaining melted butter, and sprinkle with dried dill. Bake for 12 to 15 minutes, until crisp and browned on the edges. Serve hot.

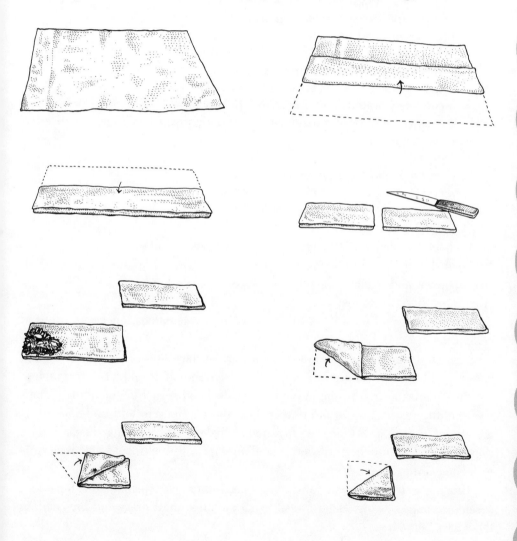

Mushrooms and Sun-Dried Tomatoes in Phyllo Dough

*S*un-dried tomatoes and smoked mozzarella cheese are an irresistible combina-tion. You can substitute 2 tablespoons minced fresh basil for the dried, but stir it in after the vegetables are cooked.

30 to 35 pastries (6 to 8 appetizer servings)

2 tablespoons canola oil
1 cup finely chopped onion (1 large onion)
5 large garlic cloves, peeled and minced
2 teaspoons dried basil
1 cup chopped green bell pepper (1 large pepper)
4 cups finely chopped mushrooms (1 pound)
½ cup chopped, drained sun-dried tomatoes in oil
½ cup finely grated Parmesan cheese (2 ounces)
½ cup grated smoked mozzarella cheese (2 ounces)
½ teaspoon salt
Pepper
1 pound phyllo dough (thawed)
½ cup (1 stick) butter or margarine, melted
Sesame or poppy seeds for garnish

Preheat the oven to 350 degrees. Grease two baking sheets.

Heat the oil in a skillet over medium heat. Sauté the onion, garlic, basil, green pepper, and mushrooms until the vegetables are tender and the liquid has evaporated, 6 to 8 minutes.

Remove the pan from the heat, and stir in the tomatoes, cheeses, salt, and pepper to taste.

Lay out a sheet of phyllo dough on a work surface and brush it with melted butter. Fold it in thirds lengthwise. Cut the dough in half, forming two rectangles.

Put 1 tablespoon of filling in the bottom left-hand corner of one of the rectan-gles. Fold the corner up to form a triangle, and continue to fold until the edges are closed (four times). Place the finished triangles on two baking sheets. For an illustration of folding the turnovers, see the recipe for Mushroom-Leek Turnovers with Blue Cheese (page 160).

Brush the triangles with any remaining butter and sprinkle the tops with sesame or poppy seeds. Bake for 12 to 15 minutes, until crisp and browned on the edges. Serve hot.

Phyllo Pizza with Three Cheeses

Cut this flaky pizza in long strips. It makes a great opener for a pasta dinner. You can substitute two thawed, well-drained, and squeezed dry 10-ounce packages of frozen spinach for the fresh.

About 36 pastries (6 to 8 appetizer servings)

2 tablespoons canola oil

8 large garlic cloves, peeled and minced

½ teaspoon dried oregano

½ teaspoon dried thyme

2 cups thinly sliced mushrooms (½ pound)

Dash of salt

12 cups coarsely chopped fresh spinach (about 2 pounds)

2 tablespoons butter or margarine, melted

6 sheets phyllo dough (thawed)

5 tablespoons finely grated Parmesan cheese (1-plus ounce)

¼ cup chopped, drained sun-dried tomatoes in oil

½ cup chopped, pitted Greek olives

¼ cup finely chopped fresh basil

½ cup thinly sliced red onion (1 medium onion)

¾ cup crumbled feta cheese (3 ounces)

¾ cup grated mozzarella cheese (3 ounces)

Heat the oil in a large skillet over medium heat. Sauté the garlic, oregano, thyme, and mushrooms until the vegetables are tender and the liquid has evaporated, 6 to 8 minutes.

Transfer the vegetables to a bowl, and stir in the salt.

Wipe out the skillet. Add the fresh spinach and ¼ cup of water. Bring it to a simmer and cook, covered, just until tender, 3 to 5 minutes. Drain, squeezing out the cooking water. (Skip this step if using frozen spinach.)

Preheat the oven to 375 degrees. Lightly brush a baking sheet with melted butter.

Place a sheet of phyllo dough on the baking sheet and brush it with butter. Sprinkle on 1 tablespoon Parmesan. Continue adding layers of phyllo dough, melted butter, and Parmesan cheese, until you have used all six sheets of dough.

Brush the top sheet with butter, and spread on the spinach, leaving a 1-inch border around the edges. Spread on the mushroom mixture, and scatter on the tomatoes, olives, basil, onion, and cheeses, in that order.

Bake for 10 minutes, until the cheese is just melted. Cut in half lengthwise, and then into long strips. Serve immediately.

Cheesy Asparagus-Dill Pastries

*F*resh asparagus and dill are combined with feta and Havarti cheese in a crisp, flaky crust.

About 36 pastries (6 to 8 appetizer servings)

2 cups thinly sliced asparagus (¾ pound)
1 cup crumbled feta cheese (4 ounces)
1 cup grated Havarti cheese (4 ounces)
2 tablespoons minced fresh dill
Dash of pepper
10 sheets phyllo dough (thawed, about ½ pound)
4 tablespoons butter or margarine, melted
1 tablespoon sesame seeds

Preheat the oven to 350 degrees. Grease two baking sheets.

Steam the asparagus just until tender, 4 to 5 minutes. Drain well.

Combine the cheeses in a medium-size bowl. Stir in the asparagus, dill, and pepper.

Cut the sheets of phyllo dough into strips 3 inches wide and 12 inches long. Brush them lightly with melted butter.

Put a heaping teaspoon of filling at the end of a dough strip, and roll it up, folding in the sides as you go. Place it on the prepared baking sheet.

Repeat until you have used all the filling.

Brush the dough packets with butter and sprinkle with sesame seeds. Bake for 20 to 25 minutes, until golden brown. Serve hot.

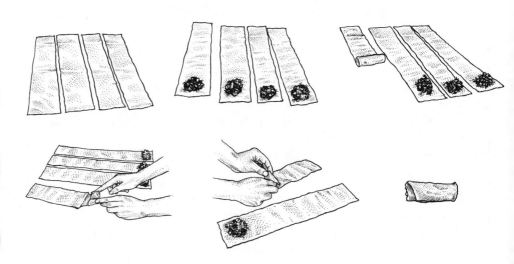

Mexican Delights

first tasted bean burritos more than twenty years ago at a tiny Mexican restaurant in the Mission district of San Francisco. They were made by an assembly line of hardworking Mexican women: the first woman patted the dough into rounds, the next one placed it in a tortilla press, the next quickly cooked it, the next filled and folded the burritos, and the last woman handed us our plates and collected our money. The place was jammed with customers, and the burritos were wonderful.

Since then I've enjoyed exploring the diverse and lively food of Mexico. Like a lot of North Americans, I've come to love it, and like a lot of vegetarians, I've found that its heavy reliance on beans makes it especially adaptable to a meatless diet. The recipes in this chapter aren't authentically Mexican but a cross of cultures, combining traditional and unconventional ingredients and techniques.

Beans are an inexpensive and versatile source of protein. Canned pinto, black, or kidney beans are a quick alternative when time is short, but I prefer to soak and cook my own whenever I can; they taste better and they cost less. Soak dried beans in water (3 cups of water for each cup of beans) for 6 to 8 hours or overnight. Then drain them and use fresh water for cooking. (The water change helps curb flatulence; if that's a problem, you might try one of the commercial products made of natural enzymes that reduce beans' gas-producing properties.)

Tortillas are another staple of Mexican cooking. Small, chewy corn tortillas are generally used in enchiladas, tostados, and tacos, while larger, softer flour tortillas are used in burritos, chimichangas, and fajitas. Tortilla making is a labor-intensive process that I don't recommend for everyday meals. Many grocery stores carry premade tortillas, and it's fairly easy to find additive-free corn tortillas. You need to shop a little harder and read labels carefully to find unadulterated flour tortillas: many brands contain preservatives and dough conditioners, and some are made with lard. Health food stores and co-ops are a good source of wholesome varieties. Both corn and flour tortillas freeze well, so stock up when you find a good brand. They break easily when frozen, though, so handle with care.

Hot peppers give Mexican food its fire. There are about two hundred varieties, but my recipes call for fresh jalapeños; they're widely available, and you can generally predict the level of hotness. Pepper juice can burn your skin, so wash your hands and equipment well when you're done chopping, and wear rubber gloves if you're handling a large amount. (Be sure not to rub your eyes when working with hot peppers!) I like to chop jalapeños in my mini food processor along with any garlic in the recipe. The membranes and seeds are the hottest part of the pepper, so you can turn down the heat by removing them.

If fresh hot peppers aren't available, you can spice your dish with cayenne after the beans and vegetables are cooked. Add it sparingly, and taste the dish carefully; the hotness can creep up on you. Dried chili peppers are another alternative; just be sure to remove them before serving. In recipes calling for cheese, jalapeño pepper Jack—cheese with hot peppers—can provide some spiciness.

Fresh cilantro adds a unique flavor and aroma to many of these recipes, and there really is no substitute. I've tried freezing cilantro and buying it dried, but have been disappointed with the results. Fortunately, fresh cilantro is inexpensive and readily available in markets. If you have a garden, it's easy to grow; let a few plants go to seed in the fall, and you'll have lots of cilantro volunteers the next spring.

Finally, a word about avocados. Although they are high in fat and calories, they contain unsaturated fat that won't clog your arteries, so enjoy them as an occasional treat. Hass avocados, with their bumpy, green or blackish-purple skin, are the most flavorful. Choose avocados that are tender to the touch but not mushy. I love the richness and smoothness they add to a dish.

Three-Bean Burritos

Burritos make a great casual meal for a big group. Have them ready to go into the oven ahead of time, and serve margaritas or sangria with corn chips, salsa, and guacamole for starters. Complete the meal with baked winter squash or sweet potatoes and a green salad.

4 generous main-course or 8 lunch servings

¾ cup dried pinto beans
¾ cup dried black beans
One 16-ounce can chick-peas, rinsed and drained
2 tablespoons canola oil
1 cup chopped onion (1 large onion)
5 large garlic cloves, peeled and minced
1 medium jalapeño pepper, minced
1 cup finely chopped carrots (2 medium carrots)
¾ cup chopped green bell pepper (1 medium pepper)
1 cup chopped zucchini (1 small zucchini)
2 teaspoons dried oregano
½ cup salsa plus extra for brushing and serving
1½ teaspoons salt
1 teaspoon ground cumin
1 teaspoon chili powder
1 large tomato, diced (1 cup)
1 cup fresh or frozen corn kernels
½ cup chopped fresh cilantro
Eight 10-inch flour tortillas
1½ cups grated jalapeño pepper Jack cheese (6 ounces)
1½ cups grated sharp Cheddar cheese (6 ounces)
Sour cream for serving

Soak pinto and black beans in 4½ cups of water for 6 to 8 hours or overnight.

Drain the beans, and put them in a large pot with 4½ cups of fresh water. Bring them to a boil, reduce the heat, and simmer, partially covered, until soft, 1½ to 2 hours, stirring occasionally.

Drain the beans, and return them to the pot, off the heat. Add the chick-peas and mash lightly.

Heat the oil in a large skillet over medium heat. Sauté the onion, garlic, jalapeño, and carrots until just tender, about 5 minutes. Stir in the green pepper, zucchini, and oregano, and cook a few minutes more.

(Continued)

Stir the cooked vegetables into the beans, along with ½ cup of the salsa, the salt, cumin, chili powder, tomato, corn, and cilantro.

Preheat the oven to 400 degrees. Grease a large baking sheet.

Lay the tortillas on a work surface. Divide the filling among them, placing about 1 cup on each. Spread the filling slightly, leaving a 3-inch border around the edges. Sprinkle with the grated cheeses.

Fold the tortillas envelope-style: sides in, bottom up, and top down. Transfer them to the prepared baking sheet, seam side down, and brush with salsa.

Bake for 10 to 15 minutes, until the edges are lightly browned. Serve hot, with sour cream and salsa.

Tempehrito

My neighbor Jennifer gave me the idea for this unconventional burrito. Since tempeh takes the place of the usual beans, it's quick to prepare.

4 to 6 servings

½ pound tempeh (three-grain or corn and jalapeño is good)
5 tablespoons canola oil
1 tablespoon tamari
5 large garlic cloves, peeled and minced
1 teaspoon dried basil
1 medium jalapeño pepper, minced
1 cup chopped onion (1 large onion)
1 cup chopped red bell pepper (1 large pepper)
1 cup chopped green bell pepper (1 large pepper)
½ pound eggplant, peeled and chopped (about 3 cups)
2 medium tomatoes, chopped (1½ cups)
¼ cup chopped fresh cilantro
½ teaspoon salt
Eight 10-inch flour tortillas
1½ cups grated jalapeño pepper Jack cheese (6 ounces)
1½ cups grated Cheddar cheese (6 ounces)
Salsa for brushing plus extra for serving
Sour cream for serving

Cut the tempeh into ½-inch chunks.

Heat 3 tablespoons of the oil in a skillet over medium heat. Cook the tempeh, stirring occasionally, until lightly brown and slightly crisp, 8 to 10 minutes. Pour in the tamari and stir quickly to combine. Transfer the tempeh to a large bowl.

Heat the remaining 2 tablespoons oil in the skillet over medium heat. Sauté the garlic, basil, jalapeño, onion, red and green peppers, and eggplant until tender, 5 or 6 minutes.

Stir the cooked vegetables into the tempeh, along with the tomatoes, cilantro, and salt.

Preheat the oven to 400 degrees. Grease a large baking sheet.

Lay the tortillas on a work surface. Divide the filling among them, placing about ½ cup on each. Spread the filling, leaving a 3-inch border around the edges, and sprinkle with the cheeses.

Fold the tortillas envelope-style: sides in, bottom up, and top down. Transfer to the prepared baking sheet, seam side down, and brush with salsa.

Bake for 10 to 15 minutes, until the edges are lightly browned. Serve hot with sour cream and additional salsa.

Guacamole and Cheese Chimichangas

These doubly crisp tortillas with their rich, creamy filling are one of those indulgences best saved for special occasions.

4 generous servings

CHEESE FILLING
- 2 cups cottage cheese
- 1 cup grated Cheddar cheese (4 ounces)
- 1 cup grated Monterey Jack cheese (4 ounces)
- 1 small jalapeño pepper, minced
- ¼ teaspoon salt
- ½ teaspoon ground coriander
- ¼ cup chopped pitted black olives

GUACAMOLE FILLING
- 2 medium avocados, peeled and seeded
- 5 large garlic cloves, peeled and minced
- ¼ cup finely chopped red onion
- 1 large tomato, diced (1 cup)
- ¼ teaspoon salt
- 1 tablespoon fresh lime or lemon juice
- 2 tablespoons minced fresh cilantro

- Eight 10-inch flour tortillas
- ¾ to 1 cup canola oil
- Sour cream for serving
- Salsa for serving

For the cheese filling, stir together the cottage cheese, Cheddar, Monterey Jack, jalapeño, salt, coriander, and olives in a medium-size bowl.

For the guacamole filling, in another bowl, mash the avocados, and stir in the garlic, onion, tomato, salt, lime juice, and cilantro.

Preheat the oven to 400 degrees.

Spread the tortillas on a work surface. Divide the cheese filling among them, placing about ⅓ cup on each. Spread the filling, leaving a 2-inch border around the edges.

Divide the guacamole among the tortillas, placing about ¼ cup on each. Spread the guacamole over the cheese filling.

Fold the tortillas envelope-style: sides in, bottom up, and top down. Fasten each one closed with two toothpicks.

Heat the oil over medium-high heat in a saucepan big enough to accommodate one filled tortilla.

Fry the tortillas, one at a time, until golden brown, about 3 minutes per side. Drain on paper towels, and remove the toothpicks.

Place the fried tortillas on baking sheets, and bake for 10 to 15 minutes, until crisp and hot. Serve immediately, with sour cream and salsa.

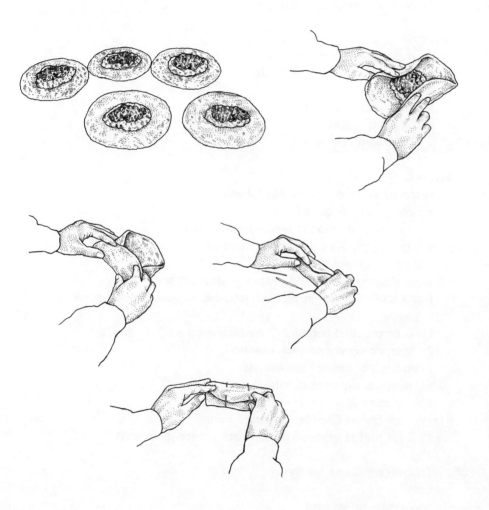

Black Bean Empanadas

Empanadas are a South of the Border turnover. The spicy bean and vegetable filling and the dough can be made in advance, but the empanadas are best fresh cooked. Serve them with salsa, sour cream, and chopped fresh cilantro on the side. Leftovers can be rewarmed in an oven.

4 to 6 servings

2 cups black beans

DOUGH

2½ cups unbleached white flour
1½ cups whole wheat pastry flour
1 teaspoon salt
½ cup (1 stick) butter or margarine, melted
⅔ cup plain yogurt
6 tablespoons cold water

FILLING

Reserved mashed, cooked black beans
2 tablespoons canola oil
¾ cup chopped onion (1 medium-large onion)
4 large garlic cloves, peeled and minced
2 teaspoons dried basil
1 cup chopped green bell pepper (1 large pepper)
1 or 2 tablespoons minced fresh jalapeño pepper (1 small-medium pepper)
1½ cups chopped zucchini (1 medium zucchini)
2 tablespoons minced fresh cilantro
1 cup fresh or frozen corn kernels
1½ teaspoons ground cumin
1 teaspoon salt
1½ cups grated Cheddar cheese (6 ounces)
1½ cups grated jalapeño pepper Jack cheese (6 ounces)

1½ cups canola oil for frying

Sour cream for serving
Salsa for serving
Chopped fresh cilantro for serving

Rinse and sort the beans, and soak them in 6 cups of water for 6 to 8 hours or overnight.

Drain the beans, and put them in a pot with 6 cups of fresh water. Bring them to a boil, reduce the heat, and simmer, partially covered, until tender, about 1½ hours. Drain the beans, and return them to the pot, off the heat. Mash them lightly and set aside.

While the beans are cooking prepare the dough. Combine the flours, salt, butter, yogurt, and water in a mixing bowl or food processor. Stir or pulse until well mixed. Turn the dough out onto a floured surface, and knead it until smooth and elastic, about 5 minutes. Cover and refrigerate.

For the filling, heat the 2 tablespoons oil in a large skillet over medium heat. Sauté the onion, garlic, basil, green and jalapeño peppers, and zucchini until tender, about 5 minutes. Remove the pan from the heat, and stir in the cilantro, corn, cumin, salt, and cheeses. Add this mixture to the reserved beans and stir well. Turn the dough out onto a floured surface, knead it lightly, and divide it into twelve balls. Roll each ball into an 8-inch circle, and place a heaping ½ cup of filling in its center. Spread the filling, leaving a 1-inch border around the edge. Fold the dough over the filling to form a half circle, and use the tines of a fork to seal it. Repeat until all twelve empanadas are filled.

Preheat the oven to 325 degrees.

Heat the 1½ cups oil in a deep, 1½- to 2-quart saucepan over medium-high heat. (To test the temperature, drop a bit of dough into the oil; it should immediately sizzle and rise to the surface. Or use a candy thermometer; it should be about 365 degrees.)

Fry the empanadas one at a time until golden brown, about 3 minutes on each side. Drain on paper towels. Place cooked empanadas on a baking sheet in the oven to keep warm until ready to serve. Serve hot garnished with sour cream, salsa, and fresh cilantro.

Southwestern Cheese and Vegetable Enchiladas

These simple, flavorful enchiladas make a great basic meal. You'll want to serve them again and again.

4 servings

Eight 6-inch corn tortillas (blue corn if available)
Butter or margarine for brushing
Salsa for brushing

FILLING
2 tablespoons canola oil
5 large garlic cloves, peeled and minced
1 teaspoon dried oregano
¾ cup chopped green bell pepper (1 medium pepper)
¾ cup chopped red bell pepper (1 medium pepper)
1 large tomato, chopped (1 cup)
¼ cup sliced pitted Greek or green olives
4 or 5 scallions, sliced
¼ teaspoon salt
1 cup grated jalapeño pepper Jack cheese (4 ounces)
1 cup grated extra-sharp Cheddar cheese (4 ounces)

SAUCE
2 tablespoons butter or margarine
2 tablespoons unbleached white flour
¾ cup salsa
½ cup heavy cream
1 teaspoon ground cumin
½ teaspoon ground coriander

Preheat the oven to 400 degrees.

Heat a skillet over medium heat. Brush the tortillas with a dab of butter and salsa, and fry them lightly, about 30 seconds on each side. Set aside.

Wipe out the skillet, and heat the oil over medium heat. Sauté the garlic, oregano, and green and red peppers until barely tender, 3 to 4 minutes. Remove the pan from the heat, and stir in the tomato, olives, scallions, and salt.

Spread the tortillas on a work surface. Divide the filling among them, placing about ¼ cup in a line down the center. Sprinkle with the cheeses.

Roll up the tortillas, and place them, seam side down, on a greased baking sheet. Bake for 10 to 15 minutes, just until the edges are crisp.

Meanwhile, for the sauce, melt the 2 tablespoons butter in a saucepan over medium heat. Whisk in the flour, and let it cook for a minute or two. Whisk in the salsa, cream, cumin, and coriander, and cook, stirring, until slightly thickened.

Serve the tortillas topped with the hot sauce.

Santa Anna Tortillas

★ **BEGINNER-FRIENDLY**

These tortillas have become a favorite with my family and friends. You can vary the vegetables to suit your taste.

4 to 6 servings

3 tablespoons canola oil
1 pound tofu, drained, pressed, and cubed
1 tablespoon tamari
¾ cup chopped onion (1 medium-large onion)
5 large garlic cloves, peeled and minced
1 medium jalapeño pepper, minced
½ cup chopped red bell pepper (1 small pepper)
½ cup chopped green bell pepper (1 small pepper)
1 medium avocado, peeled, seeded, and cut into ½-inch chunks
1 medium tomato, chopped (¾ cup)
5 scallions, sliced
¼ cup minced fresh cilantro
2 tablespoons fresh lime or lemon juice
¼ cup sour cream
½ teaspoon salt
1 teaspoon ground cumin
½ teaspoon chili powder
Cayenne
Eight 10-inch flour tortillas
2 cups grated Cheddar cheese (8 ounces)
Salsa for brushing plus extra for serving
Sour cream for serving

Heat 2 tablespoons of the oil in a skillet over medium heat. Sauté the tofu, tossing occasionally, until it browns and begins to crisp up on the edges, 10 to 12 minutes. Pour in the tamari, and stir quickly to combine. Transfer the tofu to a bowl.

Heat the remaining 1 tablespoon oil in the skillet over medium heat. Sauté the onion, garlic, jalapeño, and red and green peppers until tender, about 5 minutes.

Stir the cooked vegetables into the tofu, along with the avocado, tomato, scallions, cilantro, lime juice, sour cream, salt, cumin, chili powder, and cayenne to taste.

Preheat the oven to 400 degrees, and grease a large baking sheet.

Spread out the floured tortillas on a work surface. Divide the cheese among them in a line down the middle of each tortilla, leaving a 2-inch border on either end.

Divide the filling among the tortillas, placing about ½ cup on each one. Spread the filling over the cheese, and fold the tortillas, envelope-style: sides in, bottom up, and top down.

Place the tortillas, seam side down, on the prepared baking sheet, and brush lightly with salsa. Bake for 10 to 12 minutes, until the edges begin to brown. Serve hot with salsa and sour cream.

Broccoli, Basil, and Cheddar Tortillas

★ **BEGINNER-FRIENDLY**

Another uncommonly delicious variation on a Mexican tradition.

4 generous servings

2 tablespoons canola oil
6 large garlic cloves, peeled and minced
1 medium jalapeño pepper, minced
1 cup chopped onion (1 large onion)
6 cups chopped broccoli
1 cup chopped green bell pepper (1 large pepper)
2 large tomatoes, chopped (2 cups)
1 teaspoon salt
½ cup finely chopped fresh basil
2 tablespoons finely chopped fresh cilantro
Eight 10-inch flour tortillas
3 cups grated extra-sharp Cheddar cheese (12 ounces)
Salsa for brushing plus extra for serving
Sour cream for serving

Heat the oil in a skillet over medium heat. Sauté the garlic, jalapeño, onion, and broccoli for 1 to 2 minutes. Add the green pepper and 2 tablespoons of water. Continue to cook until the vegetables are tender, 3 to 4 minutes more.

Remove the pan from the heat. When the vegetables have cooled, stir in the tomatoes, salt, basil, and cilantro.

Preheat the oven to 400 degrees. Grease a large baking sheet.

Lay the tortillas on a work surface. Divide the filling among them, placing about 1 cup on each. Spread the filling, leaving a 3-inch border around the edges. Sprinkle with the cheese.

Fold the tortillas envelope-style: sides in, bottom up, and top down. Transfer to the prepared baking sheet, seam side down, and brush with salsa.

Bake for 10 to 15 minutes, until the edges are lightly browned. Serve hot, with salsa and sour cream.

Asparagus Tortillas

★ BEGINNER-FRIENDLY

An easy yet elegant meal.

4 servings

1 pound asparagus, tough ends removed, thinly sliced (about 3 cups)
2 tablespoons canola oil
5 or 6 large garlic cloves, peeled and minced
1 medium jalapeño pepper, minced
½ cup chopped red bell pepper (1 small pepper)
½ cup chopped green bell pepper (1 small pepper)
2 medium tomatoes, chopped (1½ cups)
3 scallions, thinly sliced
1 tablespoon fresh lime or lemon juice
2 tablespoons minced fresh cilantro
½ teaspoon salt
Eight 10-inch flour tortillas
1¼ cups grated Cheddar cheese (5 ounces)
1¼ cups grated jalapeño pepper Jack cheese (5 ounces)
Salsa for brushing plus extra for serving
Sour cream for serving

Steam the asparagus until just tender, 5 to 8 minutes. Set it aside to cool.

Heat the oil in a skillet over medium heat. Sauté the garlic, jalapeño, and red and green peppers just until tender, 3 to 4 minutes. Remove the pan from the heat, and stir in the steamed asparagus, tomatoes, scallions, lime juice, cilantro, and salt.

Preheat the oven to 400 degrees. Grease a large baking sheet.

Lay out the tortillas on a work surface. Divide the filling among them, placing about ½ cup in the center of each. Spread the filling, leaving a 3-inch border around the edges. Sprinkle on the cheeses.

Fold the tortillas envelope-style: sides in, bottom up, and top down. Place them on the prepared baking sheet, seam side down, and brush with salsa.

Bake for 10 to 15 minutes, until the edges are lightly browned. Serve with salsa and sour cream.

Enchiladas with Jalapeño and Cilantro Sauce

These enchiladas are big on flavor. You can use the simple-to-make cilantro sauce to brighten other dishes, too.

6 servings

12 corn tortillas
Butter or margarine for brushing
Salsa for brushing

FILLING
2 tablespoons canola oil
5 large garlic cloves, peeled and minced
¾ cup chopped onion (1 medium-large onion)
1 cup chopped red bell pepper (1 large pepper)
1 cup chopped green bell pepper (1 large pepper)
2 to 2¼ cups cooked brown rice
1 large tomato, diced (1 cup)
½ teaspoon salt
1 teaspoon ground cumin
1 teaspoon chili powder
1 cup grated extra-sharp Cheddar cheese (4 ounces)
1 cup grated jalapeño pepper Jack cheese (4 ounces)

SAUCE
2 large cloves garlic, peeled and coarsely chopped
1 small jalapeño pepper, sliced
½ cup chopped fresh cilantro
½ cup sour cream
½ cup plain yogurt
¼ cup salsa
¼ teaspoon salt
½ teaspoon ground cumin
2 scallions, thinly sliced

Heat a skillet over medium heat. Brush the tortillas with a dab of butter and salsa, and fry them lightly, about 30 seconds on each side. Set aside.

Preheat the oven to 400 degrees.

For the filling, heat the oil in a skillet over medium heat. Sauté the garlic, onion, and red and green peppers until tender, about 5 minutes. Remove the pan from the heat, and stir in the rice, tomato, salt, cumin, chili powder, and cheeses.

Spread the tortillas on a work surface. Divide the filling among them, placing about ⅓ cup in a line down the center of each. Spread the filling and roll up the tortillas. Place the tortillas, seam side down, on a large baking sheet. Bake for 10 to 15 minutes, until the cheese has melted.

Meanwhile, prepare the sauce. In a blender or food processor, puree the garlic, jalapeño, and cilantro with the sour cream and yogurt. Add the salsa, salt, and cumin, and process until smooth. Pour the sauce into a saucepan and stir in the scallions.

Just before serving, heat the sauce until hot and spoon it over the enchiladas and serve.

Marinated Seitan Fajitas

You can make the filling ahead, but put these flavorful fajitas together just before serving. Note that the seitan needs to marinate for several hours.

6 generous servings

½ cup plus 2 tablespoons canola oil
¼ cup fresh lime or lemon juice
2 tablespoons tamari
½ teaspoon chili powder
¼ teaspoon ground cumin
Dash of cayenne
½ pound seitan, drained and cut into thin strips
1 cup chopped onion (1 large onion)
5 large garlic cloves, peeled and minced
1 medium jalapeño pepper, minced
1 medium red bell pepper, seeded and cut into thin strips (¾ cup)
1 medium green bell pepper, seeded and cut into thin strips (¾ cup)
½ pound mushrooms, quartered (2 cups)
¼ cup minced fresh cilantro
2 medium tomatoes, chopped (1½ cups)
¼ teaspoon salt
½ teaspoon ground cumin
½ teaspoon chili powder
Twelve 8- or 9-inch whole wheat tortillas
2½ cups grated Cheddar cheese (10 ounces; optional)
1 bunch scallions, sliced
Salsa for serving

Combine ½ cup of the oil, the lime juice, tamari, chili powder, cumin, and cayenne in a lidded container. Stir in the seitan, cover, and refrigerate for 4 to 6 hours or overnight.

Drain the seitan. (Save the marinade to reuse or serve as a salad dressing.)

Heat the remaining 2 tablespoons oil in a skillet over medium heat. Sauté the onion, garlic, jalapeño pepper, and seitan for 2 to 3 minutes, stirring occasionally.

Stir in the red and green peppers and mushrooms, and cook just until tender, 3 to 4 minutes more. Remove the pan from the heat, and stir in the cilantro, tomatoes, salt, cumin, and chili powder. Drain the vegetables if they are overly juicy.

Heat the tortillas briefly in the microwave or oven until warm but still soft. (I use my toaster oven.)

Place two tortillas each on six plates or all of them on a serving platter. Divide the filling among the tortillas, spreading about ½ cup in a line down the center of each one. Top with cheese if desired, and scallions. Fold and serve, with salsa on the side.

Harvest Mexican Squash

This untraditional Mexican dish, inspired by the fall vegetable harvest, has won raves at many a potluck dinner.

6 servings

1 large butternut squash (about 2 or more pounds)
2 tablespoons canola oil
1 cup chopped onion (1 large onion)
1 cup chopped green bell pepper (1 large pepper)
1½ cups chopped zucchini (1 medium zucchini)
4 large garlic cloves, peeled and minced
1 medium jalapeño pepper, minced
1 teaspoon dried oregano
1 cup fresh or frozen corn kernels
¼ cup chopped fresh basil
3 medium tomatoes (2 chopped, 1 sliced)
1 cup chopped kale
1 cup sour cream
1 teaspoon salt
1 teaspoon ground cumin
1 teaspoon chili powder
½ teaspoon ground coriander
Pinch of ground cloves
Pinch to ¼ teaspoon cayenne
1½ cups grated jalapeño pepper Jack cheese (6 ounces)
Paprika

Preheat the oven to 425 degrees.

Cut the squash in half lengthwise, and scoop out the seeds. Place it, cut side down, in a baking pan, and pour in ½ cup of water. Bake for 45 to 50 minutes, until soft when pierced with a fork.

Remove the squash and set it aside to cool, cut side up. Reduce the oven temperature to 375 degrees.

Heat the oil in a large skillet over medium heat. Sauté the onion, green pepper, zucchini, garlic, jalapeño, and oregano until the vegetables are tender, about 5 minutes. Remove the pan from the heat.

Scoop the cooled squash from its shells and transfer it to a large bowl. Mash it until smooth, and stir in the sautéed vegetables. Add the corn, basil, chopped tomatoes, kale, sour cream, salt, cumin, chili powder, coriander, cloves, cayenne, and ½ cup of the grated cheese. Stir well.

Transfer the vegetable mixture to a 3-quart casserole. Top with the sliced tomatoes, the remaining grated cheese, and a sprinkling of paprika. Bake for 30 minutes. It should be bubbling around the edges and golden in color. Serve immediately.

Baja Black Bean and Chili Pie

*T*his hearty, spicy pie is a perfect potluck dish.

10 to 12 servings

FILLING

3 cups dried black beans
2 tablespoons canola oil
1 cup chopped onion (1 large onion)
5 large garlic cloves, peeled and minced
2 medium jalapeño peppers, minced
1 teaspoon dried oregano
1 cup chopped red bell pepper (1 large pepper)
1 cup chopped green bell pepper (1 large pepper)
1½ cups chopped zucchini (1 medium zucchini)
½ cup fresh or frozen corn kernels
One 28-ounce can chopped tomatoes with their juice
1½ teaspoons salt
1 tablespoon chili powder
1 teaspoon ground cumin
Cayenne (optional)
¾ cup minced fresh cilantro
1¼ cups grated Cheddar cheese (5 ounces)
1¼ cups grated Monterey Jack cheese (5 ounces)

CRUST

¾ cup yellow cornmeal
¾ cup unbleached white flour
2 teaspoons baking powder
½ teaspoon salt
3 tablespoons butter or margarine
1 large egg
½ cup milk
⅓ cup sour cream
1 tablespoon honey

Paprika

To make the filling, rinse and sort the beans, and soak them in 9 cups of water for 6 to 8 hours or overnight.

Drain the beans, and put them in a large pot with 9 cups of fresh water. Bring them to a boil, reduce the heat, and simmer, partially covered, until tender, about 1½ hours, stirring occasionally. Drain the beans and return them to the pot, off the heat.

Heat the oil in a skillet over medium heat. Sauté the onion, garlic, jalapeños, oregano, red and green peppers, and zucchini until tender, about 5 minutes.

Stir the cooked vegetables into the beans, along with the corn, tomatoes and their juice, salt, chili powder, and cumin. Taste the beans, and add a little cayenne if you want them hotter. Stir in the cilantro and cheeses. Set aside.

Preheat the oven to 400 degrees. Grease a large baking dish.

To make the crust, combine the cornmeal, flour, baking powder, salt, butter, egg, milk, sour cream, and honey in a food processor, and pulse just until combined. (If mixing by hand, stir together the dry ingredients, cut in the butter, and whisk together and stir in the wet ingredients.)

Transfer the beans to the prepared baking dish. Spoon on the batter, and spread it to cover the beans. Sprinkle generously with paprika, and bake for 30 minutes, until hot and bubbly, and golden on top.

Mexican Baked Beans

★ **BEGINNER-FRIENDLY**

A lively variation on Boston baked beans.

8 to 10 servings

1 pound dried Great Northern beans
2 tablespoons canola oil
2 cups chopped onions (2 large onions)
6 large garlic cloves, peeled and minced
1 or 2 medium jalapeño peppers, minced
1 cup chopped red bell pepper (1 large pepper)
1 cup chopped green bell pepper (1 large pepper)
2 tablespoons honey
2 tablespoons blackstrap molasses
2 tablespoons Dijon mustard
1 tablespoon Worcestershire sauce or vegetarian variety (see page 79)
1 tablespoon tamari
One 28-ounce can tomato sauce
1 teaspoon salt
1 teaspoon ground cumin

Rinse and sort the beans, and soak them in 8 cups of water for 6 to 8 hours or overnight.

Drain the beans, and put them in a large pot with 8 cups of fresh water. Bring them to a boil, reduce the heat to a simmer, and cook, partially covered, until tender, about 1 hour, stirring occasionally. Drain the beans, and transfer them to a large baking dish.

Preheat the oven to 350 degrees.

Heat the oil in a skillet over medium heat. Sauté the onions, garlic, jalapeños, and red and green peppers until tender, about 5 minutes.

Stir the cooked vegetables into the beans, along with the honey, molasses, mustard, Worcestershire sauce, tamari, tomato sauce, salt, and cumin.

Bake, uncovered, for about 1 hour, until most of the liquid is absorbed and the beans are bubbling around the edges. Serve hot.

Plenty of Pasta

Pasta is hard to beat for popularity, versatility, and ease; it can be the basis for so many easy and satisfying meals. In the time it takes your pasta water to boil, you can simmer up a savory sauce of tomatoes, onion, garlic, and basil. Add broccoli, capers, carrots, eggplant, mushrooms, peppers, spinach, or zucchini if you like—the "pasta-bilities" are endless. Or sauce your pasta with pesto, a cream sauce, or simply butter or olive oil, and add your favorite vegetables—and, of course, freshly grated Parmesan or Romano cheese. Toss a simple green salad, slice some crusty bread, and you're ready to eat.

The recipes in this chapter are written for dry pasta, but in most cases you can substitute fresh. (Figure about double the amount by weight, since fresh pasta doesn't expand much when cooked.) Fresh, pasta is available refrigerated in most major food stores these days. Though it's more expensive than dry, its richer taste may make it worth an occasional splurge to you. (Be aware that the freshness comes in part from eggs, if that's a health concern.)

Besides its economy, dry pasta has a long shelf life and an amazing array of shapes going for it. Look for brands made of semolina flour milled from hard durum wheat; it tastes better and won't get limp or mushy unless overcooked. There are no hard-and-fast rules about matching shapes with sauces, but I prefer thin spaghetti or angel hair pasta with tomato sauce or pesto, and broader linguine or fettuccine with thick cream sauces. I love short, colorful, vegetable-flavored pastas in spirals and other fun shapes for cold salads.

Whatever your choice, be sure to cook pasta in plenty of boiling water—at least 2 quarts for 8 ounces of dry or 16 ounces of fresh. Check it for doneness (somewhere between 8 to 12 minutes usually), and drain it when it's still a little chewy, or *al dente*—Italian for "to the tooth." There's no need to add salt or oil to the cooking water, or to rinse the cooked pasta with hot or cold water, unless you're making a pasta salad. Time your cooking so that you can serve it immediately; you don't want it getting cold and sticky while you finish the sauce. If you're making a cold pasta dish, you will want to rinse the noodles in cold water before draining, and toss them with a little oil to prevent sticking.

Tomato-Pesto Tortellini

★ BEGINNER-FRIENDLY

This tasty meal takes no time at all to prepare if you have homemade pesto on hand (see the Pesto Lasagna recipe on page 204 for directions), or use one of the many prepared varieties available. I make batch after batch of pesto each August when my garden overflows with basil, and freeze it for the long winter months ahead. It gives me a sense of kinship with the chipmunks and squirrels I see outside my kitchen window busily laying in their winter stores of seeds and nuts.

3 to 4 servings

One 16-ounce jar marinara sauce
½ cup pesto sauce
1 large tomato, chopped (1 cup)
1 pound fresh or frozen cheese tortellini
Finely grated Romano or Parmesan cheese

Heat the marinara sauce, pesto, and tomato in a saucepan, and simmer for 15 to 20 minutes, stirring occasionally.

Meanwhile, put a large pot of water on to boil.

Cook the tortellini in the boiling water just until tender, about 3 to 4 minutes for fresh pasta and 8 to 10 minutes for frozen (they'll begin to float). Drain well, and transfer to a large serving bowl.

Toss the tortellini with the sauce, top with grated cheese, and serve.

Adriatic Ravioli

ender ravioli, asparagus, and mushrooms tossed with a Dijon and basil cheese sauce make for this elegant entree, named for Italy's beautiful Adriatic coast.

4 servings

1 pound fresh asparagus
1 pound frozen small cheese ravioli
5 tablespoons butter or margarine
1 large red bell pepper, seeded and cut into thin, 2-inch-long strips (1 cup)
½ pound mushrooms, thinly sliced (about 2 cups)
4 large garlic cloves, peeled and minced
3 tablespoons unbleached white flour
2½ cups milk
¼ teaspoon salt
1 teaspoon paprika plus additional for garnish
1 tablespoon Dijon mustard
¼ cup chopped fresh basil
½ cup finely grated Romano cheese (2 ounces)
Pepper
Finely grated Parmesan cheese for serving

Put a large pot of water on to boil. Snap off and discard the tough asparagus ends, and cut the stalks into 1-inch pieces. You will have about 3 cups of asparagus. Steam until barely tender, 6 to 8 minutes, and set aside.

Begin cooking the ravioli, stirring occasionally.

Melt 1 tablespoon of the butter in a skillet over medium heat. Sauté the red pepper, mushrooms, and garlic until tender, 3 to 4 minutes. Remove the pan from the heat.

Melt the remaining 4 tablespoons butter in a large, heavy saucepan over medium heat. Whisk in the flour, and let it cook for a minute or two. Slowly pour in the milk, whisking constantly until thickened, about 3 to 5 minutes.

Add the salt, paprika, mustard, basil, Romano cheese, and pepper to taste, stirring until the cheese is melted. Reduce the heat to very low, and stir in the sautéed vegetables.

When the ravioli is tender and begins to float, after about 10 to 12 minutes, drain it well, and transfer it to a large serving bowl.

Pour on the sauce, and toss gently. Garnish with paprika, and serve with Parmesan on the side.

Garlicky Artichoke Heart, Broccoli, and Tomato Linguine

*T*his *richly flavored cheese and wine sauce can be prepared ahead and reheated in a double boiler. (Note that the artichokes must marinate for at least 2 hours.) Cook the pasta just before serving, and serve with grated Parmesan cheese on the side.*

4 generous servings

1 cup plus 2 tablespoons canola oil
½ cup cider or wine vinegar
2 tablespoons tamari
¾ cup dry white wine
One 14-ounce can artichoke hearts in water, drained and sliced
8 large garlic cloves, peeled and minced
2 teaspoons dried basil
2 cups broccoli florets and sliced stems
2 cups chopped fresh tomatoes (about 3 medium)
3 tablespoons butter or margarine
3 tablespoons unbleached white flour
¼ teaspoon salt
1½ cups milk
1 cup grated Cheddar cheese (4 ounces)
¼ cup grated Parmesan cheese (1 ounce)
1 pound dry linguine

Combine 1 cup of the oil, the vinegar, tamari, and ¼ cup of the wine in a lidded container. Add the artichoke hearts, cover, and refrigerate for at least 2 hours (overnight is best).

When you are ready to prepare the meal, put a large pot of water on to boil.

Heat the remaining 2 tablespoons oil in a skillet over medium heat. Sauté the garlic, basil, and broccoli just until tender, about 5 minutes. Remove the pan from the heat, and stir in the tomatoes.

Melt the butter in a large, heavy saucepan over medium heat. Whisk in the flour and salt, and let it cook for a minute or two. Gradually pour in the milk and the remaining ½ cup wine, whisking until thickened, about 5 minutes. Add the Cheddar and Parmesan, stirring until melted. Reduce the heat to very low, and stir occasionally.

Begin cooking the linguine in the boiling water.

Drain the artichoke hearts, saving the marinade for another time. Stir them into the cheese sauce along with the sautéed vegetables.

When the linguine is *al dente,* in 8 to 10 minutes, drain it well, and transfer it to a large serving bowl. Pour on the sauce, toss gently, and serve.

Linguine with Sun-Dried Tomato Pesto

★ BEGINNER-FRIENDLY

The sun-dried tomatoes give this pesto an intensely delicious flavor. Pesto stores well and will keep in the refrigerator for about two weeks, or in the freezer for up to a year or more, so you can make a double batch and save half for another meal.

6 generous servings

5 large garlic cloves, peeled
1 cup drained oil-packed sun-dried tomatoes
½ cup pecans
¼ cup Greek olives, pitted
¾ cup finely grated Romano cheese (3 ounces) plus extra for garnish
½ cup olive oil
Pepper
1½ pounds dry linguine
½ cup minced fresh parsley

Put a large pot of water on to boil.

Puree the garlic, tomatoes, pecans, olives, ¾ cup Romano cheese, olive oil, and pepper to taste in a blender or food processor.

Cook the linguine until *al dente,* 8 to 10 minutes. Drain well, and transfer to a serving bowl. Add the pesto and parsley, and toss. Garnish with additional Romano cheese and serve.

Linguine with Brussels Sprouts, Mushrooms, and Garlic

This wonderful dish could make a Brussels sprout lover out of you!

4 generous servings

1 pound Brussels sprouts, trimmed and halved
2 tablespoons canola oil
8 large garlic cloves, peeled and minced
1 large red bell pepper, seeded and cut into thin, 1-inch-long strips (1 cup)
½ pound mushrooms, sliced (2 cups)
¼ cup chopped fresh basil or 1 teaspoon dried
1 pound dry linguine
4 tablespoons butter or margarine
3 tablespoons unbleached white flour
½ cup heavy cream
½ cup dry white wine
¼ teaspoon salt
1 cup finely grated Parmesan cheese (4 ounces)

Steam the Brussels sprouts until just tender, 6 to 8 minutes. Set aside.

Put a large pot of water on to boil.

Heat the oil in a skillet over medium heat. Sauté the garlic, red pepper, and mushrooms (plus basil if using dried) until tender, 3 to 4 minutes. Remove the pan from the heat, and stir in the basil if using fresh.

Begin cooking the linguine.

Melt the butter in a heavy saucepan over medium heat. Whisk in the flour, and let it cook for a minute or two. Slowly pour in the cream and wine, whisking until thickened, about 5 minutes. Add the salt and Parmesan, stirring until the cheese has melted.

Reduce the heat to very low, and stir in the Brussels sprouts and the sautéed vegetables. Stir occasionally.

When the linguine is *al dente*, in 8 to 10 minutes, drain it well, and transfer to a serving dish. Add the sauce, toss well, and serve.

Spinach, Basil, and Garlic Linguine

If you prepare the marinade ahead of time, you can quickly pull together this heavenly meal. The vegetables and smoked mozzarella cheese need to marinate for at least 2 hours or overnight.

4 generous servings

8 large garlic cloves, peeled and minced
¾ cup canola oil
½ cup balsamic vinegar
2 tablespoons tamari
4 large tomatoes, diced (4 cups)
1½ cups cubed, smoked mozzarella cheese (6 ounces)
1 pound dry linguine
6 cups chopped fresh spinach leaves (lightly packed)
2 cups chopped fresh basil leaves (lightly packed)
¼ cup grated Parmesan cheese (1 ounce)
½ teaspoon salt
Pepper

Stir together the garlic, oil, vinegar, tamari, tomatoes, and mozzarella cheese in a lidded container. Cover and refrigerate for at least 2 hours or overnight.

When you are ready to proceed, put a large pot of water on to boil.

Drain the marinated vegetables and mozzarella cheese (save the marinade for another time).

Cook the linguine in the boiling water until *al dente,* about 8 to 10 minutes.

Meanwhile, steam the spinach just until wilted, 3 to 4 minutes.

Drain the cooked pasta well, and transfer it to a large serving bowl.

Add the marinated garlic, tomato, and cheese, and toss quickly so the cheese begins to melt. Add the spinach, basil, Parmesan, salt, and pepper to taste, toss again, and serve.

Double Mushroom and Tomato Cream Sauce with Linguine

★ **BEGINNER-FRIENDLY**

This sauce is as delicious as it sounds.

6 generous servings

2 tablespoons canola oil
5 large garlic cloves, peeled and minced
½ pound shiitake mushrooms, sliced (2 cups)
½ pound button mushrooms, sliced (2 cups)
One 28-ounce jar marinara sauce
¼ teaspoon salt
¼ cup finely chopped fresh basil
2 tablespoons butter or margarine
2 tablespoons unbleached white flour
1 cup heavy cream
1½ pounds dry linguine
Finely grated Parmesan cheese for serving

Put a large pot of water on to boil.

Heat the oil in a skillet over medium heat. Sauté the garlic and mushrooms until tender, 4 to 5 minutes. Remove the pan from the heat, and stir in the marinara sauce, salt, and basil.

Melt the butter in a heavy saucepan over medium heat. Whisk in the flour, and let it cook for a minute or two. Slowly add the cream, whisking until thickened, about 3 to 4 minutes. Pour in the vegetable-marinara mixture, and reduce the heat to very low, stirring occasionally.

Cook the linguine in the boiling water until *al dente*, about 8 to 10 minutes. Drain well, and transfer to a large serving bowl.

Add about half the sauce, and toss well. Serve the remaining sauce on the side, along with the Parmesan cheese.

Santa Cruz Fettuccine

This is one of those rich dishes that's well worth treating yourself to once in a while.

4 generous servings

2 tablespoons canola oil
6 large garlic cloves, peeled and minced
1 large red bell pepper, seeded and cut into thin, 1-inch-long slices (1 cup)
3 tablespoons butter or margarine
3 tablespoons unbleached white flour
1 cup heavy cream
1 cup milk
¼ cup dry white wine
1½ cups finely grated Parmesan cheese (6 ounces)
¼ teaspoon salt
Pepper
1 pound dry fettuccine
2 medium tomatoes, chopped (1½ cups)
½ cup chopped fresh basil or 2 tablespoons dried
¼ cup chopped fresh parsley or 1 tablespoon dried
2 medium avocados
1 tablespoon fresh lemon juice

Put a large pot of water on to boil.

Heat the oil in a skillet over medium heat. Sauté the garlic and red pepper until just tender, 3 to 4 minutes. (If using dried herbs, sauté them, too.) Remove the pan from the heat.

Melt the butter in a heavy saucepan over medium heat. Whisk in the flour, and let it cook for a minute or two. Slowly pour in the cream, milk, and wine, whisking until thickened, about 5 minutes.

Add the Parmesan, salt, and pepper to taste, stirring until the cheese is melted. Stir in the sautéed vegetables, reduce the heat to simmer, and cook for a few minutes until hot.

Meanwhile, begin cooking the fettuccine.

Remove the saucepan from the heat, and stir in the tomatoes, fresh basil, and fresh parsley. Cover to keep warm.

Peel, pit, and thinly slice the avocados. Toss with the lemon juice to prevent browning.

When the fettuccine is *al dente,* in 10 to 12 minutes, drain it well, and transfer it to a large serving bowl. Add the sauce and avocados, toss, and serve.

Fettuccine with Sun-Dried Tomatoes, Garlic, and Olives

★ **BEGINNER-FRIENDLY**

This deliciously quick dish combines some of my favorite ingredients—Greek olives, sun-dried tomatoes, fresh basil, and lots of garlic. You can purchase the sun-dried tomatoes in oil for this recipe or use packaged sun-dried tomatoes, which are more economical. Pour 1 cup boiling water over ½ cup packaged sun-dried tomatoes. Allow them to sit in the water and rehydrate for 10 minutes. Drain the tomatoes and press out any excess water. Chop and use in sauces and other dishes.

4 generous servings

3 tablespoons canola oil
8 large garlic cloves, peeled and minced
1 cup finely chopped onion (1 large onion)
½ cup sliced, pitted Greek olives
½ cup chopped, drained oil-packed sun-dried tomatoes
3 tablespoons olive oil
3 tablespoons butter or margarine
1 pound dry fettuccine
¼ cup finely chopped fresh basil
¼ teaspoon salt
Pepper
1 tablespoon tamari
½ cup finely grated Parmesan cheese (2 ounces) plus extra for garnish

Put a large pot of water on to boil.

Heat the canola oil in a skillet over medium heat. Sauté the garlic and onion until soft, about 5 minutes. Stir in the olives, tomatoes, olive oil, and butter. Cook until the butter is melted and the tomatoes are heated through.

Meanwhile, begin cooking the fettuccine.

Remove the skillet from the heat, and stir in the basil, salt, and pepper to taste. Cover to keep warm.

When the pasta is *al dente,* in 10 to 12 minutes, drain it well, and transfer to a large serving bowl. Add the sauce, tamari, and ½ cup Parmesan, and toss well. Serve immediately with extra Parmesan on the side.

Spinach-Ricotta Fettuccine

★ **BEGINNER-FRIENDLY**

*T*he creamy spinach and cheese sauce is uncomplicated, quick, and delightful.

4 generous servings

2 tablespoons canola oil
1 cup chopped onion (1 large onion)
8 to 10 large garlic cloves, peeled and minced
1 tablespoon dried basil
1 teaspoon dried thyme
½ cup diced red bell pepper (1 small pepper)
1 pound dry fettuccine
2 tablespoons unbleached white flour
2 cups milk
1 cup ricotta cheese
One 10-ounce package frozen chopped spinach, thawed and
    squeezed dry
½ cup finely grated Parmesan cheese (2 ounces) plus extra for garnish
½ teaspoon salt
¼ teaspoon ground nutmeg
2 tablespoons fresh lemon juice
Pepper
4 to 6 scallions, thinly sliced, for garnish

Put a large pot of water on to boil.

Heat the oil in a heavy saucepan over medium heat. Sauté the onion, garlic, basil, and thyme until the onions are soft, about 5 minutes. Stir in the red pepper, and cook until barely tender, 2 to 3 minutes more.

Begin cooking the fettuccine.

Add the flour to the sautéed vegetables, stirring quickly to combine. Slowly pour in the milk, stirring until slightly thickened, about 3 to 4 minutes. Add the ricotta, spinach, ½ cup Parmesan, salt, nutmeg, lemon juice, and pepper to taste, stirring until the cheese is melted. Reduce the heat to very low, and cover, stirring occasionally.

When the fettuccine is *al dente*, in 10 to 12 minutes, drain it well, and transfer to a large serving bowl.

Top the pasta with the sauce, garnish with scallions and additional Parmesan, and serve.

Spicy Seitan and Vegetable Stroganoff

★ **BEGINNER-FRIENDLY**

A *vegetarian Hungarian delight!*

4 servings

2 tablespoons olive oil
4 large garlic cloves, peeled and minced
1 small jalapeño pepper, minced
1 cup coarsely chopped onion (1 large onion)
½ teaspoon dried oregano
½ teaspoon dried thyme
¾ cup coarsely chopped red bell pepper (1 medium pepper)
¾ cup coarsely chopped green bell pepper (1 medium pepper)
1 cup coarsely chopped zucchini (1 small zucchini)
½ pound seitan, thinly sliced (2 cups)
One 28-ounce can ground, peeled tomatoes with their juice
¼ teaspoon salt
10 Greek olives, pitted and chopped
12 ounces wide egg noodles
Finely grated Parmesan cheese for serving (optional)

Put a large pot of water on to boil.

Heat the oil in a skillet over medium heat. Sauté the garlic, jalapeño, onion, oregano, and thyme until the onion is wilted, 2 to 3 minutes. Stir in the red and green peppers and zucchini, and cook until tender, 3 to 4 minutes more.

Stir in the seitan, tomatoes and their juice, salt, and olives. Reduce the heat to a simmer and cook, stirring occasionally.

Cook the noodles in the boiling water until *al dente*, 8 to 10 minutes. Drain well, and transfer to a large serving dish.

Top the noodles with half the sauce. Serve the rest on the side, along with Parmesan cheese if you like.

Mediterranean Pasta

★ **BEGINNER-FRIENDLY**

The chick-peas add protein and body to the sauce of this easy, low-fat dish.

4 generous servings

3 cups cooked chick-peas (rinsed and drained if canned)
Juice of 1 lemon
1/16 to 1/8 teaspoon cayenne
1 teaspoon paprika
1 teaspoon salt
2 tablespoons canola oil
1½ cups thinly sliced red onion (3 medium onions)
8 large garlic cloves, peeled and minced
½ cup chopped fresh basil (lightly packed)
4 cups diced fresh tomatoes (4 large tomatoes)
1 pound dry tubular pasta
Finely grated Romano cheese for topping

Put a large pot of water on to boil.

Mash 2 cups of the chick-peas in a medium-size bowl. Stir in the lemon juice, cayenne, paprika, salt, and remaining chick-peas.

Heat the oil in a saucepan over medium heat. Sauté the onion and garlic until soft, about 5 minutes. Stir in the chick-pea mixture, basil, and tomatoes. Reduce the heat and simmer, stirring occasionally.

Cook pasta until *al dente,* 7 to 9 minutes, drain, and transfer to a large serving bowl.

Toss the sauce with the pasta, top with Romano cheese, and serve.

Asparagus Lasagna

This light lasagna is perfect for springtime when asparagus is abundant. Use precooked lasagna noodles if you like; they're easy to handle, and cut preparation time. They can be found in the pasta section of the supermarket.

6 to 8 servings

12 dry lasagna noodles (about 12 ounces)

FILLING
1 cup boiling water
1 cup sun-dried tomatoes (not in oil)
4 cups sliced fresh asparagus, tough ends removed (1⅓ pounds)
1 pound ricotta cheese
½ teaspoon salt
¼ cup chopped fresh basil or 1 tablespoon dried
Dash of pepper
¼ teaspoon ground nutmeg

SAUCE
6 tablespoons butter or margarine (¾ stick)
⅓ cup unbleached white flour
2 cups milk
½ cup dry white wine
1½ cups grated Cheddar cheese (6 ounces)
1 tablespoon lemon juice
1 teaspoon grated lemon peel
½ teaspoon salt

1 cup finely grated Parmesan cheese (4 ounces)
Paprika for sprinkling
Chopped fresh or dried parsley for sprinkling

Bring a large pot of water to a boil, and cook the noodles until *al dente*, about 10 minutes. Drain, rinse, and cover with cold water in the pot.

For the filling, pour 1 cup of boiling water over the tomatoes, and set aside to soak for 10 minutes.

Steam the asparagus until just tender, 5 to 7 minutes.

Drain and dice the tomatoes. Discard the soaking water.

Stir together the ricotta, salt, basil, pepper, and nutmeg in a medium-size bowl. Stir in the asparagus and tomatoes.

For the sauce, melt the butter in a heavy saucepan over medium heat. Whisk in the flour, and let it cook for a minute or two. Slowly pour in the milk and wine, whisking until thickened, about 5 minutes. Add the Cheddar cheese, lemon juice, lemon peel, and salt, stirring until the cheese is melted. Remove the pan from the heat.

Preheat the oven to 400 degrees.

Drain the noodles well.

Spread a thin layer of sauce in the bottom of a 9 by 13-inch baking pan. Cover with a layer of four noodles. Spread on half the ricotta mixture. Sprinkle on ⅓ cup of the Parmesan cheese.

Repeat the layers in this order: a thin layer of sauce, a layer of four noodles, the remaining ricotta mixture, ⅓ cup Parmesan, a thin layer of sauce, a layer of four noodles, the remaining sauce, and the remaining Parmesan. Sprinkle generously with paprika and parsley.

Bake for 25 to 30 minutes, until the edges are lightly browned. Let the lasagna set for 5 to 10 minutes before cutting to serve.

Pesto Lasagna

esto replaces the traditional tomato sauce in this recipe. The fresh tomatoes add flavor and moistness, and the cheeses lend a creamy texture and flavor.

6 to 8 servings

12 dry lasagna noodles (about 12 ounces)

PESTO
6 cups fresh basil leaves (lightly packed)
10 large garlic cloves, peeled
¾ cup walnuts or pine nuts
¾ cup canola or olive oil
1 teaspoon salt
1 cup finely grated Parmesan cheese (4 ounces)

FILLING
2 pounds ricotta cheese
2 large eggs, beaten
4 large tomatoes (2 diced, 2 sliced)
½ cup finely grated Parmesan cheese
¼ teaspoon ground nutmeg
½ teaspoon salt
Pepper

3 cups grated mozzarella cheese (12 ounces)

Bring a large pot of water to a boil.

Cook the noodles in the boiling water until *al dente,* about 10 minutes. Drain, rinse, and cover with cold water in the pot.

For the pesto, puree 3 cups of the basil leaves, the garlic, nuts, oil, 1 teaspoon salt, and 1 cup Parmesan in a food processor or blender. Add the remaining basil leaves, and process until smooth.

For the filling, in a medium-size bowl, stir together the ricotta, eggs, diced tomatoes, ½ cup Parmesan, nutmeg, ½ teaspoon salt, and pepper to taste.

Drain the noodles well.

Preheat the oven to 375 degrees.

Spread a thin layer of pesto in the bottom of a 9 by 13-inch baking pan. Add a layer of four noodles, overlapping them slightly. Spread on half the ricotta filling, another thin layer of pesto, and ½ cup grated mozzarella cheese.

Repeat the layers in this order: four overlapping noodles, the remaining cheese filling, a thin layer of pesto, ½ cup grated mozzarella, four overlapping noodles, the remaining pesto, the sliced tomatoes, and the remaining 2 cups grated mozzarella.

Bake for 45 minutes to 1 hour, until the cheese is bubbling and the edges are slightly brown.

Let the lasagna set for 5 to 10 minutes before cutting to serve.

Your Own Pizzeria

You may live in an area where fresh-baked pizza is just a phone call away. Or you may live out in the country, far from the nearest pizzeria. In either case, you ought to treat yourself occasionally to homemade pizza, calzone, and focaccia. There's nothing like it.

A calzone is a sort of inside-out pizza. It's made from the same dough, but instead of a topping it has a filling tucked inside, turnover-style. Focaccia is a cross between pizza and bread that goes great with a bowl of soup or a hearty salad.

Pizza and its cousins are just the thing to make on a day when you're going to be around but have plenty to do. While the dough is rising, you can polish off a few chores or run a quick errand. If you need to be gone for more than an hour or so, you can cover and refrigerate the punch-downed dough, and just let it warm to room temperature before rolling it out.

Pizza, calzone, and focaccia are an accommodating canvas for a creative cook. You can work chopped, fresh herbs into the dough. You can experiment with flour combinations and ratios, adding rye, soy, cornmeal, or graham flour, and trying different proportions of wheat to white. (The unbleached white flour lightens the dough, so use at least half white unless you like a really wheaty, somewhat heavy crust.)

Once the dough is ready, you can fashion a topping or filling from staples, leftovers, and specialty items. Here are just a few options:

VEGETABLES

Artichoke hearts, sliced (marinated ones are extra delicious)
Asparagus, sliced and lightly steamed

Avocado, sliced
Broccoli, chopped and lightly steamed
Capers, rinsed if salted
Cauliflower, chopped and lightly steamed
Eggplant, sliced and broiled, grilled, or sautéed
Garlic, minced
Leeks, sliced and lightly sautéed
Mushrooms of all kinds (including marinated), sliced
Olives of all kinds, sliced
Onions and scallions, thinly sliced
Peppers, roasted and fresh, hot, or red, yellow, or green bell, sliced
Spinach, chopped
Tomatoes, sun-dried and fresh, red, yellow, or cherry, sliced
Zucchini and summer squash, thinly sliced

CHEESES
Blue
Cheddar
Chèvre
Feta
Fontina
Gouda
Gruyère
Monterey Jack and jalapeño pepper Jack
Mozzarella, smoked, regular, or fresh
Parmesan
Provolone
Ricotta
Romano
Soy

OTHER CHOICES
Beans, including chick-peas, pintos, and kidneys, cooked
Fresh herbs, including basil, dill, chives, oregano, marjoram, rosemary, sage, and thyme, chopped
Nuts, including walnuts, pecans, and pine nuts, chopped
Pineapple chunks or slices
Sauces, including salsa, béchamel, and pesto
Soy products, including tofu, mashed or sautéed, and tempeh, sautéed

 **PIZZA**

Chicago Pizza

*C*hicago pizza has a top and bottom crust, like a deep-dish pie. This hearty pizza has spinach, Greek olives, tomatoes, mushrooms, and a two-cheese filling wrapped in a light, whole-grain crust.

6 to 8 servings

DOUGH

2 tablespoons active dry yeast

1½ cups warm water

2 teaspoons honey

2 tablespoons olive oil

1 teaspoon salt

2 cups whole wheat flour

2 cups unbleached white flour plus extra for kneading

Cornmeal for the pan

FILLING

2 tablespoons olive oil

6 to 8 large garlic cloves, peeled and minced

2 teaspoons dried oregano

1½ cups sliced onions (3 medium onions)

2 cups sliced mushrooms (½ pound)

One 10-ounce package frozen chopped spinach, thawed and squeezed dry

½ cup chopped, pitted Greek olives

¼ cup chopped fresh basil

¼ teaspoon salt

Pepper

½ cup finely grated Parmesan cheese (2 ounces)

¾ cup marinara sauce

3 cups grated mozzarella cheese (12 ounces)

2 or 3 medium tomatoes, thinly sliced

Olive oil for brushing

To make the dough, mix the yeast and water, honey, 2 tablespoons olive oil, and the salt in a large bowl. Let it sit until foamy, 5 to 10 minutes.

Slowly work in the wheat and white flours until well mixed.

Turn the dough out onto a floured surface. Knead it, adding more flour as needed, until it's smooth and not sticky, about 5 minutes.

Wipe the bowl clean, and put the dough back in it. Cover it with plastic wrap, and let it rise in a warm place until doubled in size, about 1 hour.

Preheat the oven to 400 degrees. Grease a 12-inch pizza pan, and sprinkle it with cornmeal.

To make the filling, heat 2 tablespoons olive oil in a skillet over medium heat. Sauté the garlic, oregano, onions, and mushrooms until the vegetables are tender and the mushroom liquid has evaporated, 6 to 8 minutes.

Remove the pan from the heat, and stir in the spinach, olives, basil, ¼ teaspoon salt, pepper to taste, Parmesan cheese, and marinara sauce. Mix well.

Punch down the dough, and divide it into two balls. On a floured surface, roll each ball into a 12-inch circle.

Place one circle on the prepared pan. Spread on half the mozzarella cheese, leaving a ½-inch border around the edges. Spread on the vegetable mixture, leaving the ½-inch border clear. Layer on the sliced tomatoes, and sprinkle on the remaining mozzarella cheese.

Place the second round of dough on top of the pizza, and pinch the edges together tightly with a twisting motion. Brush the top with olive oil.

Bake for about 25 minutes, until the edges are lightly browned. Cut into wedges and serve.

Eggplant Parmigiana Pizza

Tender slices of eggplant, fresh basil, tomato, garlic, and two cheeses make a delectable topping.

4 servings

DOUGH
- 1 cup warm water
- 1 tablespoon active dry yeast
- 2 tablespoons olive oil
- ½ teaspoon salt
- 1 cup whole wheat bread flour
- 1½ cups unbleached white flour, plus extra for kneading

Cornmeal for the pan

TOPPING
- 1 pound eggplant, peeled and cut into ¼-inch-thick slices
- Olive oil for brushing
- 1 cup marinara sauce
- 3 large garlic cloves, peeled and minced
- Salt
- 1½ cups grated mozzarella cheese (6 ounces)
- 1 large tomato, thinly sliced
- ¼ cup chopped fresh basil
- ¼ cup finely grated Parmesan cheese (1 ounce)

To make the dough, mix the warm water, yeast, 2 tablespoons olive oil, and salt in a large bowl. Let it sit until foamy, 5 to 10 minutes.

Slowly work in the wheat and white flours until well mixed.

Turn the dough out onto a floured surface. Knead it, adding more flour as needed, until it's smooth and not sticky, about 5 minutes.

Wipe the bowl clean, and put the dough back in it. Cover it with plastic wrap, and let it rise in a warm place for 40 to 50 minutes, until doubled.

Preheat the oven to 425 degrees. Sprinkle a 14- or 15-inch pizza pan with cornmeal.

Brush the eggplant slices on both sides with olive oil, and spread them in a single layer on a baking sheet. Bake for about 10 minutes, until browned and tender when pierced with a fork. Turn over and bake for 3 to 4 minutes more. Set them aside to cool. (Leave the oven on.)

On a floured surface, roll the dough into a circle big enough to fit your pan. Press the dough out to the sides of the pan and pinch up the edges to form a rim. Bake for 5 to 7 minutes, until firm and barely brown.

Remove the crust from the oven, and spread the marinara sauce on it, leaving a 1-inch border for the rim. Scatter it with garlic, and layer it with the eggplant slices. Sprinkle the eggplant with salt, and top it with 1 cup of the grated mozzarella. Spread on the tomato slices, and sprinkle them with the basil. Top with Parmesan and the remaining mozzarella.

Bake for 10 minutes, until the cheese is melted and lightly browned. Cut into eight wedges and serve.

 **CALZONES**

Four-Cheese Calzone

One large calzone makes a generous main course for dinner; the smaller size is great for lunches or multicourse meals. You can freeze any leftovers. Allow calzones to cool and wrap tightly in plastic bags.

8 servings

DOUGH
> 1 cup warm water
> 1 tablespoon active dry yeast
> 1 teaspoon honey
> 1 tablespoon olive oil
> ½ teaspoon salt
> 1 teaspoon dried oregano
> 1¼ cups whole wheat flour
> 1¼ cups unbleached white flour, plus extra for kneading

FILLING
> 1½ cups ricotta cheese
> ½ cup finely grated Parmesan cheese (2 ounces)
> ½ cup grated smoked mozzarella cheese (2 ounces)
> ½ cup grated fontina cheese (2 ounces)
> 4 large garlic cloves, peeled and minced
> 2 tablespoons chopped fresh basil
> ½ teaspoon salt
> 1 medium tomato, chopped and drained (¾ cup)
> 1 roasted green chili pepper (available in cans), finely chopped

> 1 large egg, beaten with 1 teaspoon water
> 1½ cups marinara sauce

To make the dough, mix the warm water, yeast, honey, olive oil, ½ teaspoon salt, and oregano in a large bowl. Let it sit until foamy, 5 to 10 minutes.

Slowly work in the wheat and white flours until well mixed.

Turn the dough out onto a floured surface. Knead it, adding more flour as needed, until it's smooth and not sticky, about 5 minutes.

Wipe the bowl clean, and put the dough back in it. Cover it with plastic wrap, and let it rise in a warm place until doubled in size, about 1 hour.

For the filling, stir together the ricotta, Parmesan, mozzarella, fontina, garlic, basil, salt, tomato, and green chili in a medium-size bowl.

Preheat the oven to 425 degrees. Grease two baking sheets.

Turn the dough out onto a floured surface and knead it for about 5 minutes, until smooth. Divide it into eight pieces (sixteen if you're making small calzones) and form into balls. Roll each ball into a 6- to 7-inch circle (3½ inches for small ones).

Spoon about ½ cup of filling onto one side of each large dough circle (¼ cup for the small). Spread it on half the circle, leaving a ½-inch border around the edge. Fold the circles in half, and seal them well with the tines of a fork.

Place the calzones on the prepared baking sheets, and brush them with beaten egg along the top, sides, edges, and back.

Bake for 15 to 20 minutes, until lightly browned. (If filling leaks out, let the calzones cool for a few minutes and stuff it back in.)

Heat the marinara sauce in a small saucepan. Transfer the calzones to a serving platter or individual plates, top with sauce, and serve.

Broccoli-Mushroom Calzone

Smoked mozzarella adds depth to the flavorful filling.

8 servings

DOUGH

1 cup warm water
1 tablespoon active dry yeast
1 teaspoon honey
1 tablespoon olive oil
½ teaspoon salt
1 teaspoon dried oregano
1 ¼ cups whole wheat flour
1 ¼ cups unbleached white flour,

FILLING

2 tablespoons olive oil
5 large garlic cloves, peeled and minced
4 cups chopped broccoli
1 teaspoon dried oregano
1 teaspoon dried basil or 2 tablespoons minced fresh
2 cups sliced mushrooms (½ pound)
1 ½ cups grated smoked mozzarella cheese (6 ounces)
½ teaspoon salt
¼ cup finely grated Parmesan cheese (1 ounce)

1 large egg, beaten with 1 teaspoon water
1 ½ cups marinara sauce

For the dough, mix the warm water, yeast, honey, 1 tablespoon olive oil, ½ teaspoon salt, and 1 teaspoon oregano in a large bowl. Let it sit until foamy, 5 to 10 minutes.

Slowly work in the wheat and white flours until well mixed.

Turn the dough out onto a floured surface. Knead it, adding more flour as needed, until it's smooth and not sticky, about 5 minutes.

Wipe the bowl clean, and put the dough back in it. Cover it with plastic wrap, and let it rise in a warm place until doubled in size, about 1 hour.

To make the filling, heat the 2 tablespoons oil in a skillet over medium heat. Sauté the garlic, broccoli, oregano, and basil (unless using fresh basil) until the broccoli turns bright green, 3 to 4 minutes. Stir in the mushrooms, and cook until tender, 3 to 4 minutes more.

Drain the cooked vegetables, and transfer them to a medium-size bowl. Stir in the mozzarella, ½ teaspoon salt, Parmesan, and fresh basil if being used.

Preheat the oven to 425 degrees. Grease two baking sheets.

Turn the dough out onto a floured surface, and knead it for about 5 minutes, until smooth. Divide the dough into eight pieces (sixteen if you're making small calzones), and form them into balls. Roll each ball into a 6- to 7-inch circle (3½-inch circles for small calzones).

Spoon about ½ cup of filling onto one side of each large dough circle (¼ cup for small). Spread it on half the circle, leaving a ½-inch border around the edge. Fold the circles in half, and seal them well with the tines of a fork.

Place the calzones on the prepared baking sheets, and brush them with the beaten egg along the top, sides, edges, and back.

Bake for 15 to 20 minutes, until lightly browned. (If filling leaks out, let the calzones cool for a few minutes and stuff it back in.)

Heat the marinara sauce in a small saucepan. Transfer the calzones to a serving platter or individual plates, top with sauce, and serve.

Mushroom-Spinach Calzone
with Three-Cheese Filling

8 servings

DOUGH

1 cup warm water

1 tablespoon active dry yeast

1 teaspoon honey

1 tablespoon olive oil

½ teaspoon salt

1 teaspoon dried basil

1¼ cups whole wheat flour

1¼ cups unbleached white flour, plus extra for kneading

FILLING

2 tablespoons olive oil

2 cups sliced mushrooms (½ pound)

4 large garlic cloves, peeled and minced

½ cup chopped red bell pepper (1 small pepper)

1 teaspoon dried thyme

2 cups chopped fresh spinach (lightly packed)

1½ cups ricotta cheese

½ cup grated mozzarella cheese (2 ounces)

½ cup finely grated Parmesan or Romano cheese (2 ounces)

½ teaspoon salt

1 large egg, beaten with 1 teaspoon water

1½ cups marinara sauce

For the dough, mix the warm water, yeast, honey, 1 tablespoon olive oil, ½ teaspoon salt, and basil in a large bowl. Let it sit until foamy, 5 to 10 minutes.

Slowly work in the wheat and white flours until well mixed.

Turn the dough out onto a floured surface. Knead it, adding more flour as needed, until it's smooth and not sticky, about 5 minutes.

Wipe the bowl clean, and put the dough back in it. Cover it with plastic wrap, and let it rise in a warm place until doubled in size, about 1 hour.

To make the filling, heat the 2 tablespoons olive oil in a skillet over medium heat. Sauté the mushrooms, garlic, red pepper, and thyme for 2 minutes. Stir in the spinach, and cook until just tender, 2 to 3 minutes more.

Drain the vegetables, and transfer them to a medium-size bowl. Stir in the ricotta, mozzarella, Parmesan, and ½ teaspoon salt.

Preheat the oven to 425 degrees. Grease two baking sheets.

Turn the dough out onto a floured surface, and knead it for about 5 minutes, until smooth. Divide the dough into eight pieces (sixteen if you're making small calzones), and form them into balls. Roll each ball into a 6- to 7-inch circle (3½-inch circles for small calzones).

Spoon about ½ cup of filling onto one side of each large dough circle (¼ cup for small calzones). Spread it on half the circle, leaving a ½-inch border around the edge. Fold the circles in half, and seal them well with the tines of a fork.

Place the calzones on the prepared baking sheets, and brush them with beaten egg along the top, sides, edges, and back.

Bake for 15 to 20 minutes, until lightly browned. (If filling leaks out, let the calzones cool for a few minutes and stuff it back in.)

Heat the marinara sauce in a small saucepan. Transfer the calzones to a serving platter or individual plates, top with sauce, and serve.

Three-Cheese Focaccia with Sun-Dried Tomatoes, Onions, and Red Bell Pepper

*F*ocaccia *is great to bring to a potluck dinner. It also goes well with a thick, hearty soup on a cold evening.*

6 to 8 servings

DOUGH

1 cup warm water
1 tablespoon active dry yeast
1 teaspoon honey
1 teaspoon salt
¼ cup minced, drained oil-packed sun-dried tomatoes
3 tablespoons oil drained from the sun-dried tomatoes
½ cup finely grated Parmesan cheese (2 ounces)
1¾ cups unbleached white flour plus extra for kneading
1½ cups whole wheat flour

Cornmeal for the pan

TOPPING

¾ cup thinly sliced onion (1 medium-large onion)
1 large red bell pepper, seeded and thinly sliced (1 cup)
1 cup grated mozzarella cheese (4 ounces)
½ cup crumbled blue cheese (2 ounces)
¼ cup finely grated Parmesan cheese (1 ounce)

¼ teaspoon salt
½ teaspoon dried oregano
1 tablespoon olive oil

To make the dough, mix the warm water, yeast, honey, and salt in a large bowl. Let it sit until foamy, 5 to 10 minutes.

Stir in the sun-dried tomatoes and tomato oil. Add the ½ cup Parmesan cheese and the flours, and stir until well combined.

Turn the dough out onto a floured surface. Knead it, adding more flour as needed, until it's smooth and not sticky, about 5 minutes.

Wipe the bowl clean, and put the dough back in it. Cover it with plastic wrap, and let it rise in a warm place until doubled in size, about 1 hour.

Oil a 12-inch pizza pan, and sprinkle it with cornmeal.

Punch down the dough, and knead it briefly. Press it into the prepared pan, and cover it with plastic wrap. Let it rise in a warm place until doubled in size, about 1 hour.

Position an oven rack one third of the way up from the bottom. Preheat the oven to 400 degrees.

Bake the dough for 15 minutes, until lightly browned.

Meanwhile, make the topping: combine the onion, red pepper, mozzarella, blue cheese, and ¼ cup Parmesan in a bowl and toss gently.

Remove the dough from the oven, and spread on the topping. Sprinkle on the ¼ teaspoon salt and the oregano, and drizzle on the olive oil.

Return the focaccia to the oven, and bake for about 15 minutes more, until lightly browned. Serve hot or at room temperature.

A Crepe by
Any Other Name

Czechoslovakian politinkis, Eastern European blintzes, Indian chapatis, Asian moo shu pancakes, Mexican tortillas, French crepes. Thin, unleavened pancakes are known in many cultures, and are at home at any meal. The filling can be as simple as fresh berries and as elaborate as a medley of beans, vegetables, cheese, and herbs topped with a rich sauce.

Crepe batter is quick to mix and, believe it or not, easy to cook. A well-seasoned, heavy-bottomed pan is a must. (Crepe batter is at its best when it can sit for at least an hour or overnight, refrigerated, before using.) The first crepe in a batch is almost always a disaster, but soon you'll get into the rhythm of crepe making and wonder what all the fuss was about. During my café days, I would sometimes have four crepe pans going at once.

You can stack cooked crepes, but never put more than a dozen in one pile or they may stick together. You can freeze extras, separating them with waxed paper. Leftover crepes are great for wrapping fresh fruit or sautéed vegetables for an impromptu meal. I like to fix them the way my mother made her politinkis, with a simple jam filling and a sprinkling of powdered sugar on top for a sweet treat. For an unusual and pretty presentation, I sometimes fold the filled crepes in quarters rather than rolling them.

Asparagus, Potato, Cheddar, and Dill Crepes

*F*resh *dill and asparagus make this a lovely springtime dish.*

5 generous servings (10 crepes)

BATTER

3 large eggs

1¼ cups milk

2 tablespoons butter or margarine, melted

¾ cup unbleached white flour

¾ cup whole wheat pastry flour

½ teaspoon salt

2 tablespoons minced fresh dill or 2 teaspoons dried

Butter or margarine for cooking

FILLING

3 cups cubed potatoes (3 medium potatoes)

1 cup diced carrots (2 medium carrots)

2 tablespoons canola oil

1 cup chopped onion (1 large onion)

5 large garlic cloves, peeled and minced

¾ pound pencil-thin asparagus, cut into 1-inch pieces (2 cups)

2 tablespoons minced fresh dill or 2 teaspoons dried

1 teaspoon salt

½ cup fresh or frozen peas

1 tablespoon fresh lemon juice

1½ cups grated Cheddar cheese (6 ounces)

SAUCE

2 tablespoons butter or margarine

3 tablespoons unbleached white flour

1 cup milk

1 cup grated Cheddar cheese (4 ounces)

½ teaspoon dried thyme

To make the crepe batter, combine the eggs, 1¼ cups milk, 2 tablespoons melted butter, and ¼ cup of water in a blender or food processor, and process until smooth. Add the flours, ½ teaspoon salt, and dill, and process again. Refrigerate for at least 1 hour or as long as overnight.

Let the batter return to room temperature, and stir it well.

Melt a little butter in a heavy, 10-inch skillet over medium heat, and spread it over the bottom. Pour in about ¼ cup of batter, and quickly tilt the pan, swirling the batter so it covers the bottom.

Cook the crepe until lightly golden, 1 to 2 minutes. Flip it with a spatula, and cook for 30 seconds to 1 minute more. Repeat until all the crepes are cooked, adding butter to the pan as needed. Stack the cooked crepes, and set them aside.

For the filling, bring 3 cups of water to a boil in saucepan. Add the potatoes. When the water returns to a boil, add the carrots. Cook until tender, about 10 minutes all together, and drain.

Heat the oil in a skillet over medium heat. Sauté the onion, garlic, and asparagus until tender, about 5 minutes. (Sauté the dried dill, too, if using.)

Remove the pan from the heat, and stir in the cooked potatoes and carrots along with the fresh dill, salt, peas, lemon juice, and 1½ cups cheese.

Preheat the oven to 400 degrees, and grease two baking sheets.

Spread out the crepes on a work surface. Divide the filling among them, spreading ⅔ to ¾ cup in a line down the center of each. Roll up the crepes and place on the prepared baking sheets. Bake for 10 to 15 minutes, until the cheese is melted and the crepes are lightly golden.

While the crepes are baking, make the sauce. Melt the 2 tablespoons butter in a saucepan over medium heat. Whisk in the 3 tablespoons flour, and let it cook for a minute or two. Slowly add the 1 cup milk, whisking until thickened, about 3 minutes. Add the cheese and thyme, stirring until the cheese is melted.

Top the hot crepes with cheese sauce, and serve.

Cauliflower Curry Crepes

*F*resh cauliflower, chick-peas, ginger, and chutney make an enticing cultural blend.

5 generous servings (10 crepes)

CREPES
>   3 large eggs
>   1¼ cups milk
>   2 tablespoons butter, melted
>   ¾ cup whole wheat pastry flour
>   ¾ cup unbleached white flour
>   1 tablespoon curry powder
>   ½ teaspoon salt

Butter or margarine for cooking

FILLING

3 tablespoons canola oil
1 cup chopped onion (1 large onion)
1 tablespoon peeled and minced fresh ginger
¾ cup diced carrot (1 medium-large carrot)
4 cups chopped cauliflower (1 small head)
1 cup cooked chick-peas
1 large tomato, chopped (1 cup)
¼ cup mango chutney plus extra for garnish
½ cup minced fresh parsley
1 tablespoon fresh lemon juice
1 teaspoon curry powder
1 teaspoon turmeric
½ teaspoon salt
1/16 to 1/8 teaspoon cayenne

To make the crepe batter, combine the eggs, milk, 2 tablespoons melted butter, and ¼ cup of water in a blender or food processor, and process until smooth. Add the flours, 1 tablespoon curry powder, and ½ teaspoon salt, and process again. Refrigerate for at least 1 hour or as long as overnight.

Let the batter return to room temperature, and stir it well.

Melt a little butter in a heavy, 10-inch skillet over medium heat, and spread it over the bottom. Pour in about ¼ cup of batter, and quickly tilt the pan, swirling the batter so it covers the bottom.

Cook the crepe until lightly golden, 1 to 2 minutes. Flip it with a spatula, and cook for 30 seconds to 1 minute more. Repeat until all the crepes are cooked, adding butter to the pan as needed. Stack the cooked crepes, and set them aside.

To prepare the filling, heat the oil in a skillet over medium heat. Sauté the onion, ginger, carrot, and cauliflower until tender, 5 to 7 minutes, adding a tablespoon or two of water to prevent sticking.

Remove the pan from the heat, and stir in the chick-peas, tomato, ¼ cup chutney, parsley, lemon juice, 1 teaspoon curry, turmeric, ½ teaspoon salt, and cayenne to taste.

Preheat the oven to 400 degrees, and grease two baking sheets.

Lay out the crepes on a work surface. Divide the filling among them (about ½ cup for each), placing it on one quarter of the crepe. Fold the crepes in half and half again to form a pie-shaped wedge.

Transfer the crepes to the prepared baking sheets, and bake for 10 to 15 minutes, until lightly golden. Serve garnished with chutney.

Black Bean and Chili Corn Crepes

A delicate cornmeal crepe spiked with chili powder surrounds the black bean, vegetable, and cheese filling.

5 generous servings (10 crepes)

BATTER

3 large eggs

1 cup milk

2 tablespoons butter or margarine, melted

½ cup unbleached white flour

½ cup whole wheat pastry flour

½ cup yellow cornmeal

½ teaspoon salt

1 tablespoon chili powder

Butter or margarine for cooking

FILLING

2 tablespoons canola oil

1 cup chopped onion (1 large onion)

6 large garlic cloves, peeled and minced

1 medium jalapeño pepper, minced

1 cup chopped red bell pepper (1 large pepper)

½ cup diced carrot (1 medium carrot)

3½ cups cooked black beans, lightly mashed

1 small tomato, finely chopped (½ cup)

½ cup fresh or frozen corn kernels

1 teaspoon salt

1 teaspoon ground cumin

¼ cup minced fresh cilantro

3 scallions, thinly sliced

1½ cups grated sharp Cheddar cheese (6 ounces)

1½ cups grated Monterey Jack cheese (6 ounces)

Sour cream for garnish

3 scallions, thinly sliced, for garnish

To make the crepe batter, combine the eggs, milk, 2 tablespoons melted butter, and ⅓ cup of water in a blender or food processor, and process until smooth. Add the flours, cornmeal, ½ teaspoon salt, and chili powder, and process again. Refrigerate for at least 1 hour or as long as overnight.

Let the batter return to room temperature, and stir it well.

Melt a little butter in a heavy, 10-inch skillet over medium heat, and spread it over the bottom. Pour in about ¼ cup of batter, and quickly tilt the pan, swirling the batter so it covers the bottom.

Cook the crepe until lightly golden, 1 to 2 minutes. Flip it with a spatula, and cook for 30 seconds to 1 minute more. Repeat until all the crepes are cooked, adding a little butter to the pan between each one. Stack the cooked crepes, and set them aside.

To make the filling, heat the oil in a skillet over medium heat. Sauté the onion, garlic, jalapeño, red pepper, and carrot until tender, about 5 minutes. Remove the pan from the heat, and stir in the beans, tomato, corn, 1 teaspoon salt, cumin, cilantro, and the three thinly sliced scallions.

Preheat the oven to 400 degrees, and grease two baking sheets.

Lay out the crepes on a work surface. Divide the filling among them (about ½ cup for each), placing it on one quarter of the crepe. Sprinkle on the cheeses. Fold the crepes in half and half again to form a pie-shaped wedge.

Transfer the crepes to the prepared baking sheets, and bake for 10 to 15 minutes, until the cheese is melted and the crepe is lightly golden. Serve garnished with sour cream and thinly sliced scallions.

Spinach-Mushroom Crepes
with Farmer Cheese

As a time-saver, you can replace the fresh spinach with two 10-ounce boxes of
frozen spinach, thawed and squeezed dry.

5 generous servings (10 crepes)

BATTER
   3 large eggs
   ½ cup chopped fresh herbs (a combination of parsley, dill, chives,
      and/or basil)
   1¼ cups milk
   2 tablespoons butter or margarine, melted
   ¾ cup unbleached white flour
   ¾ cup whole wheat pastry flour
   ½ teaspoon salt

   Butter or margarine for cooking

FILLING
   8 cups chopped fresh spinach (lightly packed)
   2 tablespoons canola oil
   1 pound mushrooms, sliced (about 4 cups)
   6 large garlic cloves, peeled and minced
   2 cups creamy-style farmer cheese or ricotta cheese (1 pound)
   ½ cup finely grated Parmesan cheese (2 ounces)
   6 scallions, thinly sliced
   2 tablespoons minced fresh dill
   ¼ cup fresh lemon juice
   ¾ teaspoon salt
   Pepper

   Sour cream for garnish
   Chopped fresh dill for garnish

To make the crepe batter, combine the eggs, herbs, milk, melted butter, and
¼ cup of water in a blender or food processor, and process until smooth. Add the
flours and ½ teaspoon salt, and process again. Refrigerate for at least 1 hour or
as long as overnight.

Let the batter return to room temperature, and stir it well.

Melt a little butter in a heavy, 10-inch skillet over medium heat, and spread it over the bottom. Pour in about ¼ cup of batter, and quickly tilt the pan, swirling the batter so it covers the bottom.

Cook the crepe until lightly golden, 1 to 2 minutes. Flip it with a spatula, and cook for 30 seconds to 1 minute more. Repeat until all the crepes are cooked, adding a little butter to the pan between each one. Stack the cooked crepes, and set them aside.

To prepare the filling, steam the spinach lightly, and squeeze it dry.

Heat the oil in a skillet over medium heat. Sauté the mushrooms and garlic until the mushroom liquid has evaporated, 6 to 8 minutes.

Remove the pan from the heat, and stir in the spinach, farmer cheese, Parmesan, scallions, dill, lemon juice, ¾ teaspoon salt, and pepper to taste.

Preheat the oven to 400 degrees, and grease two baking sheets.

Lay out the crepes on a work surface. Divide the filling among them (about ½ cup for each), placing it on one quarter of the crepe. Fold the crepes in half and half again to form a pie-shaped wedge.

Transfer the crepes to the prepared baking sheets, and bake for 10 to 15 minutes, until the cheese is melted and the crepe is lightly golden.

Serve garnished with sour cream and a pinch of chopped fresh dill.

Tropical Dreams

Most New Englanders dream of escaping the long, cold, snowy winters, and the long, rainy, muddy springs. By the time March rolls around, it can be disheartening to know that tulips and daffodils are blooming in other Northern climes while your spring is still two months away!

Eight years ago, I was finally able to realize that tropical dream with a camping trip to the island of Tortola with a group of good friends. Since then, my family and I have made mud-season escapes whenever we can.

Long, sunny days beside sparkling Caribbean waters quickly erase all but a faint memory of winter, and the friendly islanders make you feel at home. Goats wander the beautiful, mountainous terrain, and islanders and visitors alike gather at the water's edge at the end of the day to see what the local fishermen have brought home in their nets. Watching the sun sink into the ocean gives you a sense of timelessness and peace.

Along with sunny memories, I returned from Tortola with a love for rotis, West Indian filled flat breads popular at Caribbean fairs, markets, and restaurants. Rotis go well with the relaxed lifestyle of the islands. They can be a meal in themselves, grabbed and eaten on the run, or served up nicely on a plate with spicy mango chutney, green salad, and perhaps some fritters to start. Caribbean Lime Cheesecake (page 287), Banana Cream Nut Cake (page 282), or fresh pineapple and mango slices would make a great ending to the meal.

You can use that menu for your own winter escape—a tropical dinner party complete with piña coladas, banana daiquiris, and Caribbean fruit punch. Tell your guests to wear their favorite beach garb under their down jackets, turn up the thermostat, or add an extra log to your wood stove, and cool out!

Tortolan Chick-Pea and Spinach Rotis

★ **BEGINNER-FRIENDLY**

You can substitute a 10-ounce package of chopped frozen spinach (thawed and squeezed dry) for the fresh spinach.

4 to 6 servings

1 pound coarsely chopped fresh spinach
3½ cups cooked chick-peas
2 tablespoons canola oil
1½ cups chopped onions (3 medium onions)
5 large garlic cloves, peeled and minced
2 tablespoons peeled and minced fresh ginger
1½ cups chopped zucchini (1 medium-large zucchini)
2 medium tomatoes, chopped (1½ cups)
¾ cup fresh or frozen peas
1 teaspoon salt
2 teaspoons ground cumin
2 teaspoons curry powder
1 teaspoon ground coriander
1 teaspoon turmeric
⅛ to ¼ teaspoon cayenne (to taste)
¼ cup minced fresh cilantro plus extra for garnish
Eight 8-inch whole wheat flat breads, chapatis, or tortillas
Plain yogurt for garnish
Chutney for garnish

Steam the spinach lightly, and squeeze it dry.

Puree the chick-peas in a food processor or mash them by hand until smooth.

Preheat the oven to 350 degrees.

Heat the oil in a large, heavy skillet over medium heat. Sauté the onions, garlic, and ginger until just tender, 3 to 4 minutes. (Add a tablespoon or two of water if the ginger sticks.) Stir in zucchini, and cook until just soft, 3 to 4 minutes more.

Stir in the tomatoes, steamed spinach, peas, salt, cumin, curry powder, coriander, turmeric, cayenne, ¼ cup minced cilantro, and the pureed chick-peas. Reduce the heat to low, and cook, stirring often, until steaming hot.

Meanwhile, heat the flat breads in the oven just until hot but soft to the touch.

Spread the flat breads on a work surface. Divide the filling among them, putting ¾ to 1 cup in the center of each. Fold the flat breads burrito style: sides in, bottom up, and top down.

Serve immediately, garnished with yogurt, chutney, and cilantro.

West Indian Lentil-Cheddar Rotis

★ **BEGINNER-FRIENDLY**

This creamy, gingery filling is quick to prepare and sure to please.

4 to 6 servings

2 cups dried lentils
2 cups cubed unpeeled potatoes (2 medium potatoes)
2 tablespoons canola oil
1 cup chopped onion (1 large onion)
5 large garlic cloves, peeled and minced
1½ tablespoons peeled and minced fresh ginger
1 cup diced carrots (2 medium carrots)
½ teaspoon cumin seed
1½ teaspoons salt
2 teaspoons curry powder
1 teaspoon ground coriander
⅛ to ¼ teaspoon cayenne
1 medium tomato, chopped (½ cup)
1 cup fresh or frozen peas
2 cups grated Cheddar cheese (8 ounces)
Eight 8-inch whole wheat flat breads, chapatis, or tortillas
Plain yogurt for garnish
Chutney for garnish

Bring the lentils and 4 cups of water to a boil in a saucepan. Reduce the heat to a simmer and cook, covered, for 20 minutes. Add the potatoes and cook until the lentils and potatoes are tender and the water has evaporated, about 10 minutes more.

Preheat the oven to 350 degrees.

Heat the oil in a large skillet over medium heat. Sauté the onion, garlic, ginger, carrots, and cumin seed until the onion is tender, 3 to 4 minutes. (Add a tablespoon or two of water if the ginger sticks.)

Stir in the salt, curry powder, coriander, cayenne, tomato, peas, Cheddar, and the cooked lentils and potatoes. Reduce the heat to low, and cook, stirring occasionally, until steaming hot.

Meanwhile, heat the flat breads in the oven for a minute or two, just until soft to the touch.

Spread the flat breads on a work surface. Divide the filling among them, putting about 1 cup in the center of each. Fold the flat breads burrito style: sides in, bottom up, and top down.

Serve immediately, garnished with yogurt and chutney.

Caribbean Butternut Rotis

★ BEGINNER-FRIENDLY

4 to 6 servings

2 tablespoons canola oil
5 large garlic cloves, peeled and minced
1½ tablespoons peeled and minced ginger
1 cup chopped onion (1 large onion)
1 medium jalapeño pepper, minced
½ cup chopped green bell pepper (1 small pepper)
2 cups chopped cauliflower (half a medium head)
3 cups mashed, cooked butternut squash or other winter squash
1 large tomato, chopped (1 cup)
¼ cup finely chopped fresh cilantro
1 teaspoon salt
1½ cups grated Cheddar cheese (6 ounces)
8 whole wheat flat breads, tortillas, or chapatis, 8 inches or more
   in diameter
Yogurt for garnish
Chutney for garnish

Preheat the oven to 350 degrees.

Heat the oil in a large skillet over medium heat. Sauté the garlic, ginger, onion, jalapeño, green pepper, and cauliflower until tender, 5 to 7 minutes. (Add a tablespoon or two of water if the ginger sticks.)

Stir in the squash, tomato, cilantro, salt, and cheese. Reduce the heat to low and cook, stirring often, until steaming hot.

Meanwhile, heat the flat breads in the oven for a minute or two, just until soft to the touch.

Spread the flat breads on a work surface. Divide the filling among them, putting about ¾ cup in the center of each. Fold the flat breads burrito style: sides in, bottom up, and top down.

Serve immediately, garnished with yogurt and chutney.

Eclectic Dinners

The inspiration for this chapter comes from points as far away as India, Greece, and Eastern Europe and as close as my mom's kitchen. The recipes reflect the cultural exchange so much a part of our world today that even small towns in Vermont have Indian, Chinese, Mexican, and Italian restaurants.

These dishes aren't authentic to any one culture, but represent an assimilation of cooking styles and ingredients. They're unusual, delicious, and fun to cook!

Stir-Fried Vegetables and Tempeh with Spicy Peanut Sauce

The zesty peanut sauce can be made ahead; it stores well in the refrigerator. Place leftover sauce in a tightly sealed plastic container. It will keep for two to four weeks. The recipe makes enough sauce for two meals.

4 servings

SAUCE

¼ cup garlic cloves, peeled
¼ cup coarsely chopped, peeled fresh ginger
1 cup smooth peanut butter

½ cup peanut oil
½ cup orange juice
½ cup tamari or soy sauce
⅓ cup honey
¼ cup vinegar
1 tablespoon sesame oil
1 teaspoon chili powder
⅛ to ¼ teaspoon cayenne

TO COMPLETE THE DISH

3 tablespoons canola oil
½ pound tempeh, cut into small triangles
2 tablespoons tamari or soy sauce
12 ounces dry curly pasta
4 cups chopped broccoli (florets sliced)
2 medium carrots, peeled and cut into matchstick shapes (1 cup)
2 cups sliced bok choy (4 stalks)
1 large red bell pepper, seeded and thinly sliced (1 cup)
2 cups chopped zucchini (1 large zucchini)

To prepare the sauce, process the garlic and ginger in a food processor until finely chopped. Add the peanut butter, peanut oil, orange juice, tamari, honey, vinegar, sesame oil, chili powder, and cayenne, and process until smooth. Put half the sauce in a small saucepan, and refrigerate the rest for another meal.

Put a large pot of water on to boil.

Heat 2 tablespoons of the canola oil in a skillet over medium heat. Sauté the tempeh until lightly browned on all sides, about 10 minutes. Pour on the 2 tablespoons tamari and stir quickly to distribute it. Transfer the tempeh to a large serving bowl.

Heat the peanut sauce over very low heat, stirring occasionally.

Cook the pasta in the boiling water until *al dente*, 8 to 10 minutes.

Meanwhile, heat the remaining 1 tablespoon canola oil in the skillet over medium heat. Sauté the broccoli and carrots for 2 to 3 minutes. Add the bok choy, red pepper, and zucchini, and cook until just tender, 3 to 4 minutes. Add the tempeh, and cook just until warmed through, 1 to 2 minutes more. Transfer to the serving bowl.

Drain the pasta, and toss it with the tempeh and vegetables. Add all but a few tablespoons of the hot peanut sauce, and toss again. Pour on the reserved sauce, and serve.

Greek Spinach-Potato Strudel

This potato lover's version of spanakopitta is spiked with sharp feta and Cheddar cheeses, and baked in a flaky phyllo crust.

6 servings

6 cups diced unpeeled potatoes (about 2 pounds)
1 pound chopped fresh spinach or one 10-ounce package frozen, thawed
5 tablespoons butter or margarine
2 tablespoons canola oil
1½ cups chopped onions (3 medium onions)
4 large garlic cloves, peeled and minced
2 teaspoons dried basil
1 teaspoon dried thyme
¼ teaspoon ground nutmeg
1 teaspoon salt
Pepper
¾ cup sour cream
2 cups crumbled feta cheese (8 ounces)
½ cup grated Cheddar cheese (2 ounces)
¼ cup minced fresh dill or 2 teaspoons dried
6 scallions, chopped
10 sheets phyllo dough (half a 1-pound package, thawed; see Note)
1 teaspoon sesame seeds
Sour cream for garnish
Greek olives for garnish

Bring 4 cups of water to a boil in a saucepan. Add the potatoes and cook until tender, 10 to 12 minutes.

Meanwhile, if using fresh spinach, steam it lightly. If using frozen, squeeze it dry.

Drain the cooked potatoes, and mash them in a large mixing bowl with 1 tablespoon of the butter. Stir in the spinach.

Heat the oil in a skillet over medium heat. Sauté the onions, garlic, basil, and thyme until the onions are soft, about 5 minutes. (If using dried dill, sauté it, too.)

Stir the sautéed vegetables into the mashed potatoes, along with the nutmeg, salt, pepper to taste, sour cream, feta and Cheddar cheeses, and all but 1 tablespoon each of the fresh dill and scallions. Mix very well, using your hands if needed.

Preheat the oven to 375 degrees.

Melt the remaining butter. Spread out a sheet of phyllo dough on a work surface, and brush it with butter. Stack on four more sheets of dough, brushing each with butter.

Spread half the filling over a third of the dough (dividing it the long way), leaving a 2-inch border on three edges. Fold those edges up over the filling, and roll it into a log shape. Place the filled dough on an ungreased baking sheet.

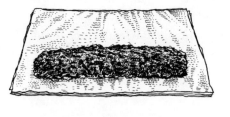

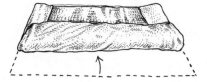
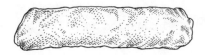

Repeat with the remaining dough and filling. Brush each log with the remaining butter, and sprinkle with sesame seeds.

Bake for 15 to 20 minutes, until golden. Serve garnished with sour cream, the reserved dill and scallions, and a few Greek olives.

Note

You need a 1-pound package of phyllo dough because the sheets in smaller packages are too small for this recipe.

Oriental Tofu Balls with Fruit Sauce, Stir-Fried Vegetables, and Rice

The crisp, spicy tofu balls are served on a bed of brown rice and stir-fried vegetables, and topped with a gingery fruit sauce. Plan this meal for a day when you're ready to have fun in the kitchen—and make it for guests who will appreciate your efforts. To speed preparation, you can make the tofu balls and fruit sauce ahead and reheat them, and cut and chill the vegetables so that they're ready for stir-frying. You can vary the fruits for the fruit sauce to suit your taste, or substitute a favorite chutney. Look for five-spice powder in the Asian section of your market.

6 servings

TOFU BALLS

- 2 tablespoons canola oil
- 1 cup diced onion (1 large onion)
- 4 large garlic cloves, peeled and minced
- 1 tablespoon peeled and minced fresh ginger
- 1 pound tofu, drained and pressed
- 2 tablespoons sesame seeds
- 3 tablespoons tahini
- 2 tablespoons tamari or soy sauce
- 2 tablespoons unbleached white flour
- 1 tablespoon five-spice powder
- 1 cup chopped sunflower or mung bean sprouts
- ½ cup chopped celery (1 stalk)
- ½ cup chopped water chestnuts
- ½ teaspoon salt

FRUIT SAUCE

- 1 cup chopped apples
- 1 cup chopped pears
- ¼ cup raisins
- ¾ cup dried apricots
- 2 tablespoons cider vinegar
- 2 tablespoons honey
- 1 tablespoon tamari or soy sauce
- 1 teaspoon five-spice powder
- 1 tablespoon peeled and chopped fresh ginger
- 2 large garlic cloves, peeled and minced

TO COMPLETE THE DISH
- 2½ cups brown rice
- ¾ cup canola oil plus 2 tablespoons for sautéing
- 2 cups broccoli florets and sliced stems
- 2 large carrots, peeled and cut into matchstick shapes (2 cups)
- 4 cups sliced bok choy (8 stalks)
- 1 medium red bell pepper, seeded and cut into thin strips (¾ cup)
- 2 cups fresh snow peas
- Tamari or soy sauce for serving (optional)

Make the tofu balls

Heat the 2 tablespoons canola oil in a skillet over medium heat. Sauté the onion, garlic, and ginger until soft, about 5 minutes. (Add a tablespoon or two of water if the ginger begins to stick.) Remove the pan from the heat.

Mash the tofu in a medium-size mixing bowl. Add the sautéed vegetables, sesame seeds, tahini, tamari, flour, and five-spice powder, and mix well. Stir in the sprouts, celery, water chestnuts, and salt.

Form the mixture into walnut-size balls (about 1 inch across). If the mixture doesn't hold together well, add a little more flour. Cover and refrigerate.

Make the sauce

Combine the apples, pears, raisins, apricots, vinegar, honey, tamari, five-spice powder, ginger, and garlic with 1 cup water in a saucepan. Bring to a boil, reduce the heat, and simmer, covered, for about 1 hour, stirring occasionally.

Complete the dish

Meanwhile, bring the rice and 5 cups of water to a boil in a saucepan. Reduce the heat and simmer, covered, until the water is absorbed and the rice is tender, 35 to 40 minutes.

About 20 minutes before the rice is done, preheat the oven to 300 degrees. Then heat the ¾ cup canola oil in a small, deep saucepan over medium-high heat. (To test the temperature, drop a bit of tofu mix into the oil; it should sizzle and rise to the top immediately.)

Fry the tofu balls, five or six at a time, until crisp and golden on one side, about 3 minutes. Turn and fry them until crisp and golden on the other side, 1 to 2 minutes more. (If the balls don't hold together, the oil needs to be hotter.) Drain on paper towels, and transfer to a baking dish. When all the tofu balls have been fried, place them in the oven to keep warm.

Just before the rice is done, heat the remaining 2 tablespoons oil in a large skillet or wok over medium-high heat. Stir-fry the broccoli and carrots for 2 to 3 minutes. Add the bok choy, red pepper, and snow peas, and stir-fry until barely tender, about 3 minutes more.

Spread the rice on a large serving platter, and mound the stir-fried vegetables in the center. Arrange the tofu balls in a ring around the vegetables, and top with half the fruit sauce.

Serve immediately, with the remaining fruit sauce on the side, along with tamari if you like.

Savory Sweet Potato Strudel

My sister-in-law Betsy first made this tempting dish for a family Christmas gathering. The sweet potatoes form a smooth, creamy background for the peppers, onions, tomato, garlic, and jalapeño pepper Jack cheese. Use Monterey Jack if you prefer a milder flavor.

8 servings

3 cups chopped, peeled sweet potatoes (2 medium potatoes)
2 tablespoons canola oil
1 cup chopped onion (1 large onion)
5 large garlic cloves, peeled and minced
1 teaspoon dried basil
2 cups sliced mushrooms (½ pound)
1 cup chopped yellow or red bell pepper (1 large pepper)
1 medium tomato, chopped (¾ cup)
1 teaspoon salt
1 tablespoon fresh lemon juice
One 1-pound package frozen puff pastry dough, thawed
1½ cups grated jalapeño pepper Jack cheese

Bring 2 cups of water to a boil in a saucepan. Add the sweet potatoes and cook until tender, about 10 minutes. Drain, and mash in a large mixing bowl.

Heat the oil in a skillet over medium heat. Sauté the onion, garlic, and basil for about 2 minutes. Stir in the mushrooms and pepper, and cook 6 to 8 minutes more, until the mushroom liquid has evaporated.

Stir the sautéed vegetables into the sweet potatoes, along with the tomato, salt, and lemon juice.

Preheat the oven to 375 degrees.

Spread a sheet of pastry dough on a floured work surface, and roll it out into a rectangle about 15 inches long and 8 inches wide.

Spread half the filling in a fat line down the middle of the dough, leaving a 2-inch border on the sides. Sprinkle on half the grated cheese. Fold the edges of the dough up over the filling, overlapping the long sides to seal. Place on an ungreased baking sheet.

Repeat with the second sheet of dough and the remaining filling and cheese.

Bake the strudel until golden brown, about 30 minutes. Let it set for 5 to 10 minutes before slicing.

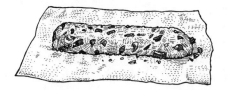

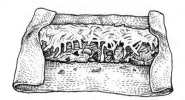

Easy Cheesy Scalloped Potatoes

★ **BEGINNER-FRIENDLY**

*S*calloped potatoes were a staple in our family when I was growing up. I've added garlic, dill, and parsley for flavor and cheese and sour cream for protein to make them into a savory main dish.

4 to 6 servings

8 cups sliced unpeeled potatoes (about 2⅓ pounds)
2 tablespoons canola oil
2 cups chopped onions (2 large onions)
5 large garlic cloves, peeled and minced
1 teaspoon dried basil
½ cup chopped green bell pepper (1 small pepper)
2 cups grated Cheddar cheese (8 ounces)
1 cup grated mozzarella cheese (4 ounces)
1½ teaspoons salt
Pepper
¼ cup minced fresh dill
¼ cup minced fresh parsley
2 tablespoons butter or margarine, melted
1 cup sour cream or yogurt
¾ cup milk
1 or 2 medium tomatoes, sliced
Paprika

Preheat the oven to 375 degrees. Grease a 2- or 3-quart baking dish.

Bring a large pot of water to a boil, and cook the potatoes just until tender, 8 to 10 minutes. Drain and transfer to a large mixing bowl.

Heat the oil in a skillet over medium heat. Sauté the onions, garlic, basil, and green pepper until tender, about 5 minutes.

Add the sautéed vegetables to the potatoes, along with 1½ cups of the Cheddar, the mozzarella, salt, pepper to taste, dill, parsley, butter, sour cream, and milk. Stir gently until well combined.

Spoon the potato mixture into the baking dish. Arrange the tomato slices on top, and sprinkle with the remaining Cheddar and the paprika.

Bake for 30 minutes, until bubbly and lightly browned, and serve.

Red and Black Basmati Rice

A *green salad and baked winter squash or sweet potatoes go well with this simple, hearty dish. Basmati is a long-grained Indian rice. Brown basmati has a slightly nutty flavor and chewy texture.*

4 to 6 servings

1½ cups dried black beans, sorted and rinsed (3 to 3½ cups cooked)
2 cups brown basmati rice
2 tablespoons canola oil
1½ cups chopped onions (3 medium onions)
5 large garlic cloves, peeled and minced
1 small jalapeño pepper, minced
1 cup chopped red bell pepper (1 large pepper)
2 teaspoons dried oregano
2 cups chopped tomatoes (2 large tomatoes)
½ cup coarsely chopped fresh basil (lightly packed)
1 teaspoon salt
½ teaspoon ground coriander
½ cup dry red wine
Sour cream, grated Cheddar cheese, and chopped sweet onion for garnish (optional)

Soak the beans in 5 cups of water for 6 hours or overnight.

Drain the beans, and bring them to a boil in a large pot with 5 cups of fresh water. Reduce the heat and simmer, partially covered, until tender, about 1½ hours. Remove the pot from the heat.

When the beans are nearly tender, bring the rice to a boil in a saucepan with 4 cups of water. Reduce the heat and simmer, covered, until the rice is tender and the water has evaporated, 30 to 35 minutes. Remove the pan from the heat.

About 10 minutes before the rice is done, heat the oil in a skillet over medium heat. Sauté the onions, garlic, jalapeño, red pepper, and oregano just until tender, about 5 minutes. Remove the pan from the heat, and stir in the tomatoes, basil, salt, coriander, and wine.

Stir the sautéed vegetables into the beans, and heat just to a simmer.

Transfer the rice to a serving dish, and top with the beans and vegetables. Garnish with sour cream, Cheddar cheese, and chopped onion if you like, and serve.

Samosas

Samosas are turnovers traditionally served in India as a first course. They're so wonderful that I always wanted more, so I decided to make them bigger and serve them as a main course. The dough can be made ahead and refrigerated overnight, but needs to be chilled for at least 2 hours before rolling it out.

About 24 samosas (6 servings)

DOUGH

1 ½ cups whole wheat flour
1 ½ cups unbleached white flour
1 teaspoon salt
½ teaspoon ground turmeric
4 tablespoons butter or margarine

FILLING

3 cups diced unpeeled potatoes (about 1 pound)
2 tablespoons plus 1 ½ cups canola oil
¾ cup finely chopped onion (1 medium-large onion)
¾ cup diced carrot (1 medium-large carrot)
2 teaspoons peeled and minced garlic
2 teaspoons peeled and minced fresh ginger
1 teaspoon mustard seed
½ teaspoon ground turmeric
1 teaspoon curry powder
¼ teaspoon ground coriander
$\frac{1}{16}$ to ⅛ teaspoon cayenne
1 teaspoon salt
1 cup fresh or frozen peas
2 teaspoons fresh lemon juice
Chutney for serving
Yogurt for serving

Make the dough

Combine the flours, salt, turmeric, and butter in a food processor, and pulse until the mixture resembles cornmeal. Slowly add ¾ to 1 cup of water, pulsing until you have a smooth dough.

Turn the dough out onto a floured surface, and knead it for 5 to 10 minutes, until smooth. Cover and chill for 2 hours. (You can refrigerate it overnight, but should take it out to warm up an hour before using.)

Make the filling

Bring 2 cups of water to a boil in a saucepan. Add the potatoes, and cook just until tender, about 10 minutes. Drain.

Heat the 2 tablespoons canola oil in a large skillet over medium heat. Sauté the onion, carrot, garlic, ginger, and mustard seed until the vegetables are tender, about 5 minutes. (Add a tablespoon or two of water if the ginger begins to stick.)

Remove the pan from the heat, and stir in the potatoes, turmeric, curry powder, coriander, cayenne, salt, peas, and lemon juice.

Complete the dish

Turn out the dough on a floured surface, and roll it to a thickness of 1/16 to 1/8 inch. Using a bowl or jar lid that's about 5 inches across, cut the dough into circles. Continue rolling and cutting until all the dough is used up. You'll have about twenty-four circles.

Spread about 2 tablespoons of filling in the center of a dough circle. Starting at the bottom of the circle, pinch the edges together about two-thirds of the way up to form an ice cream cone shape. Fold down the top of the circle, and pinch its edges to the top edges of the "cone" to form a well-sealed, triangle-shaped packet.

Repeat until you've used all the dough and filling.

Preheat the oven to 300 degrees.

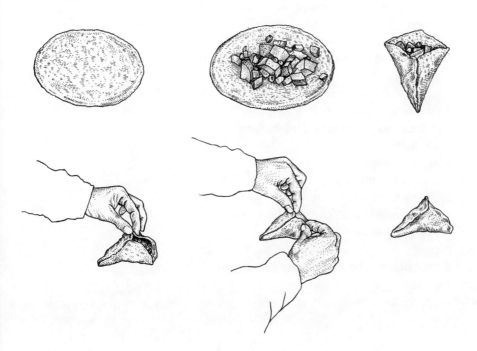

Heat the remaining 1½ cups oil in a small, deep saucepan over medium-high heat. (To test the temperature, drop a bit of dough into the oil; it should sizzle and bubble to the top immediately.)

Fry the samosas one at a time until golden, 2 to 3 minutes on each side. Keep cooked samosas warm in the oven until all are ready to be served. Serve with chutney and yogurt on the side.

Blue Potatoes

This sure-to-please dish combines potatoes, mushrooms, broccoli, garlic, and red bell pepper in a rich cheese sauce.

6 to 8 servings

2⅓ pounds potatoes, halved or quartered if large (8 cups)
½ teaspoon salt
2 tablespoons canola oil
5 large garlic cloves, peeled and minced
1½ cups chopped onions (3 medium onions)
2½ cups chopped broccoli
1 teaspoon dried thyme
1 medium red bell pepper, seeded and cut into thin, 1-inch-long strips (¾ cup)
3 cups sliced mushrooms (¾ pound)
4 tablespoons butter or margarine
4 tablespoons unbleached white flour
1 cup milk
¼ cup dry white wine
1 cup buttermilk
2 tablespoons Dijon mustard
1 cup crumbled blue cheese (4 ounces)
¼ cup minced fresh parsley
Pepper
2 cups grated Cheddar cheese (8 ounces)
Paprika

Bring 6 cups of water to a boil in a saucepan. Add the potatoes, and cook until tender, 15 to 20 minutes. Drain. When cool enough to handle, cut into slices, add the salt, and stir gently.

Heat the oil in a skillet over medium heat. Sauté the garlic, onions, broccoli, and thyme for 2 to 3 minutes. Stir in the red pepper and mushrooms, and cook until tender, 3 to 4 minutes more. Remove the pan from the heat.

Melt the butter in a saucepan over low heat. Whisk in the flour, and let it cook for a minute or two. Slowly add the milk, whisking until thickened, about 3 to 4 minutes. Add the wine, buttermilk, mustard, and blue cheese, stirring until the cheese is melted. Remove the pan from the heat, and stir in the parsley and pepper to taste.

Preheat the oven to 375 degrees. Grease a 9 by 12-inch baking dish.

Place half the potatoes in a single layer in the prepared baking dish. Top with the sautéed vegetables. Spread on half the cheese sauce, and 1 cup of the Cheddar cheese. Add the remaining potatoes in a single layer, the remaining sauce, and the remaining 1 cup Cheddar cheese. Sprinkle generously with paprika.

Bake for 40 to 45 minutes, until bubbly and lightly browned.

Cabbage, Leek, and Dill Crescents

My Czechoslovakian-born grandparents would have loved this dish. Cabbage and onions were cheap and plentiful in the old country, and were used in soups, stews, dumpling fillings, and all sorts of other dishes. Though other vegetables became available and affordable, my grandparents held fast to their old favorites. Note that the dough needs to be made at least 2 hours ahead.

4 or 6 servings

DOUGH

½ cup warm water
¼ cup canola oil
¼ cup cider vinegar
1 egg, beaten
1 teaspoon salt
1½ cups whole wheat pastry flour
1½ cups unbleached white flour

FILLING

2 tablespoons canola oil
4 large garlic cloves, peeled and minced
½ cup chopped onion (1 medium onion)
1½ cups sliced cabbage
1 medium leek, thinly sliced (1 cup)
½ teaspoon dried thyme
1 cup leftover mashed potatoes
2 tablespoons minced fresh dill plus extra for garnish
¼ teaspoon salt
1 cup grated extra-sharp Cheddar cheese (4 ounces)
Paprika
Sour cream or yogurt for garnish

Make the dough

Stir together the water, oil, vinegar, egg, and salt in a medium-size bowl, and let it sit for 10 minutes. Stir in as much of the flours as you can, and knead in the rest. Knead the dough on a floured surface until smooth, 6 to 8 minutes. Cover it with plastic wrap, and refrigerate for at least 2 hours.

Make the filling

Heat the oil in a large skillet over medium heat. Sauté the garlic, onion, cabbage, leek, and thyme until the vegetables are tender, 5 to 7 minutes.

Remove the pan from the heat, and stir in the potatoes, dill, salt, and Cheddar cheese.

Finish the dish

Preheat the oven to 350 degrees. Grease two baking sheets.

Divide the dough into sixteen balls. On a floured surface, roll each ball into a 4-inch circle.

Divide the filling among the dough circles, putting 2 to 3 tablespoonfuls in the center of each one. Pinch the edges of the circles together, and curve them slightly into a crescent shape.

Place the crescents on the prepared baking sheets, and sprinkle them generously with paprika.

Bake for about 30 minutes, until golden on the edges. Serve hot, garnished with sour cream and minced dill.

Mushroom Pot Pie with
Cheddar Cheese Sauce

When I was a child, chicken pot pie was a treat my brothers and I got to eat when our parents went out to dinner. Having our own pies seemed very grown up, and the fact that they came from the grocery store freezer made them all the more special. This vegetarian version of that sentimental favorite is chock-full of mushrooms and vegetables in a Cheddar cheese sauce, baked in a light, flaky crust. You'll need four ovenproof bowls that hold about 2 cups each for main-dish pies, or eight 1-cup containers (custard cups work well) for side dishes.

4 hearty main-course or 8 side-dish servings

FILLING

2 tablespoons canola oil
1 cup chopped onion (1 large onion)
4 large garlic cloves, peeled and minced
2 cups chopped broccoli
2 teaspoons dried thyme
2 teaspoons dried marjoram
1 tablespoon butter or margarine
1 pound mushrooms, halved, or quartered if large (4 cups)
1 cup diced carrots (2 medium carrots)
2 cups diced potatoes (2 medium potatoes)
½ teaspoon salt
1 teaspoon dried ground rosemary
½ cup fresh or frozen peas

SAUCE

3 tablespoons butter or margarine
⅓ cup unbleached white flour
1½ cups milk
1½ cups grated Cheddar cheese
2 tablespoons tamari

DOUGH

1½ cups unbleached white flour
½ cup whole wheat pastry flour
2 teaspoons baking powder
1 teaspoon baking soda
½ teaspoon salt

½ cup (1 stick) butter or margarine
⅓ cup cold milk
⅓ cup sour cream

Make the filling

Heat the oil in a skillet over medium heat. Sauté the onion, garlic, broccoli, thyme, and marjoram until the vegetables are tender, about 5 minutes. Transfer them to a mixing bowl.

Melt the 1 tablespoon butter in the skillet over medium heat, and sauté the mushrooms until tender, 3 to 4 minutes. Stir the mushrooms and their juice into the onion mixture.

Bring 3 cups of water to a boil in a saucepan. Add the carrots and potatoes, and cook just until tender, 8 to 10 minutes. Drain, and stir into the onion-mushroom mixture, along with the salt, rosemary, and peas.

Make the sauce

Melt the 3 tablespoons butter in a saucepan over low heat. Whisk in the flour, and let it cook for a minute or two. Slowly pour in the milk, whisking until thickened, about 4 to 5 minutes. Add the cheese and tamari, stirring until the cheese is melted.

Pour the sauce over the onion-mushroom mixture, and stir well.

Make the dough

Combine the flours, baking powder, baking soda, salt, and butter in a food processor. Pulse until the mixture resembles coarse cornmeal. Add the milk and sour cream, pulsing just until well combined. (Or mix the dough by hand, working the butter into the dry ingredients with a pastry blender, and stirring in the milk and sour cream.)

Finish the dish

Preheat the oven to 400 degrees.

On a floured surface, roll out the dough ½ to ¾ inch thick. Cut the dough into circles with the top of one of the bowls you'll bake the pies in. (Cut four circles for main-dish pies, eight for side dishes.)

Divide the filling among the baking containers, and top each with a dough circle. Cut any remaining dough with a biscuit cutter and bake alongside the pies.

Bake for 15 to 20 minutes, until lightly browned. Serve immediately.

Stir-Fried Vegetables with Seitan

Seitan, a wheat gluten, looks so much like meat that vegetarians like me have been known to eye it suspiciously when encountering it at a friend's dinner table or at a potluck meal! Serve it over curly noodles, shells, linguine—any pasta you like.

4 generous servings

4 tablespoons arrowroot
3 tablespoons tamari
2 tablespoons fresh lemon juice
2 tablespoons cider or white wine vinegar
2 tablespoons honey
⅛ to ¼ teaspoon cayenne
12 ounces dry pasta
2 tablespoons peanut oil
2 cups chopped fresh broccoli
2 tablespoons peeled and minced fresh ginger
6 large garlic cloves, peeled and minced
1 medium red bell pepper, seeded and thinly sliced (¾ cup)
2 cups diagonally sliced bok choy (4 stalks)
1 cup diagonally sliced snow peas
One 10-ounce can curried seitan, rinsed, drained, and diced
1 cup mung bean sprouts

Put a large pot of water on to boil.

To prepare the sauce, mix the arrowroot in ½ cup of water, and heat it in a small saucepan over low heat. When it begins to thicken, remove the pan from the heat and whisk in the tamari, lemon juice, vinegar, honey, and cayenne. Cover the pan to keep the sauce warm.

Cook the pasta until *al dente*.

Meanwhile, heat the oil in a skillet over medium heat. Sauté the broccoli, ginger, and garlic for 2 to 3 minutes. (If the ginger sticks, add a tablespoon or two of water.) Stir in the red pepper, bok choy, snow peas, and seitan, and cook until the vegetables are just tender, 3 to 4 minutes more. Remove the pan from the heat, and stir in the sprouts.

Drain the pasta, and transfer it to a large serving bowl. Add the vegetables and sauce, toss well, and serve.

Eggplant Marinara

Tender eggplant slices surround a mushroom-ricotta filling and are topped with marinara sauce and mozzarella cheese. Serve with crusty bread and a green salad for a heavenly meal. Instead of frying the eggplant slices, you can bake them on an oiled baking sheet at 400 degrees for about 10 minutes.

4 to 6 servings

1 ½ pounds eggplant, peeled and thinly sliced
Salt for eggplant plus ½ teaspoon
2 tablespoons canola oil plus extra for sautéing the eggplant
5 large garlic cloves, peeled and minced
2 cups sliced mushrooms (½ pound)
1 teaspoon dried oregano
1 pound ricotta cheese
1 egg, beaten
¼ cup minced fresh basil
½ cup finely grated Parmesan cheese (2 ounces)
2 cups grated mozzarella cheese (8 ounces)
2 cups marinara sauce (jarred or homemade)

Sprinkle the eggplant slices with salt, stack them in piles, and set aside for 30 minutes to leach out any bitterness. Wipe dry with paper towels.

Meanwhile, heat 2 tablespoons of the canola oil in a skillet over medium heat. Sauté the garlic, mushrooms, and oregano until the mushrooms are tender and their liquid has evaporated, 6 to 8 minutes.

Transfer the vegetables to a medium-size bowl, and stir in the ricotta, egg, basil, Parmesan, 1 cup of the mozzarella, and ½ teaspoon salt.

Wipe out the skillet, and heat 2 tablespoons oil over medium heat. Sauté the eggplant in batches until tender when pierced with a fork, 2 to 3 minutes per side. Add more oil to the pan as needed.

Preheat the oven to 400 degrees.

Spread about ½ cup of the marinara sauce in the bottom of a 9 by 13-inch baking pan.

Put a generous spoonful of the ricotta filling on each eggplant slice, and fold it over to form a little sandwich. Put the stuffed slices in the baking dish in a single layer, and top with the remaining sauce. Sprinkle on the remaining mozzarella cheese.

Bake for 30 minutes, until bubbly and golden.

Tomato, Eggplant, and Garlic Pie

*T*he cornmeal crust and custardy filling will melt in your mouth.

6 servings

CRUST
⅔ cup warm water
1 tablespoon active dry yeast
½ teaspoon honey
2 tablespoons olive oil
½ teaspoon salt
¾ cup unbleached white flour
½ cup whole wheat flour
¾ cup yellow cornmeal

TO FINISH THE DISH
½ pound eggplant, peeled and thinly sliced
Salt for eggplant plus ½ teaspoon
2 to 3 tablespoons olive oil for brushing
3 large eggs
½ cup heavy cream
¼ cup sour cream
1½ cups grated extra-sharp Cheddar cheese
3 scallions, sliced
¼ cup finely chopped fresh basil
Pepper
5 large garlic cloves, peeled and minced
2 or 3 large tomatoes, thinly sliced
1 teaspoon dried oregano
¼ cup fresh bread crumbs
¼ cup finely grated Parmesan cheese

Make the dough

Stir together the water, yeast, honey, and olive oil in a medium-size bowl. Let it sit until foamy, 5 to 10 minutes. Stir in the salt, flours, and cornmeal, mixing well.

Turn the dough out onto a floured surface and knead it until smooth and elastic, about 5 minutes. Cover with plastic wrap and set in a warm place to rise until doubled in size, about 1 hour.

Finish the dish

Meanwhile, sprinkle the eggplant slices with salt, and set them aside in stacks for 30 minutes to leach out any bitterness. Wipe them with dry paper towels.

Preheat the oven to 400 degrees, and grease a 10 by 15-inch baking sheet.

Punch down the dough, and roll it into a rectangle on a floured surface. Press it into the prepared baking sheet, crimping the edges to form a crust. Bake for about 10 minutes, until pale golden.

Set the crust aside to cool. Preheat the broiler.

Brush a baking sheet with olive oil, and spread on the eggplant slices. Brush them with olive oil, and broil, about 3 inches from the heat, for 4 to 5 minutes. Turn, brush again with olive oil, and broil until tender, 4 to 5 minutes more.

Beat the eggs with the cream and sour cream until smooth. Stir in the Cheddar cheese, scallions, basil, ¼ teaspoon salt, and pepper to taste.

Pour the egg mixture over the crust, spreading it evenly. Lay on the eggplant slices, and sprinkle on the garlic. Lay on the tomato slices, and sprinkle on salt and pepper to taste, the oregano, bread crumbs, and Parmesan cheese.

Bake for 15 to 20 minutes at 400 degrees, until the custard is set. Let it cool for a few minutes before cutting. Serve hot or at room temperature.

Red Bell Pepper, Olive, and Sun-Dried Tomato Quiche

★ BEGINNER-FRIENDLY

This flavorful pie won rave reviews at our neighborhood Halloween party.

6 to 8 servings

1 cup boiling water
½ cup sun-dried tomatoes (not in oil)
3 large eggs
¾ cup sour cream
2 cups grated fontina cheese (8 ounces)
1 cup grated provolone cheese (4 ounces)
¼ cup sliced pitted black olives
1 large red bell pepper, seeded and cut into 1-inch-long pieces (1 cup)
2 tablespoons chopped fresh basil
Salt and pepper
1 unbaked 10-inch pie shell (see page 256)

Pour the boiling water over the tomatoes, and let them soak for 10 to 15 minutes. Drain well, and chop coarsely.

Preheat the oven to 375 degrees.

Beat the eggs with the sour cream in a mixing bowl. Stir in the cheeses, sun-dried tomatoes, olives, red pepper, basil, and a dash of salt and pepper.

Pour the filling into the pie shell, and smooth the top.

Bake for 35 to 40 minutes, until puffy and golden. Let the pie set for 5 to 10 minutes before slicing.

Have Some Pie

Pie is a wonderfully old-fashioned dessert that makes a perfect ending to almost any meal. The filling can be as simple as a seasonal fruit or as fancy as a combination of fruits, nuts, and custard or even winter squash.

The first thing you may need to get before baking the pies in this chapter is a 10-inch pie pan. You'll get more scrumptious pie for your efforts.

For a nice, flaky piecrust, start with chilled butter or margarine. When I began making pies, I always took the butter out of the refrigerator ahead of time to soften up; I figured it would make it easier to blend it into the flour. In fact, it made for sticky, unmanageable dough that cracked and fell apart when I tried to roll it out. I only learned better when someone at the café mistakenly put my room-temperature butter back into the fridge. I grumbled as I started cutting in the cold butter, but I quickly saw how much better it blended, and how much more easily the dough rolled out. It was easy as pie!

Ready-made pie dough and crusts are widely available, but most contain additives and come only in a 9-inch size. If you haven't made your own before, it really is worth it to struggle through rolling out your first crust or two. They will get simpler to make with time and practice, and soon will be no trouble at all.

Most pies need to set for an hour or two after baking to firm up; they'll still be loose enough to meld nicely with a scoop of ice cream. Unless the pie is supposed to be chilled, don't serve it straight out the refrigerator; it will look stiff and unappealing. It's easy to warm slices for a few minutes in the microwave or oven.

When choosing a pie, consider the meal it will follow. A fruit pie goes well after almost anything except perhaps another pie, such as quiche. Something rich like Chocolate Hazelnut Pie (page 268) or Sweet Georgia Cream Pie (page 264) is best after a relatively light meal that will leave your guests with lots of room!

Piecrust

You can mix pie dough by hand as described or with the pulsing action of your food processor, both to cut in the butter and incorporate the water. Be sure not to overmix it; light handling is the key to a flaky crust. For a single-crust pie, cut this recipe in half, or save half of the dry mix before the water has been added for another time. Wrap and refrigerate for up to a week, or freeze it for a month or more.

Dough for one 2-crust, 10-inch pie or two 1-crust, 10-inch pies

1 cup unbleached white flour
1 cup whole wheat pastry flour
Dash of salt
⅔ cup butter, chilled
5 to 6 tablespoons ice water

Stir the flours and salt together in a medium-size bowl. Cut in the butter using a pastry blender or two knives. A food processor will do this job beautifully. Continue working the dough (use your fingers if you like) just until the butter is broken into small pieces—about the size of a pea.

Mix in the water, a tablespoon at a time, until the dough holds together but is not sticky.

Divide the dough into two balls, wrap them in plastic wrap, and refrigerate for at least 30 minutes. (If you're pressed for time, put them in the freezer for 10 minutes.)

On a floured surface, roll one dough ball into a circle that's about 2 inches bigger around than your pie plate—enough for the sides of the pan plus a 1-inch overhang. (Hold the plate over the dough to check the size.) Gently fit the dough into the pie pan.

For a single-crust pie, fold the extra dough under, even with the lip of the pan. Use the thumb and index finger of one hand and the index finger of the other to push the dough in while you pinch the edges into a fluted pattern all around the pan.

For a double-crust pie, let the edge of the bottom crust hang over the edge of the pan. Spoon in the filling. Roll the second dough ball into a circle that's about 1 inch bigger around than your pie plate. Center it on top of the filling. Trim the edges of the top and bottom crusts if they're uneven. Press them together, fold them under, and flute. Use a sharp knife to cut a few slits in the top crust so the steam can escape.

Blueberry Cheese Pie

T his two-layered fruit and cream cheese pie goes together quickly. You can sub-stitute raspberries, cherries, or sliced peaches with equally delightful results.

8 to 10 servings

Dough for a 1-crust, 10-inch pie (page 256)
5 cups fresh or frozen blueberries (thawed if frozen)
¾ cup honey
2 tablespoons unbleached white flour
3 tablespoons arrowroot
8 ounces cream cheese or Neufchâtel (light) cheese
1 teaspoon vanilla extract
2 large eggs
½ cup heavy cream

Preheat the oven to 425 degrees.

Roll out and prepare the dough as directed in the Piecrust recipe.

Combine the blueberries with ½ cup of the honey, the flour, and arrowroot in a mixing bowl. Stir gently but well. Spoon the filling into the pie shell and bake for 20 minutes. Remove the pie from the oven, and lower the temperature to 350 degrees.

Meanwhile, in a clean bowl, beat the cream cheese with the remaining ¼ cup honey and the vanilla until smooth. Add the eggs and cream, and beat well.

Pour the cream cheese mixture over the blueberries, and bake for about 30 minutes more, until almost set.

Let the pie cool for at least 1 hour before serving.

Cherry Pie

★ BEGINNER-FRIENDLY

Cherries are in season for such a short time that I try to make the most of them while I can. Serve this pie with a touch of vanilla ice cream or frozen yogurt.

8 to 10 servings

4 tablespoons arrowroot
3 tablespoons cold water
¾ cup honey
7 cups halved, pitted cherries
2 tablespoons unbleached white flour
1 tablespoon fresh lemon juice
Dough for a 2-crust, 10-inch pie (page 256)

Stir the arrowroot into the water in a small dish.

Heat the honey in a 2-quart saucepan over medium-high heat. When it comes to a boil, pour in the arrowroot mixture, and whisk until thick, 2 to 3 minutes.

Remove the pan from the heat, and stir in the cherries, flour, and lemon juice.

Preheat the oven to 425 degrees.

Roll out and prepare the dough for the bottom crust as directed in the Piecrust recipe. Pour in the cherry filling.

Roll out and finish the top crust as directed, cutting slits to vent the steam.

Bake for 10 minutes. Lower the oven temperature to 375 degrees, and bake for about 25 minutes more, until the crust is lightly browned on the edges.

Let the pie cool and set for at least 1 hour before cutting.

Plum Pie

★ BEGINNER-FRIENDLY

*T*he plums turn a beautiful cherry red when baked.

8 to 10 servings

3 tablespoons arrowroot
3 tablespoons cold water
7 cups sliced, pitted Italian prune plums
⅔ cup honey
3 tablespoons unbleached white flour
¼ teaspoon ground nutmeg
2 tablespoons fresh lemon juice
Dough for a 2-crust, 10-inch pie (page 256)

Dissolve the arrowroot in the water.

Stir together the plums, honey, flour, nutmeg, and lemon juice in a large saucepan. Bring it to a boil, stir in the arrowroot mixture, and reduce the heat to a simmer. Stir constantly until thickened, 3 to 5 minutes. Remove the pan from the heat.

Preheat the oven to 375 degrees.

Roll out and prepare the dough for the bottom crust as directed in the Piecrust recipe. Pour in the filling. Roll out and finish the top crust as directed, cutting slits to vent the steam.

Bake for about 45 minutes, until the edges are golden brown. Let the pie cool and set for at least 1 hour before serving.

Peach-Rhubarb Pie

*R*hubarb *is almost a weed in Vermont. Just about every old house has a patch of it in the backyard. Once rhubarb takes hold of the earth, it never lets go. It produces prolifically in the spring before almost anything else edible is growing, and it adds a delicious, tart flavor to pies and sweet breads. This pie, made with a flaky phyllo crust, is especially good with a scoop of vanilla ice cream.*

8 to 10 servings

4 cups sliced rhubarb (1-inch pieces)
2 cups fresh or frozen sliced, unpeeled peaches (thawed if frozen)
2 tablespoons unbleached white flour
1 cup honey
6 tablespoons arrowroot
½ teaspoon ground cinnamon
½ of a 1-pound package phyllo dough (12 or 13 sheets, thawed; see Note)
¼ cup (½ stick) butter or margarine, melted

Toss the rhubarb and peaches with the flour in a medium-size bowl.

Heat the honey, arrowroot, and cinnamon in a saucepan over low heat, whisking until it begins to thicken, 4 to 5 minutes. Pour the syrup over the fruit and mix gently.

Preheat the oven to 325 degrees.

Spread a piece of phyllo dough on a work surface. Brush it lightly with melted butter, and place it in a 10-inch pie plate. Repeat with four more sheets of dough, letting the edges hang over the pan. Gently press the dough layers into the pie pan, and roll up the edges to form a crust. Pour in the filling.

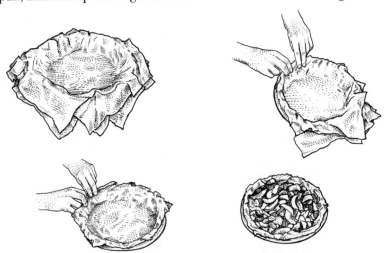

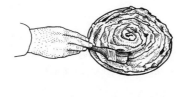

Brush another sheet of dough with butter. Fold it over and over lengthwise to form a ½-inch- to ¾-inch-thick rope. Place the dough rope on top of the filling in a circle around the edge. Repeat, buttering and rolling enough phyllo dough to form a continuous coil that covers the top of the pie. (You will need seven or eight sheets of dough.) Brush the top with any remaining butter.

Bake for 45 minutes, until the crust is lightly golden.

Let the pie cool and set for 2 hours before serving. (You can warm it for 5 to 10 minutes in a 325-degree oven.)

Note

You need a 1-pound package because the dough sheets in smaller packages aren't big enough for this recipe.

Ginger Pear Pie

★ **BEGINNER-FRIENDLY**

Ginger and citrus give this pear pie a bold flavor. If you prefer a milder taste, cut back on the ginger by half.

8 to 10 servings

½ **cup honey**
1 **tablespoon grated orange rind**
1 **tablespoon fresh lemon juice**
1 **tablespoon peeled and minced fresh ginger**
¾ **teaspoon ground cinnamon**
½ **teaspoon ground nutmeg**
2 **tablespoons unbleached white flour**
7 **cups sliced, unpeeled fresh pears**
Dough for a 2-crust, 10-inch pie (page 256)

Stir together the honey, orange rind, lemon juice, ginger, cinnamon, nutmeg, and flour in a medium-size bowl. Add the pears, and mix gently but well.

Preheat the oven to 375 degrees.

Roll out and prepare the bottom crust as directed in the Piecrust recipe. Pour in the filling. Roll out and finish the top crust as directed, cutting slits to vent the steam.

Bake for 40 to 45 minutes, until the edges are golden brown. Let the pie cool and set for at least 1 hour before serving.

Peach Custard Pie

★ BEGINNER-FRIENDLY

A *delightful summer pie that's best served chilled.*

8 to 10 servings

Dough for a 1-crust, 10-inch pie (page 256)
2 large eggs
⅔ cup plus 1 tablespoon honey
1 cup heavy cream
½ cup sour cream
2 tablespoons unbleached white flour
1 teaspoon vanilla extract plus a dash for the whipped cream
½ teaspoon ground cinnamon
6 cups sliced, unpeeled fresh peaches

Roll out the dough and prepare the crust as directed in the Piecrust recipe. Preheat the oven to 350 degrees.

Beat the eggs with ⅔ cup of the honey, ½ cup of the heavy cream, the sour cream, flour, vanilla, and cinnamon until smooth.

Arrange the peach slices in a circular pattern in the piecrust. Pour the egg mixture over them. (If any peach slices peek out, smooth the custard over them with a rubber spatula.)

Bake for 50 to 55 minutes, until the top is set and the crust is lightly browned.

Let the pie cool to room temperature, and refrigerate it until chilled, about 2 hours total, or overnight is fine.

Just before serving, beat the remaining ½ cup heavy cream, 1 tablespoon honey, and dash of vanilla with an electric mixer until thick. Garnish the pie with the whipped cream and serve.

Sweet Georgia Cream Pie

*T*his *irresistible pairing of peanut butter filling and chocolate crust is my Vermont variation on a Southern favorite. If you aren't a chocolate lover, substitute graham crackers in the crust. The pie is best when it's been allowed to set overnight in the refrigerator.*

8 to 10 servings

CRUST
4 tablespoons (½ stick) butter or margarine
2 tablespoons honey
2 cups chocolate cookie crumbs

FILLING
1 cup smooth peanut butter
8 ounces cream cheese or Neufchâtel
½ cup honey
1 teaspoon vanilla extract
½ cup heavy cream
2 tablespoons maple syrup

½ cup heavy cream
2 tablespoons maple syrup
Bittersweet or semisweet chocolate shavings for garnish

Preheat the oven to 350 degrees.

To prepare the crust, melt the butter in a saucepan over low heat, and stir in the honey. Remove the pan from the heat, and stir in the cookie crumbs.

Press the crumb mixture evenly over the bottom and up the sides of a 10-inch pie pan. (It will slip down a bit during baking, so press it up over the lip of the pan.)

Bake the crust for 10 minutes, and set it aside on a rack to cool.

In a medium-size bowl, beat the peanut butter, cream cheese, honey, and vanilla for several minutes until soft and fluffy.

Clean the beaters, and in a separate bowl beat the ½ cup heavy cream with the 2 tablespoons maple syrup until stiff.

Fold the whipped cream into the peanut butter mixture until well blended. Pour the filling into the cooled crust, and refrigerate for at least 2 hours. Overnight is best.

Just before serving, whip the ½ cup heavy cream with the 2 tablespoons maple syrup until stiff. Spread it over the pie, and garnish with chocolate shavings.

Pumpkin Rum Custard Pie

The rum and molasses give this rich, spicy pie a distinctive New England flavor. It's terrific for Thanksgiving.

10 to 12 servings

Dough for a 1-crust, 10-inch pie (page 256)
2 cups pureed pumpkin or winter squash
1 cup plus 1 tablespoon honey
4 large eggs
4 tablespoons (½ stick) butter or margarine, melted
½ cup sour cream
1 cup heavy cream
¼ cup molasses
2 tablespoons rum
1 teaspoon vanilla extract
2 teaspoons ground cinnamon
1 teaspoon ground allspice
1 teaspoon ground nutmeg
½ teaspoon ground ginger
½ teaspoon salt

Roll out the dough and prepare the crust as directed in the Piecrust recipe. (This makes a very tall pie, so bring the dough to the very top of your pie plate, and build up a high fluted edge.)

Preheat the oven to 400 degrees.

Process the pumpkin, 1 cup of the honey, the eggs, and melted butter in a food processor or with an electric mixer until smooth. Add the sour cream, ½ cup of the heavy cream, the molasses, rum, vanilla, cinnamon, allspice, nutmeg, ginger, and salt, and mix well.

Pour the filling into the piecrust. Bake for 55 to 60 minutes, until the filling is set, and a knife inserted in the center comes out clean.

Let the pie cool for at least 2 hours before cutting.

Just before serving, beat the remaining ½ cup heavy cream and 1 tablespoon honey until stiff. Garnish the pie and serve.

Chocolate Cream Pie

A chocolate lover's dream come true. Allow the pie to set in the refrigerator for at least 2 hours before serving.

10 servings

CRUST
> 4 tablespoons (½ stick) butter or margarine
> 2 tablespoons honey
> 2 cups chocolate cookie crumbs

FILLING
> 2 large eggs
> 1 teaspoon vanilla extract
> ⅔ cup honey
> 3 ounces (3 squares) unsweetened chocolate
> 2 tablespoons arrowroot
> 1¼ cups milk
> ½ cup heavy cream
>
> ½ cup heavy cream
> 1 tablespoon honey
> Dash of vanilla extract
> Bittersweet or semisweet chocolate shavings for garnish

Preheat the oven to 350 degrees.

To prepare the crust, melt the butter in a saucepan over low heat, and stir in the 2 tablespoons honey. Remove the pan from the heat, and stir in the cookie crumbs.

Press the crumb mixture evenly over the bottom and up the sides of a 10-inch pie pan. (It will slip down a bit during baking, so press up over the lip of the pan.)

Bake the crust for 10 minutes, and set it aside on a rack to cool. (Leave the oven on.)

Process the eggs, 1 teaspoon vanilla, and ⅔ cup honey in a food processor or blender until smooth.

Melt the chocolate in a small saucepan over very low heat, and set aside.

Dissolve the arrowroot in ¼ cup of the milk.

Heat the remaining 1 cup milk and the ½ cup heavy cream in a large saucepan over medium heat, stirring. When the milk just begins to bubble, whisk in the melted chocolate. Add the arrowroot mixture, and whisk until smooth and thick, 3 to 5 minutes.

Remove the pan from the heat, and whisk in the egg mixture until well blended.

Pour the filling into the cooled crust, and bake for 40 to 45 minutes, until a knife inserted in the center comes out clean.

Let the pie cool to room temperature, and then chill in the refrigerator, about 2 hours or overnight.

Just before serving, beat the ½ cup heavy cream with the 1 tablespoon honey and dash of vanilla until stiff. Garnish the pie with the whipped cream and chocolate shavings.

Chocolate Hazelnut Pie

A *wonderfully rich and attractive pie that's perfect for a special celebration. It's a bit fussy to make, but well worth the effort.*

6 to 8 servings

CRUST
- ½ cup unbleached white flour
- ½ cup whole wheat pastry flour
- 6 tablespoons butter or margarine, chilled
- 1 tablespoon honey
- ¼ teaspoon salt

FILLING
- 1 cup shelled hazelnuts (also called filberts)
- ⅓ cup honey
- 2 teaspoons vanilla extract
- 3 large eggs, at room temperature
- 2 tablespoons unbleached white flour
- 6 ounces good-quality bittersweet chocolate
- 4 tablespoons (½ stick) butter or margarine

- ½ cup heavy cream
- 1 tablespoon honey
- Dash of vanilla extract
- 1 cup fresh raspberries for garnish

For the crust, combine the flours, butter, honey, and salt in a food processor, and pulse just until blended. (To mix by hand, combine the flours into a medium bowl and cut in the butter with a pastry blender until the mixture resembles cornmeal. Add the honey and salt and mix well.) Form the dough into a ball, cover it with plastic wrap, and refrigerate for 30 minutes.

Preheat the oven to 350 degrees, and grease an 8-inch cake pan.

On a floured surface, roll the chilled dough into a circle that's 2 to 3 inches bigger around than the cake pan. Gently place the crust in the prepared pan. If it cracks, just press it back together. Fold under and flute the edges.

Prick the bottom of the crust all over with the tines of a fork, and bake for 10 minutes. Set it on a rack to cool. (Leave the oven on.)

While the crust is cooling, grind the nuts into a fine powder in a food processor or blender. Add the honey, vanilla, 1 egg, and flour, and process until smooth. Gently spread the nut paste into the shell.

Bake for 20 minutes, and return it to the rack to cool.

While the pie is baking, melt the chocolate and butter in a saucepan over very low heat, and set aside to cool.

In a mixing bowl, whisk the 2 remaining eggs until triple in volume. (The eggs won't expand enough if they're cold; if you forget to take them out of the refrigerator in time, crack them into the top of a double boiler and warm them quickly over hot water.)

Fold the chocolate into the eggs, and pour the mixture over the nut filling.

Place the cake pan inside a baking dish, and put it on the oven rack. Pour hot water into the baking dish about halfway up the side of the cake pan. Bake for about 15 minutes, until set.

Let the pie cool to room temperature, and chill it in the refrigerator, about 2 hours total.

Just before serving, beat the ½ cup cream with the honey and dash of vanilla. Garnish the pie with the whipped cream and raspberries and serve.

Apple-Raspberry Custard Tart

*T*art apples and sweet, fragrant raspberries bake up in a delectable custard. Use ½ cup raisins if raspberries are not available, or substitute 6 cups blueberries for the apples and raspberries to make a blueberry tart.

8 to 10 servings

CRUST
- ¾ cup unbleached white flour
- ½ cup whole wheat pastry flour
- Dash of salt
- 7 tablespoons butter or margarine, chilled
- 2 teaspoons honey
- 3 tablespoons ice water

FILLING
- 5 cups sliced, unpeeled tart apples (5 large apples)
- 2 tablespoons fresh lemon juice
- ½ cup honey
- 3 egg yolks
- 1 cup heavy cream
- 1 teaspoon vanilla extract
- ½ teaspoon ground cinnamon
- 1 cup fresh or frozen raspberries

To prepare the crust, mix the flours and salt in a food processor. Add the butter, and pulse until the mixture resembles coarse cornmeal. Add the honey and water, and process just until blended. (To mix by hand, cut in the butter with a pastry blender, and stir in the liquid.) Form the dough into a ball, cover with plastic wrap, and refrigerate for 30 minutes.

Preheat the oven to 375 degrees.

Roll out the dough on a floured surface, and fit it into a 10-inch tart pan. Fold under and flute the edges, and gently press a piece of aluminum foil over the bottom and up the sides.

Cover the bottom with dried beans, rice, or pie weights and bake for 10 minutes. Remove the beans and foil, and bake for about 5 minutes more, until lightly golden in color.

Set the crust on a rack to cool. Lower the oven temperature to 350 degrees.

For the filling, toss the apples with the lemon juice and honey, and arrange in a spiral pattern in the bottom of the cooled pie shell.

Whisk together the egg yolks, cream, vanilla, and cinnamon. Gently stir in the raspberries. Pour over the apples.

Bake for 40 to 45 minutes, until the tart is set and the apples are soft. Let it cool for at least an hour before serving.

Cranberry Walnut Tart

*T*he cranberries add tang to this deliciously sweet tart, which makes a festive *Thanksgiving or Christmas dessert.*

8 to 10 servings

CRUST
>   ¾ cup unbleached white flour
>   ½ cup whole wheat pastry flour
>   Dash of salt
>   7 tablespoons butter or margarine, chilled
>   2 teaspoons honey
>   3 tablespoons ice water

FILLING
>   3 large eggs
>   1 cup honey
>   4 tablespoons (½ stick) butter or margarine, melted
>   ¼ teaspoon salt
>   1 teaspoon vanilla extract
>   1½ cups coarsely chopped cranberries
>   1 cup coarsely chopped walnuts

To make the crust, mix the flours and salt in a food processor. Add the butter, and pulse until the mixture resembles coarse cornmeal. Add the honey and water, and process just until blended. (To mix by hand, cut in the butter with a pastry blender, and stir in the liquid.) Form the dough into a ball, cover with plastic wrap, and refrigerate for 30 minutes.

Preheat the oven to 375 degrees.

Roll out the dough on a floured surface and fit into a 10-inch tart pan. Flute the edges and gently press a piece of aluminum foil over the bottom and up the sides.

Cover the bottom with dried beans, rice, or pie weights and bake for 10 minutes. Remove the beans and foil, and bake for about 5 minutes more. The crust should be lightly golden in color.

Set the crust on a rack to cool, and lower the oven to 350 degrees.

To prepare the filling, beat the eggs until creamy and lemon-colored. Beat in the honey, melted butter, salt, and vanilla. Stir in the cranberries and walnuts.

Pour the filling into the cooled crust, and bake for 30 to 35 minutes, until set. Let the pie cool for an hour before serving.

Company's Here: Cakes

We usually skip dessert at our house, except for the occasional cookie, unless we have company. In my mind, cake is a special dessert for special occasions, from birthdays and anniversaries to gatherings around the kitchen table with good friends.

You'll find three kinds of cakes in this chapter: "celebration" cakes like Orange Poppy Seed (page 274) and German Chocolate (page 276) that are just the thing for a party; "anytime" cakes like Chocolate Zucchini (page 283) and Applesauce-Raisin Spice Cake with Maple Cream Frosting (page 284) that you'll want to slice warm from the oven and serve casually to family and friends; and cheesecakes like Caribbean Lime Cheesecake (page 287), luscious concoctions that are the perfect ending to an elegant meal. (They're so rich that they're best served in small portions and only once in a great while!)

Cakes require special handling, so follow the directions carefully. Grease and flour your pans well, and don't overmix the batter. Be sure to bake them on the center rack of the oven, and keep a close eye on them so they don't get overdone and dry. Check for doneness when the cake has pulled away slightly from the sides of the pan. First press down the top gently with a fork to see if it springs back. (Don't do this with cheesecakes!) Then stick a toothpick in the center to see if it comes out clean. A few crumbs clinging to the toothpick is fine; if you see gooey batter the cake isn't done yet. A cheesecake is done when it's still slightly jiggly, but tests clean with a knife.

Sometimes a cake baked in a large rectangular or springform pan will brown on the outside before it's done in the middle. (That usually happens because the oven doesn't regulate its heat well.) The solution is to bake the batter in two small square or round pans the next time, and cut back on the baking time.

You can make cupcakes from many of the "celebration" and "anytime" recipes in this chapter. Just reduce the baking time by about one-third. I like to use paper cupcake liners; the cupcakes are easier to remove and transport, and cleanup is so much quicker.

Except for cheesecakes, which are fine after sitting overnight in the fridge, cakes are best served the day they're made. Take your cheesecake out about 30 minutes before serving; just like ice cream, it tastes better when it's not ice cold.

Don't rush dessert onto the table after a big meal. Let your guests relax over a cup of coffee or tea, or even stretch out in the living room for a while. That way they'll have more room—and appreciation—for your special creation.

⭐ CELEBRATION CAKES

Orange Poppy Seed Cake

Triple-orange liqueur gives this cake its wonderful flavor. Buy a small bottle of triple sec, and use it to make Orange French Toast (page 33) and Apricot Cheesecake with Chocolate Crust (page 288), too.

10 to 12 servings

CAKE
1 cup unbleached white flour
1 cup whole wheat pastry flour
½ teaspoon salt
1 teaspoon baking soda
½ teaspoon baking powder
½ cup poppy seeds
¾ cup (1½ sticks) butter or margarine, softened
4 large eggs, separated
1 cup honey
2 tablespoons grated orange peel
¾ cup sour cream
1 teaspoon vanilla extract
¼ teaspoon cream of tartar

FROSTING

> 8 ounces cream cheese or Neufchâtel, softened
> 2 tablespoons butter, softened
> ⅓ cup honey
> 2 tablespoons triple sec liqueur
>
> 1 tablespoon grated orange peel for garnish

Preheat the oven to 350 degrees. Grease and flour a 10-inch springform pan.

For the cake, stir together the flours, salt, baking soda, baking powder, and poppy seeds in a medium-size bowl.

In another bowl, beat the butter and egg yolks with an electric mixer until smooth. Beat in the honey, orange peel, sour cream, and vanilla.

Wash the beaters well, and beat the egg whites until they begin to stiffen. Add the cream of tartar, and continue beating until the egg whites hold a peak.

Mix the dry ingredients into the butter mixture. Fold in the egg whites just until well combined.

Pour the batter into the prepared pan, and bake for 50 to 55 minutes, until a toothpick inserted in the center comes out clean. Set the cake on a cooling rack.

When the cake is cool, prepare the frosting. Beat the cream cheese and butter with the honey and orange liqueur until fluffy.

Remove the cake from the pan, and cut it horizontally into two rounds. Place one round on a serving plate, and frost its top. Place the other round on top, and frost the top and sides of the cake. Garnish with the grated orange peel and serve.

German Chocolate Cake

Amoist, rich cake that's well worth the extra time (it takes about 2 hours to make). Dazzle your guests with it after a simple dinner.

12 servings

CAKE
4 ounces semisweet chocolate
½ cup sour cream
½ cup buttermilk
1 teaspoon vanilla extract
1¼ cups whole wheat pastry flour
1¼ cups unbleached white flour
1 teaspoon baking soda
½ teaspoon salt
1 cup (2 sticks) butter or margarine, softened
1½ cups honey
4 large eggs, separated

FILLING
4 tablespoons (½ stick) butter or margarine
½ cup heavy cream
½ cup honey
2 egg yolks, beaten
2 tablespoons unbleached white flour
1 teaspoon vanilla extract
¾ cup shredded coconut
¾ cup coarsely chopped pecans

GLAZE
4 ounces semisweet chocolate
2 tablespoons butter or margarine
2 tablespoons honey

Coarsely chopped pecans for garnish
Shredded coconut for garnish

Preheat the oven to 350 degrees. Grease and flour two 9- or 10-inch cake pans.

For the cake, melt the chocolate in a small saucepan over very low heat, and set it aside to cool.

Stir the sour cream, buttermilk, and vanilla together in a measuring cup.

Stir the flours, baking soda, and salt together in a medium-size bowl.

In a large bowl, cream the butter with the honey until light and fluffy. Beat in the melted chocolate and then the four egg yolks.

Beat in the flour mixture alternately with the buttermilk mixture and the egg yolk mixture, adding about one third of each at a time.

Wash the beaters well, and beat the egg whites until stiff. Fold into the batter.

Divide the batter between the prepared pans, and bake for 30 to 40 minutes, until a toothpick inserted in the middle comes out clean. Set the cakes on a rack to cool.

Prepare the filling next. Melt the 4 tablespoons butter in a heavy saucepan over very low heat. Stir in the cream and honey. Whisk a little of this hot mixture into the egg yolks and pour back into the pan. Stir in the flour, and simmer, stirring, until thickened, about 10 minutes. (Don't let it boil.) Remove the pan from the heat, and stir in the vanilla, coconut, and pecans.

While the filling is cooling, prepare the glaze. Melt the chocolate and 2 tablespoons butter in the top of a double boiler over boiling water until smooth and melted. Stir in the honey and 2 tablespoons of water, and simmer for a few minutes. Take the top off the double boiler, and set the glaze aside to cool.

To assemble the cake, invert one of the layers onto a serving plate, and spread the coconut filling on top. Place the second layer on the filling, and spread the chocolate glaze on top. (If the glaze has hardened, rewarm it in the double boiler.) Garnish with chopped pecans and shredded coconut and serve.

Hazelnut Torte with Chocolate Glaze

This tall, rich, yet exceptionally light cake should be sliced thin; it can easily serve more than a dozen guests.

12 to 16 servings

CAKE
2 cups ground hazelnuts (filberts)
½ cup fresh whole wheat bread crumbs
½ cup unbleached white flour
2 teaspoons baking powder
¼ teaspoon salt
6 large eggs, separated
1 teaspoon vanilla extract
1 tablespoon fresh lemon juice
1 cup honey

CHOCOLATE GLAZE
2 ounces (2 squares) unsweetened chocolate
2 ounces semisweet chocolate
4 tablespoons (½ stick) butter or margarine
2 tablespoons honey

WHIPPED CREAM
1 cup heavy cream
1 teaspoon vanilla extract
1 teaspoon honey

Preheat the oven to 325 degrees. Grease and flour three 9- or 10-inch cake pans. (Nonstick pans are best for this cake.)

To prepare the cake, stir together the hazelnuts, bread crumbs, flour, baking powder, and salt.

In a large mixing bowl, beat the egg yolks with an electric mixer until thick and creamy. Beat in the vanilla, lemon juice, and honey.

Wash the beaters well, and beat the egg whites until stiff.

Stir the dry ingredients into the egg yolk mixture. Gently fold in the egg whites in three additions.

Divide the batter among the prepared pans, and bake for 20 to 25 minutes, until a toothpick inserted in the center comes out clean.

Run a knife around the edges of the cakes, and immediately invert them onto cooling racks. If the cake sticks, run a spatula gently under its edges. (Any tears will be covered up with whipped cream or chocolate glaze.)

While the cakes are cooling, prepare the glaze. Melt the unsweetened and semisweet chocolate and the butter in a heavy saucepan over very low heat. Stir in the honey, and remove from the heat.

Wash the beaters well, and beat the cream until thick. Beat in the vanilla and honey.

Transfer one of the cooled cake layers to a serving plate, and spread half the whipped cream on top. Place a second on the first, and cover its top with the rest of the whipped cream. Add the third layer, and spread its top with the chocolate glaze, letting it drip over the edges. (Set the pan of glaze in cold water if it's too warm and runny.)

Refrigerate for an hour or more before serving to set the glaze.

Boston Cream Pie

oston cream pie is not in fact a pie, but a luscious chocolate-glazed, custard-filled cake that originated at Boston's famous Parker Hotel.

10 to 12 servings

CAKE
- 1½ cups heavy cream
- 3 large eggs
- 1½ teaspoons vanilla extract
- ¾ cup honey
- 2¼ cups unbleached white flour
- 2 teaspoons baking powder
- ½ teaspoon salt

CUSTARD FILLING
- ¼ cup unbleached white flour
- 2 large eggs
- 1¼ cups milk
- ½ cup honey
- 2 teaspoons vanilla extract

CHOCOLATE GLAZE
- 2 ounces (2 squares) unsweetened chocolate
- 4 tablespoons (½ stick) butter or margarine
- ¼ cup honey

Preheat the oven to 350 degrees. Grease and flour two 9-inch cake pans.

To prepare the cake, beat the cream in a medium-size bowl with an electric mixer until stiff.

In another bowl, beat the eggs until thick and lemon-colored. Beat in the vanilla and honey. Fold into the whipped cream.

Stir together the flour, baking powder, and salt, and fold into the whipped cream mixture just until blended.

Pour the batter into the prepared pans, and bake for about 15 minutes, until a toothpick inserted in the center comes out clean. Let the cakes cool on a rack for 15 minutes before removing them from the pan.

While the cake is cooling, prepare the custard. Process the flour and eggs in a food processor or blender until smooth.

Heat the milk, honey, and vanilla in a heavy saucepan over medium heat, stirring, until it begins to bubble (don't scald it). Add the egg mixture, and whisk until nicely thickened, about 5 minutes.

Set the custard aside to cool, stirring it occasionally to prevent a skin from forming. (Let it cool completely before assembling the cake.)

While the custard is cooling, make the glaze. Melt the chocolate and butter in the top of a double boiler over boiling water, and stir in the honey.

Remove the top from the double boiler, and set the glaze aside to cool slightly while you assemble the cake.

Remove the cooled cakes from the pans, and place one on a serving plate. Spread the cooled custard over it. Gently place the second cake on top of the custard. Pour on the chocolate glaze, and spread it over the top of the cake, allowing it to drip over the edges where it wants to. Cut and serve.

Banana Cream Nut Cake

Caribbean islanders make many versions of banana cake. This one is wonderfully light, and especially delicious topped with whipped cream, bananas, and walnuts. Serve it after a West Indian roti dinner for an authentic island meal.

12 to 14 servings

1½ cups unbleached white flour
1½ cups whole wheat pastry flour
2 teaspoons baking powder
2 teaspoons baking soda
½ teaspoon salt
1 cup (2 sticks) butter or margarine, softened
1¼ cups honey
1 teaspoon vanilla extract
3 large eggs
5 ripe bananas (4 mashed, about 2 cups; 1 whole)
¼ cup milk
1 cup chopped walnuts
1 cup heavy cream
1 tablespoon maple syrup or honey

Preheat the oven to 350 degrees. Grease and flour two 9- or 10-inch cake pans.

To prepare the cake, stir together the flours, baking powder, baking soda, and salt in a medium-size bowl.

In another bowl, cream the butter with the honey until light and fluffy. Beat in the vanilla, eggs, mashed bananas, and milk. Beat in the dry ingredients in three or four additions. Stir in ¾ cup of the chopped walnuts.

Pour the batter in the prepared pans, and bake for 30 to 40 minutes, until a toothpick inserted in the center comes out clean. Set the pans on cooling racks for 10 minutes, and then turn the cakes out on the racks.

When the cakes are cool, whip the cream until stiff, and beat in the maple syrup.

Place one cake layer on a serving plate, and cover the top with half the whipped cream. Add the second layer, and spread the rest of the whipped cream on top.

Slice the remaining banana into fourths lengthwise, and cut crosswise into small chunks. Sprinkle the banana and the remaining walnuts on top of the cake, and serve immediately.

Chocolate Zucchini Cake

★ BEGINNER-FRIENDLY

This large, moist, coffee-style cake is a good way to use up some of the summer's never-ending surplus of zucchini. Kids don't seem to notice the green stuff hidden inside the yummy chocolate.

12 to 16 servings

1½ cups unbleached white flour
1½ cups whole wheat pastry flour
1 tablespoon baking powder
1 teaspoon salt
1 teaspoon ground cinnamon
¾ cup cocoa powder
¾ cup (1½ sticks) butter or margarine, softened
1½ cups honey
4 large eggs
¼ cup milk
2 teaspoons vanilla extract
2½ cups grated zucchini
¾ cup chopped walnuts (optional)

Preheat the oven to 350 degrees. Grease and flour a 10-inch tube pan (springform, Bundt, or angel food).

Stir together the flours, baking powder, salt, cinnamon, and cocoa powder in a medium-size bowl.

In another bowl, cream the butter with the honey until light and fluffy. Beat in the eggs, milk, and vanilla. Beat in the dry ingredients in three or four additions. Stir in the zucchini and ½ cup of the walnuts if desired.

Pour the batter into the prepared pan, and sprinkle on the remaining walnuts if you are using them. Bake for about 1 hour, until a toothpick inserted in the center comes out clean. Allow the cake to cool for 10 to 15 minutes and serve.

Applesauce-Raisin Spice Cake with Maple Cream Frosting

This wonderful old-fashioned cake is the kind your grandmother—and even some grandfathers—might have made! Real maple syrup is a must.

12 to 16 servings

CAKE
¾ cup (1½ sticks) butter or margarine, softened
1 cup honey
2 large eggs
2 cups unsweetened applesauce
1 teaspoon vanilla extract
1½ cups whole wheat pastry flour
1½ cups unbleached white flour
½ cup rolled oats
1 tablespoon baking soda
1½ teaspoons ground cinnamon
1 teaspoon ground nutmeg
½ teaspoon cardamom
¼ teaspoon ground cloves
¾ cup raisins

GLAZE
1 cup maple syrup
½ cup heavy cream
2 tablespoons unbleached white flour

Preheat the oven to 350 degrees. Grease and flour two 9- or 10-inch cake pans.

For the cake, in a medium-size bowl, cream the butter with the honey until light and fluffy. Beat in the eggs, applesauce, and vanilla.

In another bowl, stir together the flours, oats, baking soda, cinnamon, nutmeg, cardamom, and cloves.

Beat the dry ingredients into the wet in three additions. Stir in the raisins.

Pour the batter into the prepared pans, and bake for 25 to 30 minutes, until a toothpick inserted in the center comes out clean. Place the cakes on cooling racks for 10 minutes, and then turn them out onto the racks.

To prepare the glaze, heat the maple syrup, cream, and flour in a saucepan over low heat, whisking until it begins to simmer and thickens slightly, about 5 minutes. Cool the glaze in the refrigerator until the cake is cool.

Place one of the cake layers on a serving plate, and spread half the glaze on top. Add the second layer, and spread the remaining glaze on top, swirling it in a decorative pattern. Cut and serve.

Carolina Peach-Pecan Kitchen Cake

★ **BEGINNER-FRIENDLY**

Enjoy this sweet, moist cake at the kitchen table with friends. Add a dab of whipped cream for an extra treat!

12 servings

1½ cups whole wheat pastry flour
1½ cups unbleached white flour
1½ teaspoons baking powder
1 teaspoon ground ginger
1 teaspoon ground cinnamon
½ teaspoon ground nutmeg
1/16 teaspoon ground cloves
¾ cup (1½ sticks) butter or margarine, softened
1¼ cups honey
3 large eggs
1 teaspoon vanilla extract
¼ cup buttermilk or yogurt
6 cups fresh or frozen sliced, unpeeled peaches (thawed if frozen)
1 tablespoon fresh lemon juice
¾ cup chopped pecans

Preheat the oven to 350 degrees. Grease and flour a 9 by 13-inch cake pan.

Stir together the flours, baking powder, ginger, cinnamon, nutmeg, and cloves in a medium-size bowl.

In another bowl, cream the butter with the honey until light and fluffy. Beat in the eggs, vanilla, and buttermilk. Beat in the dry ingredients in two additions. Stir in the peaches and lemon juice.

Pour the batter into the prepared pan, spreading it into the corners. Sprinkle with pecans, and bake for 50 to 55 minutes, until a toothpick inserted in the center comes out clean.

Let the cake cool on a rack for 10 to 15 minutes before serving.

 **CHEESECAKE**

Marbled Pumpkin Cheesecake

*T*his spicy, multilayered cheesecake is especially good with a pot of mint tea. *Chill for at least 8 hours before serving.*

12 servings

CRUST
1½ cups graham cracker crumbs
5 tablespoons butter or margarine, melted
1 tablespoon honey
1 tablespoon unbleached white flour
1 teaspoon vanilla extract

FILLING
Two 8-ounce packages cream cheese or Neufchâtel, softened
¾ cup honey
1 teaspoon vanilla extract
3 large eggs
1 cup pumpkin puree
¾ teaspoon ground cinnamon
¼ teaspoon ground nutmeg
½ teaspoon ground ginger

Preheat the oven to 325 degrees. Grease a 10-inch springform pan.

Stir together the graham cracker crumbs, butter, honey, flour, and vanilla in a small bowl. Press over the bottom and 2 or 3 inches up the side of the prepared pan.

Bake the crust for 10 minutes, until lightly golden, and set it on a rack to cool. Raise the oven temperature to 350 degrees.

Beat the cream cheese, ½ cup of the honey, and the vanilla until smooth. Beat in the eggs, one at a time. Set aside 1 cup of the mixture. Beat in the pumpkin, the remaining ¼ cup honey, and the cinnamon, nutmeg, and ginger.

Pour half the pumpkin mixture into the crust. Top it with ½ cup of the reserved cream cheese mixture. Repeat. For a marbled effect, swirl a knife through the layers a few times.

Bake for 50 to 55 minutes, until a knife inserted in the center comes out clean. Cool it on a rack to room temperature. Loosen the sides of the pan, cover, and chill for at least 8 hours before serving.

Caribbean Lime Cheesecake

This rich, sweet-tart cheesecake goes especially well after a hot and spicy dinner. It needs to chill for at least 8 hours before being devoured!

12 servings

CRUST

1 ½ cups graham crackers

4 tablespoons (½ stick) butter or margarine, melted

1 tablespoon honey

1 tablespoon unbleached white flour

FILLING

Two 8-ounce packages cream cheese or Neufchâtel, softened

⅔ cup honey

1 cup sour cream or plain yogurt

4 tablespoons unbleached white flour

½ cup fresh lime juice

1 teaspoon vanilla

3 large eggs

1 lime, sliced, for garnish

Preheat the oven to 325 degrees. Grease a 10-inch springform pan.

To prepare the crust, stir together the graham cracker crumbs, butter, honey, and flour in a small bowl. Press over the bottom and 2 to 3 inches up the side of the prepared pan.

Bake the crust for 10 minutes, until golden around the edges. Set it on a rack to cool. Raise the oven temperature to 375 degrees.

For the filling, beat the cream cheese and honey until smooth with an electric mixer or in a food processor. Beat in the sour cream, flour, lime juice, vanilla, and eggs.

Pour the filling into the cooled crust, and bake for 15 minutes. Reduce the temperature to 250 degrees, and bake for 50 minutes more, until a knife inserted in the center comes out clean.

Cool on a rack to room temperature. Loosen the sides of the pan, cover, and chill for at least 8 hours before serving. Garnish with fresh lime slices and serve.

Apricot Cheesecake with Chocolate Crust

*A*pricots and brandy lend a mellow, fruity flavor to this cheesecake. The cream cheese topping and chocolate crust make it simply irresistible. (You could substitute graham crackers for the chocolate cookie crumbs if you prefer.) Allow the cheesecake to chill for at least 8 hours before serving.

12 servings

CRUST
1½ cups chocolate cookie crumbs
4 tablespoons (½ stick) butter or margarine, melted

FILLING
1 cup dried apricots
Two 8-ounce packages cream cheese or Neufchâtel, softened
¾ cup honey
2 tablespoons apricot or triple sec brandy
3 large eggs

TOPPING
1 cup sour cream
1 teaspoon vanilla extract
2 tablespoons honey

Preheat the oven to 325 degrees. Grease a 10-inch springform pan.

For the crust, stir together the cookie crumbs and butter in a small bowl. Press over the bottom and 2 to 3 inches up the side of the prepared pan.

Bake the crust for 10 minutes. It should be golden in color around the edges. Set it on a rack to cool. Raise the oven temperature to 350 degrees.

Bring the apricots and 1 cup water to a boil in a saucepan. Reduce the heat and simmer, stirring occasionally, until the water has evaporated, about 10 minutes.

Puree the apricots in a food processor. Add the cream cheese, honey, brandy, and eggs, and process until smooth, stopping to scrape the sides once or twice.

Pour the filling into the cooled crust, and bake for 45 to 50 minutes, until the cake has puffed up and is lightly golden.

Take the cake out, and let it cool for 5 minutes. (Leave the oven on.)

To prepare the topping, stir together the sour cream, vanilla, and honey, and gently spread over the top of the cheesecake. Return to the oven and bake for 5 minutes more.

Cool on a rack to room temperature. Loosen the sides of the pan, cover, and chill for at least 8 hours before serving.

More Temptations

Desserts are temptations, and the key to enjoying them without guilt is having them only occasionally. Moderation will allow you to maintain a healthy diet without feeling like an ascetic.

This chapter is a catchall for favorite sweets that aren't pies, cakes, or cookies. They are generally more casual and less labor intensive than other desserts in the book.

That's especially true of the cobbler, fruit strudels, and shortbread, which can be put together easily. Enjoy the fruit desserts like Peach and Two-Berry Cobbler (page 291) as summer fruits come into season.

The turnovers, baked in a flaky phyllo crust, are infinitely lighter than commercial varieties. Make them when you have company enough to eat them all, so there won't be any left to tempt you tomorrow!

The three sauces—Hot Fudge (page 301), Mocha Fudge (page 300), and Peanut Butter (page 301)—are rich indulgences that I can't resist making now and then. Their flavor and purity are vastly superior to commercial brands. They store well in the refrigerator and will last for weeks, and turn a simple dessert like ice cream or frozen yogurt into a special treat.

Peach and Two-Berry Cobbler

★ **BEGINNER-FRIENDLY**

Fruit cobbler is so simple to put together and so difficult to resist that it's one of my favorite summertime desserts.

12 servings

    4 cups sliced unpeeled peaches
    1½ cups fresh raspberries
    1½ cups fresh blueberries
    ½ cup honey
    1 tablespoon fresh lemon juice
    2 tablespoons plus 1 cup unbleached white flour
    1 cup whole wheat pastry flour
    2 teaspoons baking powder
    ½ cup (1 stick) butter or margarine, softened
    1 large egg
    ½ teaspoon ground cinnamon

Preheat the oven to 400 degrees. Grease and flour a 9 by 13-inch cake pan.

In a medium-size bowl, gently stir together the peaches, raspberries, blueberries, ¼ cup of the honey, the lemon juice, and 2 tablespoons of the unbleached flour.

In another bowl, stir together the remaining 1 cup unbleached flour, the pastry flour, and baking powder. Beat in the butter, egg, and remaining ¼ cup honey until smooth and no longer sticky.

Spread the fruit mixture in the prepared pan, and sprinkle with cinnamon. Pick up a handful of the dough, flatten gently, and place on top of the filling. Repeat until you have a patchwork with some fruit peeking out.

Bake for 25 to 30 minutes, until lightly browned. Cool for 30 minutes before serving.

Austrian Plum Strudel

I *talian prune plums, available in late summer and fall, are best for this wonderfully sweet-tart treat. They are deep purple and give up their pits easily. If they aren't in season, you can use another variety, and gently slice the fruit from the pits.*

8 to 10 servings

5 cups sliced Italian prune plums (25 to 30 plums)
1 tablespoon fresh lemon juice
½ cup honey
¼ teaspoon ground allspice
¼ teaspoon ground cinnamon
¼ teaspoon ground nutmeg
2 tablespoons unbleached white flour
¾ cup fresh whole wheat bread crumbs
10 sheets phyllo dough (half of a 1-pound package)
4 tablespoons (½ stick) butter or margarine, melted
1 teaspoon raw sugar

Preheat the oven to 350 degrees. Grease a large cookie sheet.

Stir together the plums, lemon juice, honey, allspice, cinnamon, nutmeg, flour, and bread crumbs in a medium-size bowl.

Spread a sheet of phyllo dough on a work surface, and brush it lightly with melted butter. Place a second sheet on top of the first, and brush with butter. Repeat, using three more sheets.

Stir the filling again, and spread half of it lengthwise onto the dough, leaving a 2-inch border on both ends and one side. Fold the ends of the dough up over the filling, roll it into a log, and place it on the prepared cookie sheet. (See Greek Spinach-Potato Strudel, page 234, for an illustration showing how to put the strudel together.)

Repeat with the remaining phyllo dough, butter, and filling.

Brush the dough logs with the remaining butter, and sprinkle them with the sugar. Bake for 20 to 25 minutes, until golden brown.

Cool on a rack for 30 minutes before slicing.

Apple-Cranberry-Raisin Strudel

For the filling, substitute 4 cups sliced, unpeeled green apples (such as Granny Smith), and stir them together with 1½ cups fresh cranberries, ½ cup raisins, ½ cup honey, 1 tablespoon fresh lemon juice, 1 teaspoon ground cinnamon, ½ teaspoon ground nutmeg, and ½ cup fresh bread crumbs. Assemble and bake the strudel as directed above.

Almond-Lemon Poppy Seed Shortbread

★ **BEGINNER-FRIENDLY**

Each time someone walks by this yummy shortbread, a little piece will disappear, and before you know it, it will all be gone!

12 to 16 servings

1 cup (2 sticks) butter or margarine, softened
1 cup honey
1 tablespoon grated lemon peel
1 tablespoon fresh lemon juice
1 teaspoon vanilla extract
¼ cup poppy seeds
1½ cups unbleached white flour
1¼ cups whole wheat pastry flour
½ teaspoon salt
1 cup ground almonds

Preheat the oven to 325 degrees. Grease and flour a 9 by 13-inch cake pan.

In a medium-size bowl, cream the butter with the honey until light and fluffy. Beat in the lemon peel, lemon juice, vanilla, and poppy seeds.

In another bowl, stir together the flours and salt.

Beat the dry ingredients into the wet, mixing just until well combined. Stir in the ground almonds.

Spread the batter in the prepared pan, and bake for 30 to 35 minutes, until the edges are lightly browned and a toothpick inserted in the center comes out clean.

Cool on a rack for 10 minutes before cutting.

Pear Almond Medley

This delightful cross between a cobbler and a crisp is especially good with a scoop of vanilla ice cream. You may substitute peaches, plums, nectarines, or apples for the pears.

8 servings

4 cups sliced unpeeled pears (4 large pears)
2 tablespoons fresh lemon juice
½ cup ground almonds
¼ cup milk
¼ cup sour cream or plain yogurt
3 large eggs
7 tablespoons butter or margarine, melted
1 teaspoon vanilla extract
1 teaspoon almond extract
½ cup honey
½ cup whole wheat pastry flour
½ cup unbleached white flour
⅛ teaspoon salt
1 teaspoon ground cinnamon
¼ cup sliced almonds
1 tablespoon raw sugar

Preheat the oven to 400 degrees. Grease a 2-quart baking dish.

Toss the pears with the lemon juice, and spread them in the prepared pan.

In a food processor or blender, process the ground almonds, milk, sour cream, and eggs until smooth. Add 6 tablespoons of the melted butter, the vanilla, almond extract, and honey, and mix well.

Stir together the flours, salt, and cinnamon. Add the flour mixture to the liquid, and process until smooth.

Pour the batter over the fruit. Drizzle on the remaining 1 tablespoon melted butter. Sprinkle on the sliced almonds and sugar.

Bake for about 40 minutes, until firm and golden. Cool for at least 30 minutes before serving.

Double Chocolate Peanut Butter Brownies

Guaranteed to satisfy that chocolate craving. The smell of these brownies baking will entice noses from a good distance away!

12 large brownies

¾ cup (1½ sticks) butter or margarine, softened
1 cup smooth peanut butter
1½ cups honey
4 large eggs
2 teaspoons vanilla extract
6 ounces (¾ cup) cream cheese, softened
4 ounces (4 squares) unsweetened chocolate
¾ cup unbleached white flour
½ cup whole wheat pastry flour
1 teaspoon baking powder
½ cup chocolate chips

Preheat the oven to 350 degrees. Grease a 9 by 13-inch baking pan.

Beat ¼ cup of the butter, the peanut butter, ½ cup of the honey, 1 egg, 1 teaspoon vanilla, and the cream cheese with an electric mixer until smooth.

Melt the unsweetened chocolate in a saucepan over very low heat, stirring occasionally.

In a medium-size bowl, beat the melted chocolate into the remaining ½ cup butter. Add the remaining 3 eggs, 1 cup honey, and 1 teaspoon vanilla, and mix well.

In another bowl, stir together the flours and baking powder. Beat the flour mixture into the chocolate mixture, and stir in the chocolate chips.

Pour the chocolate batter into the prepared pan, spreading it to the edges and into the corners. Pour on the peanut butter batter, gently swirling the top to create a marble pattern.

Bake for 40 to 45 minutes, until the top is firm and lightly browned, and a toothpick inserted in the center comes out clean. Allow brownies to cool for 15 minutes before serving.

Peanut Butter–Chocolate Chip Cupcakes

★ **BEGINNER-FRIENDLY**

Cupcakes bring back memories of childhood birthday parties, when we got dressed up in stiff new clothes, wore silly hats, and blew noisemakers. These cupcakes, which combine two of most kids' favorite tastes, are great birthday or school party fare.

12 cupcakes

1 cup unbleached white flour
1 cup whole wheat pastry flour
1 tablespoon baking powder
⅛ teaspoon salt
¾ cup honey
½ cup smooth peanut butter
6 tablespoons (¾ stick) butter or margarine, softened
2 large eggs
1 teaspoon vanilla extract
½ cup milk
2½ cups chocolate chips
½ cup heavy cream

Preheat the oven to 350 degrees. Line twelve muffin cups with paper cupcake liners.

Stir together the flours, baking powder, and salt in a medium-size bowl.

In another bowl, beat the honey, peanut butter, and butter until smooth. Beat in the eggs, vanilla, and milk.

Beat the wet ingredients into the dry in two additions. Stir in 1 cup of the chocolate chips.

Spoon the batter into the prepared muffin cups, and bake for 20 to 25 minutes, until a toothpick inserted in the center comes out clean. Set the cupcakes on a rack to cool.

Meanwhile, heat the cream in a small saucepan over medium heat just until it begins to boil. Remove the pan from the heat, and stir in the remaining 1½ cups chocolate chips. Using a whisk, beat until smooth and fluffy.

Let the frosting cool, whisk again, and spread on the cooled cupcakes.

 TURNOVERS

These turnovers are made with phyllo dough. It's easy to work with if you take a couple of precautions. First, make sure the package is undamaged; a crushed or mangled package means cracked or broken dough that will be torture to work with. Second, defrost the package in the refrigerator to prevent sticky dough. If sheets stick together, separate them gently.

Blueberry Turnovers

Big, juicy, sweet blueberries wrapped in a flaky crust. These are irresistible, especially right out of the oven!

8 turnovers

½ cup honey
4 tablespoons arrowroot
½ teaspoon ground cinnamon
4 cups fresh blueberries
1 tablespoon fresh lemon juice
2 tablespoons unbleached white flour
16 sheets phyllo dough (1-pound package, thawed)
4 tablespoons (½ stick) butter or margarine, melted
1 tablespoon raw sugar

Preheat the oven to 350 degrees. Grease a large cookie sheet.

Heat the honey, arrowroot, and cinnamon in a small saucepan over medium heat, stirring, until it begins to thicken. Remove the pan from the heat.

In a medium-size bowl, toss the blueberries with the lemon juice and flour. Pour the honey mixture over the berries, and mix gently but well.

Lay a sheet of phyllo dough on a work surface, and brush it lightly with melted butter. Place a second sheet on top of the first, and brush with butter. Fold in half lengthwise. Place ½ cup of filling in the bottom left-hand corner, and fold the dough up over it to form a triangle. Continue folding, like a flag, up the length of the dough until you have a closed triangle.

Place the turnover on the prepared baking sheet, and repeat until you have used all the filling and dough. Brush with the remaining butter, and sprinkle with raw sugar. Bake for 15 to 20 minutes, until lightly golden. Serve warm.

Peach-Raspberry Turnovers

For the filling, substitute 3 cups sliced unpeeled peaches, and stir them together with 1 cup fresh raspberries, ½ teaspoon ground cinnamon, 1 table-spoon fresh lemon juice, ¼ cup unbleached white flour, and ½ cup honey. Fill and bake as directed above.

Apple-Raisin Turnovers

For the filling, substitute 4 cups sliced unpeeled apples, and stir them together with ½ cup raisins, ½ teaspoon ground cinnamon, ¼ teaspoon ground nutmeg, 1 tablespoon fresh lemon juice, and ½ cup honey. Fill and bake as directed above.

Apple-Cheddar Turnovers

For the filling, substitute 1 cup grated sharp Cheddar cheese for the raisins in the Apple-Raisin variation.

Chocolate-Cherry Cream Cheese Turnovers

Black Forest cake lovers will swoon over these! For the filling, substitute 2 ounces semisweet chocolate melted over low heat. Beat in 8 ounces cream cheese, ½ cup ground walnuts, ½ teaspoon vanilla extract, and ½ cup honey until smooth. Stir in 1 cup pitted cherries (rinsed and drained if canned). Fill and bake as directed above, using ¼ cup of filling per turnover.

 **SAUCES**

Mocha Fudge Sauce

★ **BEGINNER-FRIENDLY**

Bittersweet chocolate, coffee, and coffee-flavored liqueur combine in this intensely flavored sauce. If you use espresso coffee granules, reduce the amount to 2 tablespoons.

2 cups

¾ cup honey
3 tablespoons instant coffee granules
1 ½ ounces bittersweet chocolate
¾ cup heavy cream
2 tablespoons unbleached white flour
¼ cup cocoa powder
1 tablespoon coffee-flavored liqueur (such as Kahlúa)

Heat the honey and coffee granules in a saucepan over low heat until the coffee dissolves. Add the chocolate, and whisk until melted. Add the cream, flour, and cocoa powder, and whisk until smooth. Stir in the liqueur, and heat just until hot and steamy.

Serve immediately, or reheat over a double boiler.

Peanut Butter Sauce

★ BEGINNER-FRIENDLY

A *little dab will do you! Serve over vanilla, coffee, or chocolate ice cream.*

2 cups

½ cup honey
2 tablespoons butter or margarine
¾ cup smooth peanut butter
½ cup heavy cream
1 teaspoon vanilla extract

Heat the honey and butter, stirring, in a heavy saucepan over medium heat. When it begins to boil, reduce the heat to a simmer, and add the peanut butter, whisking until smooth. Stir in the cream and vanilla, and heat just until hot and steamy.

Serve hot, or reheat over a double boiler.

Hot Fudge Sauce

★ BEGINNER-FRIENDLY

B *e sure to use good quality chocolate for this rich sauce—a true chocolate lover's delight. Serve it over ice cream, brownies, or cake. It will keep in the refrigerator for weeks—if it lasts that long!*

2½ cups

2 ounces bittersweet chocolate, chopped
½ cup (1 stick) unsalted butter
½ cup cocoa powder
¾ cup honey
¾ cup heavy cream

Melt the chocolate and butter in a heavy saucepan over low heat, stirring occasionally. Add the cocoa powder, honey, and cream, whisking until smooth. Cook, stirring, just until it begins to boil.

Serve immediately, or reheat over a double boiler.

Comforting Cookies

There's something so comforting about homemade cookies warm from the oven. Maybe it goes back to the milk and cookies many of us looked forward to after school when we were growing up. One thing's for sure: I don't know many grown-ups who aren't still kids at heart when it comes to cookies.

Homemade cookies are so much fresher and better than the store-bought variety that there's no comparison. Many commercial cookies are overly sweetened, and are made with cheap shortenings such as highly saturated palm and coconut oils. When you bake at home you can control the level of sweetness, and use wholesome ingredients such as whole-grain and organically grown flours.

If you're not a baker, cookies are the place to start. They're easy and almost foolproof to make. A few simple rules will guarantee success:

- Don't overmix the dough or your cookies will be tough. This is a good rule to follow for most baked goods.

- Make sure your oven temperature is accurate. Check it with an oven thermometer; if it's off, have it adjusted professionally, or compensate for the difference when you set the temperature.

- Bake one sheet of cookies at a time for best results. If you want to bake two, switch them, top to bottom and front to back, halfway through baking to ensure even browning.

- Make sure your baking sheets aren't too big for your oven. There should be a few inches on each side to allow the heat to circulate.

- Preheat the oven before you put your cookies in, and check them 2 to 3 minutes before the stated baking time has elapsed.

- Use a kitchen timer. The most common mistake when baking cookies is burning them, especially the last pan! One tray of black, smoking cookies will teach an important lesson you won't soon forget.

Cookies freeze well. I always make a double recipe and put half in the freezer with good results. Make sure the cookies are completely cool before storing them. Wrap them tightly in foil or in plastic wrap, and put them in a sturdy container to protect them from cracking or breaking. Allow them to thaw in their container at room temperature.

I love the soft texture and mellow sweetness that honey gives cookies, but for crisper results you can substitute an equal amount of sugar. Cut back on the flour by ¼ to ½ cup to make up for the reduced liquid.

When your first pan of cookies comes out of the oven, be sure to sit down and enjoy a few with a cup of tea or the traditional glass of milk. That's the best part!

Dream Cookies

★ **BEGINNER-FRIENDLY**

These cookies are wonderful with either carob powder and carob chips or cocoa powder and chocolate chips. The sour cream adds a smoothness and the almonds lend a delightful crunch.

3 dozen large cookies

1½ cups (3 sticks) butter or margarine, softened
¾ cup honey
½ teaspoon almond extract
½ cup sour cream
1½ cups whole wheat pastry flour
1 cup unbleached white flour
1 teaspoon baking powder
2 tablespoons cocoa or carob powder
1 cup chopped almonds
1 cup chocolate or carob chips

Preheat the oven to 350 degrees, and grease your cookie sheets.

In a medium-size bowl, cream the butter, honey, and almond extract until light and fluffy. Beat in the sour cream.

In another bowl, stir together the flours, baking powder, and cocoa.

Stir the flour mixture into the butter mixture, and fold in the almonds and chips.

Drop the dough onto the cookie sheets in heaping tablespoonfuls about 2 inches apart.

Bake for 10 to 12 minutes, until lightly golden. Let the cookies cool in the pan for a few minutes before transferring them to cooling racks.

Oatmeal Chocolate Chip Cookies

★ **BEGINNER-FRIENDLY**

*T*hese are one of my favorite cookies, especially warm from the oven. If there are nut haters in your family as there are in mine, make half the cookies without nuts, and stir half the amount of nuts (¼ cup for this recipe) into the remaining dough.

2 dozen large cookies

½ cup (1 stick) butter or margarine, softened
1 cup honey
1 large egg
1 teaspoon vanilla extract
¾ cup unbleached white flour
1 cup whole wheat pastry flour
2 cups rolled oats
½ teaspoon baking soda
⅛ teaspoon salt
1 cup chocolate chips
½ cup chopped walnuts (optional)

Preheat the oven to 350 degrees, and grease your cookie sheets.

In a medium-size bowl, cream the butter with the honey until light and fluffy. Beat in the egg and vanilla.

In another bowl, stir together the flours, oats, baking soda, and salt.

Stir the dry ingredients into the wet, mixing well. Fold in the chocolate chips and nuts if desired.

Drop the dough onto cookie sheets in heaping tablespoonfuls about 2 inches apart.

Bake for 12 to 15 minutes, until light golden on top. Let the cookies cool in the pan for a few minutes before transferring them to cooling racks.

Lemon Walnut Cookies

★ BEGINNER-FRIENDLY

These double nutty cookies have both ground and chopped walnuts in them. The lemon juice and peel add a pleasing touch of tartness. You can grind the nuts in a food processor.

3 dozen cookies

1 cup (2 sticks) butter or margarine, softened
¾ cup honey
½ teaspoon vanilla extract
Grated peel of 1 lemon
3 tablespoons fresh lemon juice
½ cup ground walnuts
½ cup chopped walnuts
1 cup whole wheat pastry flour
1 cup unbleached white flour

Preheat the oven to 325 degrees, and grease your cookie sheets.

In a medium-size bowl, cream the butter with the honey until light and fluffy. Beat in the vanilla, lemon peel, and lemon juice.

In another bowl, stir together the ground and chopped walnuts and the flours. Stir the dry ingredients into the wet, mixing well.

Roll the dough into walnut-size balls. Place them about 2 inches apart on cookie sheets, and press them down slightly.

Bake for 10 to 12 minutes, until lightly browned on the edges.

Let the cookies cool in the pan for a few minutes before transferring them to cooling racks.

Molasses Spice Cookies

The dough for these old-fashioned favorites needs to chill for at least 2 hours. It's rolled in raw sugar before baking to give a sweet crunch to each bite.

4 dozen cookies

¾ cup (1½ sticks) butter or margarine, softened
⅓ cup blackstrap molasses
1 cup honey
1 large egg
1¾ cups unbleached white flour
1¾ cups whole wheat pastry flour
1½ teaspoons baking soda
1½ tablespoons ground cinnamon
1½ tablespoons ground ginger
1 tablespoon ground cloves
1 teaspoon ground mace or allspice
¼ teaspoon salt
½ cup raw sugar

In a medium-size bowl, cream the butter with the molasses and honey until light and fluffy. Beat in the egg.

In another bowl, stir together the flours, baking soda, cinnamon, ginger, cloves, mace, and salt.

Beat the dry ingredients into the wet. Cover the dough with plastic wrap, and chill for at least 2 hours or overnight.

Preheat the oven to 350 degrees, and grease your cookie sheets.

Roll the dough into balls about 1½ inches across. Roll the balls in the sugar, and place them about 3 inches apart on the cookie sheets. Flatten them slightly.

Bake for 12 to 15 minutes, until lightly browned on the edges. Let the cookies cool in the pan for a few minutes before transferring them to cooling racks.

Oatmeal-Carrot-Raisin Cookies

★ BEGINNER-FRIENDLY

Oats and raisins add a chewy texture and carrots add sweetness and flecks of color to these wholesome cookies.

3 dozen cookies

¾ cup (1 ½ sticks) butter or margarine
1 cup honey
1 large egg
1 teaspoon vanilla extract
1 cup whole wheat pastry flour
1 cup unbleached white flour
2 cups rolled oats
1 teaspoon baking powder
¼ teaspoon baking soda
⅛ teaspoon salt
1 teaspoon ground cinnamon
1 cup grated carrots (2 medium carrots)
½ cup raisins

Preheat the oven to 375 degrees, and grease your cookie sheets.

In a medium-size bowl, cream the butter with the honey until light and fluffy. Beat in the egg and vanilla.

In another bowl, stir together the flours, oats, baking powder, baking soda, salt, and cinnamon.

Stir the dry ingredients into the wet, mixing well. Stir in the carrots and raisins.

Drop the dough onto cookie sheets in heaping tablespoonfuls about 2 inches apart.

Bake for about 10 minutes, until lightly browned on the edges.

Let the cookies cool in the pan for a few minutes before transferring them to cooling racks.

Everything Cookies

★ **BEGINNER-FRIENDLY**

*C*hock-full of goodies from the pantry, Everything Cookies are highly flexible. Substitute your favorite nuts, dried fruits, nut butter, and chips, and savor the results.

3 dozen large cookies

1 cup (2 sticks) butter or margarine, softened
½ cup smooth peanut or almond butter
1 cup honey
2 large eggs
1 cup whole wheat pastry flour
1½ cups unbleached white flour
1½ cups rolled oats
1 teaspoon baking soda
⅛ teaspoon salt
½ cup chopped walnuts
½ cup raisins
½ cup coconut flakes
1 cup chocolate chips

Preheat the oven to 375 degrees, and grease your cookie sheets.

In a medium-size bowl, cream the butter with the peanut butter and honey until light and fluffy. Beat in the eggs.

In another bowl, stir together the flours, oats, baking soda, and salt.

Mix the dry ingredients into the wet. Stir in the nuts, raisins, coconut, and chocolate chips.

Drop the dough onto cookie sheets in heaping tablespoonfuls about 3 inches apart. Flatten slightly.

Bake for about 10 minutes, until lightly browned on the edges.

Let the cookies cool in the pan for a few minutes before transferring them to cooling racks.

Hazelnut Chocolate Cookies

hese cookies are somewhat labor intensive, but they're so delicious and beautiful that your friends and family will be happy you went to the trouble. The dough needs to chill for at least 2 hours, and can be made a day ahead. Toast the hazelnuts in a 375-degree oven for about 5 minutes.

4½ to 5 dozen small cookies

1 cup (2 sticks) butter or margarine, softened
1 cup honey
1 large egg
1 teaspoon vanilla extract
1¼ cups unbleached white flour
1 cup whole wheat pastry flour
1 teaspoon baking powder
½ teaspoon salt
¾ cup toasted hazelnuts
½ cup cocoa powder

In a medium-size bowl, cream the butter with the honey until light and fluffy. Beat in the egg and vanilla.

In another bowl, stir together 1 cup of the unbleached flour with the whole wheat flour, baking powder, and salt.

Beat the dry ingredients into the wet just until well combined.

Divide the dough in half. Work the hazelnuts and remaining ¼ cup flour into one half, and the cocoa into the other. The dough will be sticky. Wrap separately in plastic wrap, and refrigerate for at least 2 hours or overnight.

Preheat the oven to 350 degrees, and grease your cookie sheets.

Scoop up a teaspoonful of each dough, and roll them together into a ball. Place the balls on cookie sheets about 2 inches apart, and flatten gently with your fingers until about ¼ inch thick.

Bake for 12 to 15 minutes, until lightly browned on the edges. Let the cookies cool in the pan for a few minutes before transferring them to cooling racks.

Lemon-Coconut-Almond Cookies

Chill the dough for at least 2 hours before forming and baking these lemony delights. You can grind the almonds in a food processor.

2½ dozen cookies

1 cup (2 sticks) butter or margarine, softened
¾ cup honey
1 tablespoon grated lemon peel
1 tablespoon fresh lemon juice
1 teaspoon vanilla extract
1 cup unbleached white flour
1 cup whole wheat pastry flour
⅛ teaspoon salt
1 cup shredded coconut
½ cup ground almonds

In a medium-size bowl, cream the butter with the honey until light and fluffy. Beat in the lemon peel, lemon juice, and vanilla.

In another bowl, stir together the flours and salt.

Beat the dry ingredients into the wet. Stir in the coconut and almonds. Cover and chill for at least 2 hours or overnight.

Preheat the oven to 325 degrees, and grease your cookie sheets.

Scoop up the dough by the tablespoonful, and form it into balls. Place the balls about 2 inches apart on the cookie sheets, and gently flatten them to a thickness of about ⅜ inch.

Bake for about 15 minutes, until golden brown on the edges. Let the cookies cool in the pan for a few minutes before transferring them to cooling racks.

Chocolate-Covered
Peanut Butter–Raspberry Cookies

*T*his *peanut butter cookie filled with raspberry jam and glazed with chocolate is irresistible. The dough needs a quick 30-minute chill in the refrigerator.*

2½ dozen cookies

COOKIES
> 1⅓ cups chunky peanut butter
> 1 cup honey
> ⅔ cup butter or margarine, softened
> 1 teaspoon vanilla extract
> 1⅓ cups unbleached white flour
> 1⅓ cups whole wheat pastry flour
> ⅓ cup toasted wheat germ
> ½ teaspoon salt

FILLING AND GLAZE
> ½ cup raspberry preserves
> 2 ounces (2 squares) unsweetened chocolate
> 4 tablespoons (½ stick) butter or margarine
> ¼ cup honey

In a medium-size bowl, beat the peanut butter, honey, butter, and vanilla until smooth.

In another bowl, stir together the flours, wheat germ, and salt.

Mix the dry ingredients into the wet. Cover and chill for at least 30 minutes.

Preheat the oven to 350 degrees, and grease your cookie sheets.

Scoop up the dough, a heaping tablespoonful at a time, and roll it into balls. Place the balls about 3 inches apart on the cookie sheets, and flatten gently using the greased tines of a fork to form a crisscross pattern.

Using your thumb, press down in the center of each cookie to form an indentation deep enough to hold about ½ teaspoon of raspberry jam. Spoon jam onto each cookie.

Bake for 10 to 12 minutes, until lightly browned on the edges. Let the cookies cool in the pan for a few minutes before transferring them to cooling racks.

While the last pan of cookies is baking, melt the chocolate and butter in a small saucepan over low heat. Stir in the honey, and set aside to cool and thicken slightly.

When the last pan of cookies is baked and slightly cooled, place all the cookies close together on one or two baking sheets.

Spoon on the chocolate glaze in a swirling pattern, covering the preserves. Let the glaze set for 10 to 15 minutes before serving.

Suggested Menus

Like cooking, meal planning can be creative and fun. Everyday meals often get put together on the run, but for special occasions, it's a treat to sit down with your favorite cookbooks and recipe files, and search out just the right combination of dishes: an entree to anchor the meal, accompaniments to add variety and balance, and a dessert to finish things off with a flourish.

The first thing to ask yourself is what's in season, whether in your garden or market. Then you need to factor in cost, your guests' preferences (try not to serve them the same thing twice in a row!), and the amount of time you'll have to cook. Your guests may help you out here by offering to bring something; I rarely say no. Knowing that someone else is making a dip, salad, or dessert can be a big help, and your guests will have the satisfaction of knowing that they contributed to the meal. Just be sure to return the favor when they invite you for dinner!

Paging through this book will no doubt give you plenty of menu ideas; here are a few to get you started:

BRUNCHES

Fresh fruit (grapefruit halves, berries, grapes, or mixed fruit)
Asparagus Frittata (page 14)
Sweet Carolina Cranberry Muffins (page 43)
Tea, coffee, juices

Black Bean Huevos Rancheros (page 22)
Two-Berry Coffee Cake (page 38)
Fresh sliced pineapple
Fruit spritzers or mimosas

Baked Blueberry French Toast (page 35)
New England Red Flannel Home Fries (page 10)
Fresh fruit
Hot cocoa, tea, or coffee

Melon slices
Stuffed Hash Browns (page 8)
Peach Pecan Muffins (page 41)
Tea, coffee, juices

Tropical Fruit Salad (page 118)
Nanny Cay Pancakes (page 32)
Fresh limeade or orange juice

Grapefruit halves
Deluxe Hash Brown Potatoes (page 9)
Raisin Cinnamon Biscuits (page 54)
Sparkling cider or mimosas

Artichoke Frittata (page 17)
Doubly Red Potato Salad (page 104)
Lemon Raspberry Muffins (page 42)
Fresh carrot or orange juice

Fresh berries or grapes
Florentine Eggs (page 11)
Rhubarb-Walnut-Buttermilk Coffee Cake (page 39)
Coffee, tea, juices

Broccoli, Cauliflower, Walnut, and Avocado Salad (page 117)
Sunday Morning Biscuit Pizza (page 12)
Sparkling juices or mimosas

Red Potato and Three-Pepper Breakfast Burritos (page 21)
Black-Eyed Pea Salad (page 105)
Gingerbread Walnut Muffins (page 48)
Fruit juices, tea, coffee

BASIC MEALS

Four-Bean Chili (page 71)
Cornmeal and Cheddar Buttermilk Biscuits (page 57)
Ice-cold lemonade or beer

Egg Salad Sandwiches with Sun-Dried Tomatoes (page 129)
Black-and-White Soup (page 92)
Fruit juice, tea, coffee

Sesame Noodles (page 152)
Shiitake Mushroom and Seitan Soup (page 88)
Chinese tea

Barley-Lentil Salad (page 107)
Pumpkin Pecan Muffins (page 47)
Hot or iced tea or coffee

Monterey Chowder (page 74)
Oatmeal Date Scones (page 52)
Juice spritzers

Texas Tofu Temptation (page 130)
Potato-Carrot-Spinach Soup (page 91)
Hot cocoa, tea, or coffee

Zesty Cabbage Salad (page 115)
Greek Stuffed Potatoes (page 140)
Milk or fruit juice

Butternut Chili (page 72)
Dill-Chive Bread (page 64)
Green salad with Mexican Vinaigrette (page 123)
Ice-cold beer, sangria, or limeade

Barley-Feta Salad (page 110)
Pita bread
Chilled white wine or sparkling cider

Crispy Ginger and Tofu Fritters (page 143)
Hot and Sour Soup (page 95)
Chinese tea

Cherry Tomato Gazpacho (page 99)
French Bread with Two Cheeses and Vegetables (page 125)
Iced tea or coffee

Garden Tomato, Basil, and Mozzarella Salad (page 118)
Fresh crusty bread
Chilled white wine or juice spritzers

Three-Cheese Focaccia with Sun-Dried Tomatoes, Onions, and
Red Bell Pepper (page 218)
Mushroom Garlic Bisque (page 76)
Red wine or grape juice

CASUAL MAIN MEALS TO SHARE

Chilled or Hot Ginger-Carrot Soup (page 97)
West Indian Lentil-Cheddar Rotis (page 230)
Green salad with Creamy Dill Dressing (page 121)
Lemon Walnut Cookies (page 306)
Ice water or beer; tea or coffee with dessert

Chicago Pizza (page 208)
Green salad with Artichoke-Parmesan Dressing (page 119)
Vanilla ice cream with Hot Fudge Sauce (page 301)
Ice water, juice spritzers, or red wine

Black Bean and Lime Chili (page 70)
Monterey Tortillas (page 135)
Baked winter squash
Fresh pineapple
Ice water, beer, or sangria

Fettuccine with Sun-Dried Tomatoes, Garlic, and Olives (page 198)
French bread
Green salad with Creamy Lemon-Chive Dressing (page 122)
Ice water, sparkling cider, or white wine

Tomato-Pesto Tortellini (page 190)
Marinated Artichoke and Vegetable Salad (page 116)
French bread
Fresh berries
Iced coffee or tea

Creamy Asparagus Soup (page 80)
Mushroom-Spinach Calzone with Three-Cheese Filling (page 216)
Oatmeal Chocolate Chip Cookies (page 305)
Ice water or white wine

Eggplant Parmigiana Pizza (page 210)
Green salad with Pesto Dressing (page 120)
Ice cream with Mocha Fudge Sauce (page 300)
Sparkling cider, red wine, or ice water

Blue Potatoes (page 244)
Green salad with Dilly Lemon-Dijon Dressing (page 120)
Carolina Peach-Pecan Kitchen Cake (page 285)
Ice water, beer, or juice

Cauliflower–Black Bean Salad with Buttermilk-Parmesan Dressing (page 106)
Oatmeal-Molasses Soda Bread (page 61)
Steamed fresh asparagus
Ice water, iced tea, or coffee

Red and Black Basmati Rice (page 241)
Steamed collard greens
Peach and Two-Berry Cobbler (page 291)
Ice water, iced tea, or coffee

Chilled Ginger-Carrot Soup (page 97)
Fresh bread
Asparagus, Rice, and Black Bean Salad (page 108)
Iced lemonade or limeade, or chilled white wine

Mexican Baked Beans (page 188)
Cheddar, Scallion, and Jalapeño Corn Bread (page 63)
Green salad with Mexican Vinaigrette (page 123)
Iced water, beer, or juice spritzers

Tempehrito (page 172)
Green salad with Avocado Vinaigrette (page 121)
Baked winter squash or sweet potatoes
Molasses Spice Cookies (page 307)
Iced lemonade or limeade, sangria, or water

Double Mushroom and Tomato Cream Sauce with Linguine (page 196)
Garlic bread
Green salad with Dilly Lemon-Dijon Dressing (page 120)
Ice cream or frozen yogurt
Ice water, red wine, or sparkling grape juice

MAIN MEALS FOR ENTERTAINING

Nepal Country Vegetable Soup (page 89)
Cauliflower Curry Crepes (page 222)
Green salad with Creamy Sesame Dressing (page 119)
Peach Custard Pie (page 263)
Ice water and chilled white wine

Gingery Vegetable-Barley Egg Rolls (page 158)
Stir-Fried Vegetables and Tempeh with Spicy Peanut Sauce (page 232)
Apricot Cheesecake with Chocolate Crust (page 288)
Ice water and beer; tea and coffee with dessert

Szechuan Eggplant Dip (page 149) with vegetable dippers
Oriental Tofu Balls with Fruit Sauce, Stir-Fried Vegetables, and Rice (page 236)
Peach-Rhubarb Pie (page 260)
Ice water or Chinese tea

Mushroom-Leek Turnovers with Blue Cheese (page 160)
Spicy Seitan and Vegetable Stroganoff (page 200)
Steamed fresh broccoli or asparagus
Apple-Cranberry-Raisin Strudel (page 293) with vanilla ice cream
Ice water, red wine, or sparkling cider

Baked Black Bean Dip (page 147) with corn chips
Southwestern Cheese and Vegetable Enchiladas (page 174)
Baked winter squash or potatoes
Broccoli, Cauliflower, Walnut, and Avocado Salad (page 117)
Chocolate Cream Pie (page 266)
Ice water, cold beer, or limeade

Hot Cheese and Chili Pepper Dip (page 151) with corn chips
Three-Bean Burritos (page 167)
Baked winter squash or sweet potatoes
Green salad with Avocado Vinaigrette (page 121)
Peach-Rhubarb Pie (page 260)
Beer, ice water, or juice spritzers

Mushrooms and Sun-Dried Tomatoes in Phyllo Dough (page 162)
Tomato, Eggplant, and Garlic Pie (page 252)
Marinated Artichoke and Vegetable Salad (page 116)
Steamed fresh asparagus
Cherry Pie (page 258)
Ice water, red wine, or sparkling cider

Cheesy Asparagus-Dill Pastries (page 164)
Pesto Lasagna (page 204)
Garlic bread
Green salad with Creamy Lemon-Chive Dressing (page 122)
Apple-Raspberry Custard Tart (page 270)
Red wine, ice water, or sparkling grape juice

Black Bean, Corn, and Cheddar Fritters (page 142)
Harvest Mexican Squash (page 184)
Green salad with Mexican Vinaigrette (page 123)
Chocolate Hazelnut Pie (page 268)
Ice water, beer, or juice spritzers

Caribbean Fritters (page 144)
Tortolan Chick-Pea and Spinach Rotis (page 229)
Green salad with Creamy Dill Dressing (page 121)
Caribbean Lime Cheesecake (page 287)
Limeade, ice water, or beer

Asian Stuffed Mushrooms (page 153)
Adriatic Ravioli (page 191)
Green salad with Pesto Dressing (page 120)
French bread
Ginger Pear Pie (page 262)
Ice water, wine, or sparkling grape juice

Cauliflower-Mushroom-Cheddar Soup (page 79)
Cornmeal and Cheddar Buttermilk Biscuits (page 57)
Greek Spinach-Potato Strudel (page 234)
Steamed fresh Brussels sprouts or asparagus
Cranberry Walnut Tart (page 272)
Juice spritzers or chilled white wine

Chilled Avocado-Zucchini Soup with Jalapeño Pepper (page 98)
Black Bean Empanadas (page 172)
Green salad with Mexican Vinaigrette (page 123)
Pumpkin Rum Custard Pie (page 265)
Limeade, sangria, or ice water

Pesto Cheese Dip (page 148)
Mushroom Pot Pie with Cheddar Cheese Sauce (page 248)
Steamed fresh asparagus, green beans, or broccoli
Green salad with Creamy Sesame Dressing (page 119)
Plum (page 259) or Cherry Pie (page 258)
Ice water, chilled white wine, or sparkling cider

Index

323